D1610558

A WORD FROM THE LEGENDS

"To lift the Webb Ellis Cup after winning the Rugby World Cup is the greatest honour you can achieve as a player for your country, but to be the first person to have the honour is extra special. Captaining the All Blacks to success in the inaugural Rugby World Cup in 1987 was the pinnacle of my rugby career and thank you John for bringing so many wonderful memories back to me in your magnificent book."
David Kirk, 1987 Rugby World Cup winner with New Zealand

"This is a truly wonderfully crafted book which is quite simply a treasure trove of all things Rugby World Cup. From the first page to the last, John will amaze you with so many wonderful entries and facts you may not have previously known. All-in-all a superb read."
Nick Farr-Jones, 1991 Rugby World Cup winning captain with Australia

"I will never forget winning the 1995 Rugby World Cup on home soil in front of our Rainbow Nation, experiencing how the tournament brought our nation together, indescribable. We were one team playing for one country. John's book brings back so many memories of that wonderful time."
Francois Pienaar, 1995 Rugby World Cup winning captain with South Africa

"To win the Rugby World Cup is the dream of every rugby player, and I was no different. To achieve this, on home soil in 1995, in the presence of the great man himself, Nelson Mandela, is something that will live with me forever. And thanks to John I can relive that very special moment time and time again in his wonderful book."
Joel Stransky, 1995 Rugby World Cup winner with South Africa

"I will never forget my nation's path to Rugby World Cup glory in 1995. The entire Rainbow Nation was United as One behind us and spurred us on to victory. John's book tells our story and the story of every Rugby World Cup tournament."
Chester Williams, 1995 Rugby World Cup winner with South Africa

"This is a book which will teach you everything you need to know about the history of the sport's greatest competition, the Rugby World Cup. Well done John on producing such an excellent insight into the history of this event."

George Gregan, 1999 Rugby World Cup winner with Australia

"Winning the Rugby World Cup is the pinnacle of any player's or coach's career. When I held the Webb Ellis Cup in my hands as coach of the winning England side in 2003, I was so proud of my team's achievement. John's book rekindled that memory along with many other outstanding moments from previous Rugby World Cups. John has produced a very comprehensive book which all rugby fans, regardless of what country they support, will thoroughly enjoy reading."

Sir Clive Woodward OBE, 2003 England Rugby World Cup winning coach

"Winning the Rugby World Cup with England down under in 2003 was the best moment of my 18-year rugby career. I actually forgot so many things that happened during that tournament but John has brought them so vividly back to me in his superb book."

Lawrence Dallaglio OBE, 2003 Rugby World Cup winner with England

"I was 17 when the Rainbow Nation won the Rugby World Cup in 1995 and after watching President Mandela present the famous Webb Ellis Cup to Francois Pienaar I dreamt that one day I would follow in my countryman's footsteps as a Rugby World Cup winning captain. So you can imagine my joy when 12 years later I captained my country to Rugby World Cup glory. John's book is superb and reveals so many Rugby World Cup moments I never knew about until now."

John Smit, captain of South Africa's 2007 Rugby World Cup winning side

"John's Rugby World Cup Miscellany is one of those books which when you start reading it you will find difficult to set down. It is jam-packed with Rugby World Cup facts, figures and trivia."

Sir Graham Henry, 2011 New Zealand Rugby World Cup winning coach

A MISCELLANY OF
RUGBY'S WORLD CUP

FACTS · HISTORY

1987 2019

STATISTICS · TRIVIA

A MISCELLANY OF
RUGBY'S WORLD CUP

JOHN WHITE

FOREWORD BY JASON LEONARD OBE

First published by Pitch Publishing, 2019

Pitch Publishing
A2 Yeoman Gate
Yeoman Way
Worthing
Sussex
BN13 3QZ
www.pitchpublishing.co.uk
info@pitchpublishing.co.uk

A CIP catalogue record is available for this book
from the British Library.

ISBN 978 1 78531 561 9

Typesetting and origination by Pitch Publishing

Printed and bound in India by Replika Press Pvt. Ltd.

Contents

DEDICATION

I am dedicating my book to three very good friends of mine who are big rugby fans:

Bill Clarkson and Mike Hartley from Dukinfield, Cheshire, England and Victor Coard from east Belfast, Northern Ireland.

Your friend always,

John

ACKNOWLEDGEMENTS

I wish to express my thanks to a number of people for their assistance in the writing of this book.

First of all, to Jason Leonard OBE for his wonderful Foreword.

Secondly, to the rugby legends who so very kindly gave me a supportive quote for my book: Lawrence Dallaglio OBE, George Gregan, Sir Graham Henry, Nick Farr-Jones, David Kirk MBE, Francois Pienaar, John Smit, Joel Stransky, Chester Williams and Sir Clive Woodward OBE.

And to the following websites:

http://rugbyfootballhistory.com/originsofrugby.htm - Nigel.
https://www.rugbyschool.co.uk/ – Amanda and Tracey.
http://www.talkingrugbyunion.co.uk/ - Austin and Max.
https://nzhistory.govt.nz/keyword/sport - Martha.
https://www.sahistory.org.za/ - Omar.
http://www.twickenham-museum.org.uk/ - Ed.

Finally, I owe a very big Thank You to Victor for proofreading my book.

Thank you.
John

INTRODUCTION

Rugby fans around the world flock to their local stadiums every weekend to watch their favourite club or their country play. Their passion for rugby is unrivalled and unmatched, but just why do so many want to watch one of the most rigorous and physically demanding of sports? The fans go in expectation, full of hopes and dreams. They go to the games for the promise of greatness. They go to the games to be seduced by genius. They go to the games for the love of the sport.

The Rugby World Cup finals is one of the biggest sporting events on the planet, a quadrennial festival of rugby union which brings the fans of 20 nations together as one and unites all rugby supporters as the games are beamed to a worldwide television audience. Fans watch in awe as century-old rivalries are played out in a 'Clash of Titans' between the great antipodean rivals, Australia and New Zealand, the old foes from the northern hemisphere and double world champions, South Africa. The tournament always produces the odd shock result, treats us to some magnificent games, witnesses individual battles on the field of play, gives us magical solo performances and mesmerises us with some magnificent tries. Villains will appear and new heroes will emerge. But in the end only one nation will celebrate glory and hold aloft the sport's most iconic and prestigious trophy, the coveted Webb Ellis Cup.

There are two quotes from famous sportsmen who never played rugby that sum up the game of rugby and the players for me.

'Sportsmanship for me is when a guy walks off the court and you really can't tell whether he won or lost, when he carries himself with pride either way.'

Jim Courier, grand slam-winning tennis champion.

'Champions aren't made in the gyms. Champions are made from something they have deep inside them – a desire, a dream, a vision.'

Muhammad Ali, world heavyweight boxing champion.

And so to my book.

This is sport.

This is captivating.

This is epic.

This is war.

This is legendary.

This is the Rugby World Cup.

The Rugby World Cup finals is where the legends of the future are born from the shadows of the past and where the history of rugby union is written one game at a time.

To the victors, the spoils.

John White

FOREWORD

I was surprised, but extremely pleased, when John contacted me and asked me to write the foreword to this book. After all, aren't the English and Irish supposed to be continually at war with one another? Well, that is what the historians would lead us to believe. But whilst the English and the Irish may be at 'rugby war' every time their respective XVs pull on their international jerseys to confront one another, the bond between these two fierce nations is evident in the respect of the fans. What I love so much about rugby is the fact that segregation amongst fans is non-existent. Why? Respect. Rugby fans love the game and respect their opposition from kick-off to conversions/penalties, to the final whistle. That's true sport. That's camaraderie. That's true sportsmanship which is not always present in other sporting codes. That's rugby.

I was born in Barking, London on 14 August 1968, and attended Warren Comprehensive, which was primarily a football school given its close proximity to West Ham United FC. I loved playing different sports at school but I knew I didn't have the physique to become a professional footballer. So, not long after my 14th birthday, I walked into my local club, Barking RFC, one Sunday morning and said I wanted to be a rugby player. When I left school aged 15, I began work as a carpenter alongside my father, dovetailing this at weekends with playing for Barking RFC's Under-19 side. When we won the Essex Cup, I started to take rugby, which at the time was still an amateur sport, seriously. I knew playing rugby as a prop forward was my destiny in life. I devoted myself to the sport and set out to be fitter and stronger than anyone else. I knew I did not have the pace to dazzle opponents, score tries, win games or grab the headlines. But I also knew that I possessed the determination and ability to wrap my arms around my teammates and stand firm in the front row regardless of the opposition. I suppose you could say I was cut out for the trench warfare of rugby, ready to go over the top when necessary and prepared to fall. My teammates knew what they were going to get from me: nothing fancy, I just did what it said on the tin as prop forward.

In 1989, Saracens showed some interest in me and I signed for them. After a year, and 19 games for Saracens, I moved on to Harlequins where I remained until I decided it was time to hang up my boots at the end of the 2003/04 season, some 290 games later. Little did I know when I started my professional career that one day I would play for my country let alone win four grand slams (1991, 1992, 1995 and 2003) and the Rugby World Cup (2003). I also endured the pain of losing the 1991 Rugby World Cup Final to Australia on home soil, a match I still cannot watch to this day. I will never forget my international debut, winning my first cap aged 20, England's youngest Test debutant at the time, in a friendly versus Argentina in Buenos Aires on 28 July 1990. A friendly? In my first ruck I was punched on the jaw by an Argentina forward but my big teammate, Wade Dooley, sorted him out. Before the game the partisan home crowd (it was just eight years after the Falklands War had ended) were burning Union Jack flags in two of the stands. The national anthem was being played on an old gramophone and halfway through it you just heard this screech as someone ripped the record off. People were throwing oranges on to the field. We found an empty whisky bottle someone had thrown, a pair of scissors and a huge bath tap! It was a baptism of fire but one I thoroughly enjoyed especially after we won the game 25-12.

I was nicknamed 'The Fun Bus' during my England career. I trundled on to the training pitch one day wearing a red shirt leading my teammate, Martin Bayfield, to comment that I looked as big as a London bus! But whilst Sir Cliff Richard had his *Summer Holiday* in the movie of the same name in 1963, I was so pleased to be a passenger on the England bus which drove us to Rugby World Cup glory 40 years later when we beat Australia 20-17 after extra time in the 2003 final.

When I retired in May 2004, I did so with a record 114 caps for England, a record I am so proud of. I was also capped five times by the British and Irish Lions. But one of my proudest moments in an England shirt has to be the first time I captained my country. Ironically, it was against the side I won my first cap against, Argentina. The game was played at Twickenham Stadium, London on 14 December 1996. It was a tough game and nothing separated the two teams at half-time as the score stood at 9-9. The second half panned out like the previous 40 minutes, a bruising encounter dominated by the opposing kickers. Towards the end of the game the visitors took an 18-12 lead when their fly-half, Gonzalo Quesada, scored his sixth penalty. From a rolling maul, I scored a try to reduce the deficit to 18-17 and a Mike Catt penalty, his fifth of the game, secured a 20-18 victory. What was I saying about me never being able to win games? The try will live with me forever, not least because it is the only one I ever scored for England! Mind you, I only scored four points for Saracens and nine for Harlequins.

Every four years since the inaugural World Cup tournament in 1987, rugby fans across the globe have been treated to a festival of rugby when the top 20 nations do battle to be crowned world champions. I was honoured to have represented England at four Rugby World Cup finals in 1991, 1995, 1999 and 2003. John's book has managed to bring back so many wonderful memories of my four finals campaigns. He brings the tournament to life with stories about some outstanding individual performances and some truly magnificent games. I can still see the late, great Jonah Lomu swatting Rob Andrew, Will Carling and Tony Underwood aside and then running over the top of Mike Catt to score against us in the All Blacks' 45-29 semi-final win in the 1995 Rugby World Cup at Newlands, Cape Town, South Africa. If you watch the TV footage of the try you will see I almost made it to Jonah before he crossed the line. And of course, I will always remember Jonny Wilkinson as he dropped-kicked us to glory in the 2003 Rugby World Cup Final in the last seconds of extra time.

This is a book for all rugby fans, regardless of what nation you will be supporting at the 2019 Rugby World Cup finals in Japan. I know who I will be following and I know John will be hoping that Ireland can take their magnificent performances from 2018 on to the world stage and bring the world's most famous rugby trophy, the Webb Ellis Cup, back to the northern hemisphere for the first time in 16 years.

Jason Leonard OBE

THE RUGBY WORLD CUP
MISCELLANY

THE WEBB ELLIS CUP

The winners of the Rugby World Cup are presented with the Webb Ellis Cup. According to a popular legend it was William Webb Ellis who invented the game of rugby when he was a schoolboy at Rugby School. It is said that during a game of football he picked up the ball and started to run with it.

The Webb Ellis Cup is 38 centimetres high and weighs 4.5kg. It was crafted from solid sterling silver and 24 carat gold plate and has two cast scroll handles. On one handle there is the head of a satyr and on the other the head of a nymph. The words 'International Rugby Football Board' and 'The Webb Ellis Cup' are engraved on the face of the trophy.

There are two official Webb Ellis Cups, which are used interchangeably. The original cup was made in 1906 by Carrington & Co. London. It was a Victorian design of a cup from the 1740s made by Paul de Lamerie. The second is a replica which was made in 1986.

Did You Know That?
The Webb Ellis Cup is often referred to as 'Bill', a nickname coined by the 1991 winners, Australia.

A HISTORY LESSON

At least two centuries of rugby's history are written in the stones and other monuments to tradition at Rugby School that stand around the School Close, where in 1823, local lad William Webb Ellis, 'with a fine disregard for the rules of football', took the ball in his arms and ran with it, originating the game of rugby football. The players then were more numerous: in 1839, when Queen Adelaide visited the school, it was School House (75) versus the Rest (225). Today, innumerable tourists visit the 'Home of the Game' and rugby teams from all over the world can be seen training against the distinctive backdrop of Butterfield's Chapel. At the top of the Close stands the King's Oak, planted by Edward VII in 1909, beneath which the heads of school watch the pupils file into chapel every morning. Behind it rises the battlemented skyline of School House where the headmaster has his study – he still sits at Bishop Percival's desk – which pupils can enter by a spiral staircase at the foot of a tower. Rugby's greatest headmaster Dr

Thomas Arnold (1828–42) instigated this practice so that boys could see him privately and the tradition continues today.

Arnold is famed for ridding the school of its 'Flashmans' and emphasising subjects that were a good 'preparation for power'. He treated his senior boys as gentlemen, increasing their power and duties so that they shared responsibility for moral tone and discipline with him. As Arnold put it: 'First religious and moral principle, second gentlemanly conduct, third academic ability.' Masters were expected to supervise as well as teach; the dames' houses were abolished and pastoral care was born.

If Arnold's educational initiatives had not assured Rugby's fame, his political intervention certainly would have done. His 1829 pamphlet on the issue of Catholic Emancipation attracted widespread criticism, and though the storm of publicity had subsided by the late 1830s, Rugby School and its remarkable headmaster were now national news and the school was growing rapidly. Not only did the 260 boys Arnold inherited become 360 by the time he died, but his disciples spread his ideas throughout the United Kingdom and Empire. No fewer than 23 of his assistant masters became headmasters of other public schools between 1842 and 1899. This trend has continued ever since.

Arnold's ideas – or at least Thomas Hughes's version of them, as written in *Tom Brown's School Days* – found fertile ground in France and in the mind of one French boy in particular. Pierre de Coubertin was 12 years old when he first encountered Thomas Arnold in the pages of Hughes's book. By the time the novel was translated into French in 1875, Arnold had become something of a legend. Inspired by what he had read, de Coubertin visited Rugby several times during the 1880s and concluded that organised sport could be used to raise the aspirations and improve the behaviour of young people. This idea fuelled his vision for universal amateur athletics which culminated, in 1896, in the first modern Olympic Games in Athens. As one world expert on Olympic history says, 'Thomas Arnold was the single most important influence on the life and thought of Pierre de Coubertin.' Arnold's influential role in the Olympic Games is commemorated in a plaque on the school's Doctor's Wall, unveiled by Lord Sebastian Coe in 2009. In July 2012, the Olympic torch came to Rugby School on its route towards the Olympic Stadium and paused at the plaque to acknowledge the importance of Thomas Arnold, who would certainly have enjoyed the school's re-enactment of a 19th-century game of rugby with the boys wearing kit of the time.

Arnold was succeeded by a number of formidable figures, notably Frederick Temple (1858–69), under whom the tercentenary buildings of the New Quad were begun; John Percival (1877–95), who had made his name as the founder of Clifton College; and Herbert Armitage James (1895–1910), whose nickname 'The Bodger' has since become part of Rugbeian argot. Numbers further increased in the 20th century from 580 under James to 620 under W. W. Vaughan (1921–31), passed 700 under Sir Arthur fforde (1948–57) and topped 800 under Brian Rees in the early 1980s. Having resounded to Arnold's passionate sermons, the chapel is now his resting place, beneath the chancel steps. The walls boast tablets in memory of renowned Rugbeian writers such as Lewis Carroll, Rupert Brooke and the Victorian poets – Matthew Arnold, Arthur Hugh Clough and Walter Savage Landor. The Boomer, a 3¼-ton bell raised in July 1914 and rung at noon every day in the First World War, still calls the school to chapel. In 2001, a new award-winning organ was inaugurated in the chapel. The smaller Memorial Chapel, where the BBC has recorded *Songs of Praise* more than once, was dedicated in 1922. Old Quad was built before even the first chapel. A drainpipe proclaims the date 1809 of this oldest part of the school, designed by Henry Hakewill, who was also responsible for School House and the first chapel (1820). Here is the trough where Tom Brown was 'ducked' and, inside, the fire where he was 'roasted'. Looking up one sees Upper Bench where Arnold taught Thucydides and looked down severely upon moral turpitude. On the town side, a splendid oriel window, with stained glass portraits of successive headmasters, looks out over the main school gate and down the High Street to where the school began, 200 yards away.

In 2006, William Webb Ellis and Rugby School became the first two inductees of the newly established World Rugby Hall of Fame.

Did You Know That?

On 1 November 1923, Rugby School celebrated the centenary of William Webb Ellis's 'fine disregard for the rules of rugby' with a match between an England/Wales XV and an Ireland/Scotland XV. The Rugby Football Union, the sport's governing body, wanted the match to be played at Twickenham Stadium, London where a larger crowd could see it, but the school remained steadfast and hosted the match at the Close. A crowd of 2,000 spectators, which included players from the first ever international match (Scotland beat England 1-0 on 27 March 1871 at Raeburn Place, Edinburgh, Scotland), watched the England/Wales XV triumph 21-16. The schoolboys sat on tarpaulins whilst one of the many former Rugbeians at the game was Adrian Stoop, the English international after whom the Harlequins' ground is named. The post-match dinner took place at The Great Central Hotel in London.

INAUGURAL RUGBY WORLD CUP UNDER THREAT

In mid-1986 a nervous International Rugby Union Football Board (IRFB), concerned at slow progress the co-host nations, Australia and New Zealand, were making with planning the inaugural Rugby World Cup finals in 1987, considered taking over the tournament (sponsors were not secured until shortly before the tournament kicked off). Indeed, a proposal to do so was lost only on the chairman's casting vote. The IRFB spent a year arguing over the distribution of profits, which were yet to be made. Knowing they had the old guard (IRFB) over a barrel, the host unions held out for the best terms they could get. The deal reached in March 1986 gave Australia and New Zealand all their net gate takings. They would also share 48% of the income generated by the tournament representatives (the commercial company that would manage the event). The other 14 unions taking part would share most of the rest. The same March 1986 meeting appointed the British sports marketing company, West Nally, as the tournament representatives. West Nally had suggested a Rugby World Cup several years earlier. They trumped rival bidders by offering US$5 million upfront for the rights. The Australians' insistence on payment in advance was to prove wise in view of the stock market crash on 19 October 1987, known as 'Black Monday'. Potential sponsors demanded stadiums that were 'clean' (free of all other advertising). Because of this, and Australian rugby politics, the traditional New South Wales Test venue, the Sydney Cricket Ground, was unavailable. Auckland's Eden Park would host the final, and both semi-finals would be played in Australia. Brisbane's Ballymore Oval could readily stage one (New Zealand beat Wales 49-6). The Sydney semi-final was allocated to the small Concord Oval, which the New South Wales Rugby Union was developing as its base (Australia lost 30-24 to France). With rugby weak outside these two cities, only one pool would be contested in Australia (Pool 1 comprising Australia, England, Japan and USA – won by Australia). Eight venues in New Zealand would host the other three pools, namely Athletic Park, Wellington; Carisbrook, Dunedin; Lancaster Park, Christchurch; McLean Park, Napier; Rotorua International Stadium, Rotorua; Rugby Park, Hamilton; Rugby Park Stadium, Invercargill; and Showgrounds Oval, Palmerston North.

Rugby World Cup Proprietary Ltd, the company set up in Australia to handle the financial side of organising the tournament, appointed a New Zealand judge, Sir Desmond Sullivan, as its chief executive officer. When he was appointed to the Waitangi Tribunal, he was replaced by management consultant Jim Campbell (the father of TV3 broadcaster John Campbell). Both men found it tough going. The host unions had only a handful of employees between them, and much of the work was done by committees headed by the respected rugby identities Sir Nicholas Shehadie (in Australia) and Dick Littlejohn (in New Zealand). Sponsors were not secured until shortly before the tournament kicked off. When they were announced, the wisdom of including Japan and the USA in the tournament was justified. KDD, a Japanese telecommunications company, was the main sponsor. The others were Mazda, Rank Xerox and New Zealand Breweries. Commercialism was suddenly everywhere. The name of a New Zealand beer, Steinlager, was even painted on the small buckets in which sand was carried out to place-kickers. Despite a stern circular from the New Zealand Rugby Football Union (NZRFU), this ruse was repeated in the final. In rugby's brave new world, even official sponsors were not above a little guerrilla marketing. The host television rights were shared by public broadcasters, the Australian Broadcasting Corporation and Television New Zealand. At the last minute, the British Broadcasting Corporation decided to pay £1 million to cover the tournament meaning it would be shown live in 17 countries. This fee looked excessive, but by the 1991 World Cup it would seem the bargain of the century.

There were other problems too. The New Zealand Cavalier tour of South Africa, an unofficial venture in which key rugby figures in both countries were heavily involved, had just ended. All but two (David Kirk and John Kirwan) of the 30 players selected for the cancelled 1985 All Black tour of South Africa had taken part. The IRFB expressed its disapproval. The Cavalier tour disrupted the All Blacks' preparation for the 1987 Rugby World Cup finals. The rebels were let off very lightly, being banned for just two Tests. They were then blended uneasily with their temporary replacements, the 'Baby Blacks' and more than half the team that played in the 1987 World Cup Final were former Cavaliers. A week before the All Blacks' first game against Italy, Prime Minister David Lange announced a boycott of his team's matches, prompted by the presence in the squad of many of the Cavaliers. Many people in New Zealand were extremely angry that their star sportsmen had broken ranks on the stance against apartheid and made large sums of money from doing so.

Lange had been elected to office in 1984 at the age of 41 (New Zealand's youngest prime minister), and had inherited a country in the midst of an economic and political crisis. In September 1986, Lange was at loggerheads with France over nuclear testing and the sinking of *Rainbow Warrior* on 10 July 1985. The sinking of the *Rainbow Warrior*, codenamed '*Opération Satanique*', was organised by the 'Action Branch' of the French foreign intelligence services, the

Direction Générale de la Sécurité Extérieure (DGSE). The boat was the flagship of the Greenpeace fleet and was bombed at the Port of Auckland, New Zealand, on its way to a protest against a planned French nuclear test in Moruroa, French Polynesia in the southern Pacific Ocean.

The New Zealand government refused to invite overseas dignitaries to attend the 1987 Rugby World Cup finals or to host functions for the visiting players and administrators. Just two days before the opening match, the captain of the All Blacks, Andy Dalton, pulled a hamstring, which ruled him out of the tournament. However, when Prime Minister Lange boycotted matches, some of his ministers were more than delighted to take his place in the VIP section at Eden Park, Auckland. Despite the political tensions, the fraught build-up and the loss of their inspirational captain, the All Blacks rallied and roused themselves, resulting in David Kirk lifting the Webb Ellis Cup following the All Blacks' 29-9 win over, of all nations, France, in the final played at Eden Park on 20 June 1987.

Did You Know That?
The total attendance at the 1987 Rugby World Cup finals was 600,000.

The Ball
An original rugby ball was round and changed shape over a period of time to the oval it is today. They varied in size depending on the pig's bladder they were made from. Gilberts, a local boot maker near Rugby School, took up ball-making to supply the school. Others, notably London, also supplied balls and it was this maker that invented the inflatable inner and the pump.

Uniform, Teams and Rules
Rugby School played in white and, because the committee of the Rugby Football Union (RFU) in 1871 was composed largely of Old Rugbeians (ORs), England played in white too. School House at Rugby School was the first team to play in a uniform kit (long flannels, shirts and caps), because it was the only house to play as a single group until 1850. Before this, the boys at Rugby School played in their ordinary school clothes in teams made up from various houses. In 1867, the first 'foreign' match was played against ORs and a team from the town of Rugby. The teams were now down to 20 players, and then 15 by 1876. Internal teams stayed at 20 until 1888. The first inter-school match was against Cheltenham in 1896 and half the players in the first England international team were ORs. The RFU was formed (largely of ORs)

in 1871 and the first national code was introduced. The boys at Rugby School kept their own rules, and even modified them, until the late 1880s. There were no referees in the early days and boys would wear sharpened boots with nails in them for extra hacking. Boys considered good enough to play for the main teams were given 'following up' caps, which later developed into the international cap awarded to the country's top players.

Rugby School and the Calcutta Cup

The Calcutta Rugby Football Club was established by former students of Rugby School in January 1873. However, with the departure of a local British army regiment (and perhaps more crucially the cancellation of the free bar at the club!), interest in rugby diminished in the area and sports such as tennis and polo began to thrive as they were better suited to the Indian climate. Whilst the Calcutta (Rugby) Football Club was disbanded in 1878, members decided to keep the memory of the club alive by having the remaining 270 silver rupees in their bank account melted down to be made into a trophy. The trophy was then presented to the (RFU) to use as 'the best means of doing some lasting good for the cause of Rugby Football'. The Calcutta Cup continues today as the trophy that is presented to the winner of the England versus Scotland rugby union match which takes place during the annual Six Nations Championship.

Rules of the Game

In 1845, the first codified rules of the game were drawn up by the levee [Rugby School prefects] and included the following: No. 5 'Try at goal' (a touchdown doesn't count unless it is converted; so it's a try or attempt at goal). No. 18 'A player having touched the ball straight for a tree, and touched the tree with it, may drop from either side if he can, but the opposite side may oblige him to go to his own side of the tree.' No. 20 'All matches are drawn after five days, but after three if no goal has been kicked.' No. 25 'No stranger, in any match, may have a place kick at goal.' No. 33 'The Island is all in goal.'

Rugby Football Union

The first five Rugby Football Union presidents were Old Rugbeians, as well as the first England captain. An OR introduced the game to Cambridge University. When first played some passers-by ran on to the pitch thinking they were breaking up a brawl!

Origins of Half-Time

Half-time originated at Rugby School. After some 40 minutes the school captain stopped the game and announced it was hardly fair as his team was playing with a strong following wind. He offered the opposition the chance of playing the rest of the match with the breeze. They changed ends and half-time was born. Forty minutes each way was first mentioned in the 1926 Rules.

International Caps

The international cap originates from Rugby School, as well as the distinctive posts that go up well above the cross bar. It became near impossible to kick the ball between the posts due to the number of young men who packed the goal mouth. Hence the kickers began to kick over the crossbar.

Kit

England's original white shirt and shorts with black socks is from Rugby School and Oxbridge's 'blue' also comes from the school's XV.

Terminology

The terminology in the original rules can still be found in the laws today: knock-on, onside/offside, fair catch, try, goal, place kick, 25-yard (22m) line, touch judge, charge, scrummage and in-goal.

THE SOMME CUP

The closest thing to a Rugby World Cup before the inaugural tournament in 1987 was an event organised at the end of the First World War (1914–18). In late 1916 and early 1917, a team made up of New Zealand soldiers played seven matches in Britain against teams made up from local military regiments. The New Zealand Division, organised by Colonel Arthur Plugge, scored a total of 292 points across the seven games and conceded only nine. In another game, they beat a Welsh Division XV 3-0 in Belgium, a game played with the sound of German shells exploding in the distance. In 1917, the Paris newspaper, *Le Journal*, donated a trophy, the Somme Cup, which was contested by teams from the English, French, Irish, New Zealand and Welsh military who were serving on the Western Front. The final saw the home side, the French Service, play the New Zealand Division at Vincennes on 8 April 1917 before a crowd estimated at 25,000. The military All Blacks demolished their allies 40-0, scoring nine tries, five conversions and a penalty goal on a bright Easter Sunday afternoon in Paris. Two of the French players were airmen who had taken part in bombing raids the day before whilst three members of their team left the trenches to play. A rival newspaper, *L'Image*, wrote the following about the game: 'Our men ... had to bow to world champions ... The result of 40-0 was nevertheless honourable and was proclaimed in a storm of cheers and a burst of fraternal esteem.' Three months after the match, All Black

Reg Taylor was killed in action in Messines, West Flanders, Belgium on 20 June 1917; Maori All Black Tom French was severely wounded on 4 October 1917 resulting in his left arm being amputated; and George Scott lost the sight in both eyes at Passchendaele, West Flanders. The French captain, Maurice Jean-Paul Boyau, an outstanding pilot, was shot down and killed on 16 September 1918. He earned the *Médaille militaire* and *Légion d'honneur* for his aerial exploits in 1917 and 1918.

Did You Know That?

The Somme Cup is not a cup. It is a statue created by the French sculptor Georges Chauvel, and it was presented to the New Zealand captain, George Murray. The statue depicts a French soldier in the act of throwing a hand grenade and was originally called *Le Lanceur de Grenades*. However, the French and New Zealand soldiers dubbed it the *'Coupe de la Somme'*.

RUGBY'S MOST FAMOUS WHISTLE

From the inaugural Rugby World Cup in Australia and New Zealand in 1987 to the 2011 edition hosted by New Zealand, the opening game of every tournament was started by the same whistle. Welsh referee Gil Evans used the sterling silver whistle when the original All Blacks played England at Crystal Palace, London on 2 December 1905, a match the All Blacks won 15-0. Evans then passed it on to another Welsh referee, Albert E. Freethy, who is believed to have used it in the rugby union final at the 1924 Summer Olympics in Paris, when the United States of America beat the hosts 17-13 at the Colombes Stadium, the last occasion the 15-a-side version of the sport featured in the Games. On 3 January 1925, Freethy famously blew the whistle to dismiss the All Blacks' Cyril Brownlie in the Test between New Zealand and England at Twickenham Stadium, London, making him the first player to be sent off in an international match. The tourists won the game 17-11. Freethy then presented it to Stan Dean, the manager of the 1924/25 All Black Invincibles, who then presented it to John Sinclair, one of the founders of the New Zealand Rugby Museum, on 16 April 1969 for the museum's opening ceremony. Dean also served as the chairman of the New Zealand Rugby Football Union for many years.

For the 2015 Rugby World Cup hosted by England, the sport's governing body, World Rugby, took the decision not to continue the trend and so the famous whistle remained in its display case in the museum located in Palmerston. The whistle bears an inscription saying it was used by Gil Evans in the famous 1905 Test match. Bob Fordham (Australia) was the first to blow it at a Rugby World Cup when he kicked off the 1987 tournament, a 70-6 rout of Italy by New

Zealand at Eden Park, Auckland. Since then the whistle has been used by Jim Fleming (Scotland, 1991), Derek Bevan (Wales, 1995), Paddy O'Brien (New Zealand, 1999), Paul Honiss (New Zealand, 2003), Tony Spreadbury (England, 2007) and George Clancy (Ireland, 2011). In 1996, the whistle was also used to start the first professional rugby match between the Hurricanes and the Blues at the Palmerston North Showgrounds, a five-minute walk from the museum.

The referee of the 1924 Test between England and the All Blacks did not have a coin on him to toss prior to kick-off and so Hector Gray, a New Zealand fan who was sitting on the touchline and following his country's 1924/25 tour, offered him a florin. Mr Gray was given the coin back and he later had a rose embossed on one side and a silver fern on the other and presented it to the museum in 1973. The coin was tossed prior to the Hurricanes and the Blues match.

Did You Know That?

In season 1885/86, referees were allowed to use a whistle to stop the game for the first time in the sport's history, while umpires (now known as assistant referees) were given sticks.

RUGBY WORLD CUP QUOTES

'I have had some of the most intimate moments of my life with Madiba (Nelson Mandela). There is a sincerity and openness about him that affected millions. Our relationship was incredible. It grew enormously after 1995. That was the start of the journey, not the end. He was a special, special person. I wish I had the words now to give a fitting tribute but I can't find them, I just can't.'

Francois Pienaar, 1995 Rugby World Cup winning captain of South Africa

TOP OF THE POPS 1987

When New Zealand won the inaugural Rugby World Cup Final on 20 June 1987, the No.1 song in the UK pop charts was *Star Trekkin* by The Firm. This was a novelty song parodying the characters of *Star Trek*, the long-running TV series. It spent two weeks in the top slot before being ousted by The Pet Shop Boys with *It's A Sin*.

LA BAJADA

Dr Francisco Ocampo pioneered this unorthodox scrum technique back in the 1960s in Argentina. His twin loves of physics and scrummaging combined to devastating effect to create the '*Bajada*', Argentina's classic set-piece counter-drive. The locks bind round the props' hips with their outside arms, rather than through the legs as standard. Pinning the props inwards towards the hooker, all the power shoots through the centre of the front row.

A BLESSING IN DISGUISE

Argentina coach Pablo Bouza said the Pumas would not have made the semi-finals of the 2015 Rugby World Cup had they joined the Six Nations, as originally planned, instead of the Rugby Championship. The Pumas, who petitioned the tournament organisers for inclusion in the Six Nations competition following their Rugby World Cup semi-final appearance in 2007, had their application to compete in the European competition with games in San Sebastian, Spain, dismissed out of hand.

Instead Argentina joined New Zealand, Australia, and South Africa's annual Tri-Nations tournament in 2012, their inclusion the catalyst for the competition's rebranding into the Rugby Championship in 2012. When he was asked, in October 2015, if Argentina would be as strong had they joined the Six Nations in 2012 and not the Rugby Championship, Bouza said: 'I cannot be sure, but I don't think so, they are quite different styles. Last year when we finished playing the championships, we struggled, we came back here and we lost against Scotland. But they are such different styles, when you play here in autumn, November, the pitches are slow, the breakdown is tough, it's tough to have quick ball to play. When you have quick ball, for us it's very positive. I think playing in the Rugby Championship for us has been great.' Argentina lost their semi-final 29-15 to Australia followed by a 24-13 defeat to South Africa in the bronze final match.

Did You Know That?

For the first time in Rugby World Cup history no teams from the northern hemisphere reached the semi-final stage following Argentina's 43-20 win over Ireland in the quarter-finals of the 2015 tournament.

FROM RUSSIA WITH LOVE

Vasily Artemyev (78 caps, 2009–present) was born in Moscow, Russia on 24 July 1987 and is his country's record try scorer with 28. He went to school at Blackrock College in County Dublin, Ireland and won schools' Junior Cup and Senior Cup medals. He also attended University College Dublin where he studied law and played for their successful rugby team in 2007, winning the League and Metro Cup, and was also part of the Intervarsity Team which won the Conroy Cup in 2006 and 2007. He played for Russia in the 2011 World Cup finals and has won 17 international caps and scored five tries.

1987 RUGBY WORLD CUP VENUES

Athletic Park, Wellington, New Zealand
Ballymore Stadium, Brisbane, Australia
Carisbrook, Dunedin, New Zealand
Concord Oval, Sydney, Australia
Eden Park, Auckland, New Zealand
Lancaster Park, Christchurch, New Zealand
McLean Park, Napier, New Zealand
Rotorua International Stadium, Rotorua, New Zealand
Rugby Park, Hamilton, New Zealand
Rugby Park Stadium, Invercargill, New Zealand
Showgrounds Oval, Palmerston North, New Zealand
Pool 1 was played in Australia
Pool 2 was played with five matches held in New Zealand and one in Australia
Pool 3 was played in New Zealand
Pool 4 was played in New Zealand

THE 1987 RUGBY WORLD CUP FINALS

Pool 1	Pool 2	Pool 3	Pool 4
Australia,	Canada,	Argentina,	France,
England,	Ireland,	Fiji,	Romania,
Japan,	Tonga,	Italy,	Scotland,
United States	Wales	New Zealand	Zimbabwe

Pool Winners – Australia, Wales, New Zealand, France
Runners-Up – England, Ireland, Fiji, Scotland

Quarter-finals

New Zealand	30	3	Scotland	Christchurch	6 Jun 1987
Fiji	16	31	France	Auckland	7 Jun 1987
Australia	33	15	Ireland	Sydney	7 Jun 1987
England	3	16	Wales	Brisbane	8 Jun 1987

Semi-finals

| Australia | 24 | 30 | France | Sydney | 13 Jun 1987 |
| New Zealand | 49 | 6 | Wales | Brisbane | 14 Jun 1987 |

Third Place Play-off

| Australia | 21 | 22 | Wales | Rotorua | 18 Jun 1987 |

Final – 20 June 1987
Eden Park, Auckland, New Zealand
New Zealand 29-9 France

New Zealand went into the 1987 tournament as the overwhelming favourites to be crowned the first ever Rugby World Cup winners. The All Blacks won all three of their pool games racking up 130 points, conceding just 34 points and scored 30 tries. In the quarter-finals they saw off Scotland with a 30-3 victory and then in the semi-finals they cruised to a 49-6 victory over Wales. Their opponents in the final, France, were the best side in the northern hemisphere having won the Five Nations Grand Slam two months previously, which included away wins over England and Ireland. However, *Les Bleus* only just pipped Scotland to winning their pool by scoring 25 tries to the Scots' 20. The pair drew their Pool 4 encounter 20-20. In the quarter-finals the French beat Fiji 31-16 and then defeated Australia 30-24 in the semi-finals in what is still one of the greatest games in the history of the competition.

However, when it came to the final France just seemed to have run out of steam as New Zealand dominated the game from start to finish to run out 29-9 winners before a home partisan crowd at Eden Park, Auckland. Grant Fox scored 17 points for the All Blacks in the final and ended the tournament as the leading points scorer with 126. His teammates, Craig Green and John Kirwan, were the leading try scorers with six each.

New Zealand: John Gallagher; John Kirwan, Warwick Taylor, Joe Stanley, Craig Green; Grant Fox, David Kirk; John Drake, Sean Fitzpatrick, Steven McDowell, Murray Pierce, Gary Whetton, Michael Jones, Alan Whetton, Buck Shelford.

France: Serge Blanco; Patrice Lagisquet, Philippe Sella, Denis Charvet, Didier Camberabero; Frank Mesnel, Pierre Berbizier; Jean-Pierre Garuet-Lempirou, Daniel Dubroca, Pascal Ondarts, Jean Condom, Alain Lorieux, Eric Champ, Dominique Erbani, Laurent Rodriguez.

New Zealand	France
Tries Jones, Kirk, Kirwan	Try Berbizier
Con Fox	Con Camberabero
Pens Fox 4	Pen Camberabero
Drop Goal Fox	Drop Goals None

Referee: Kerry Fitzgerald (Australia)
Attendance: 48,035

Did You Know That?

New Zealand full-back John Gallagher was back on his policeman's beat the morning after he won a Rugby World Cup winners' medal.

SOUTH AFRICA'S POCKET ROCKET

Going into the third place match at the 2015 Rugby World Cup, South Africa's Bryan Habana was on the verge of making tournament history. The 32-year-old was seeking to score his 16th try at a Rugby World Cup finals which would see him become the tournament's all-time leading try scorer (he was level with New Zealand's Jonah Lomu on 15 tries).

Bryan Gary Habana was born on 12 June 1983 in Johannesburg, South Africa. At school he played at centre and as a scrum-half before being switched to the wing to utilise the electric speed he possessed. Not surprisingly, he was nicknamed 'the Pocket Rocket'. In 2003, he signed for his local team, the Golden Lions, and was a member of the South Africa Sevens side which took part in the 2003/04 World Sevens Series (finishing in fifth place). At the 2004 IRB Under-21 World Championships he was the top try scorer and later that same year, on 20 November 2004, he made his Test debut for the Springboks against England, scoring a try with his first touch of the ball. However, the visitors lost the match 32-16 at Twickenham Stadium, London.

'When I got the ball I knew that nothing was going to stop me. It was incredible. I had never played on the wing before and I found myself scoring a try with my first touch of international rugby,' said Habana, when asked about his try.

In 2005, he played in all 12 of South Africa's international matches and scored 12 tries and was named South African Player of the Year (he also won the award in 2007 and 2012). His two long-range tries against Australia in Perth on 20 August 2005 helped the Springboks win their first Tri-Nations match overseas since 1998. Habana was a member of South Africa's 2007 Rugby World Cup squad, scoring four tries in a

59-7 win over Samoa and two against the USA in a 64-15 win to help the Springboks win Pool A. His two tries versus Argentina in the semi-finals tied Jonah Lomu's record of eight tries at a Rugby World Cup finals tournament (1999 Rugby World Cup). Although Habana didn't score in the 2007 Rugby World Cup Final versus England he played his part in his nation's 15-6 victory in Paris, France on 20 October 2007. After collecting his winners' medal, he was asked about his failure to add to his tally of tries in the final. 'I just wanted to help the team effort. Everyone in the squad made a contribution from number one to number 30. Every player who's represented the country in the last four years made a contribution. The 1995 victory planted the seed that made me want to be a part of this great game,' was the star winger's measured response.

The very next day he was named the 2007 IRB Player of the Year.

Habana was selected for the South Africa squad which would play three Tests versus the 2009 touring British and Irish Lions. He played in the first game at Durban which the Springboks won 26-21 but was not among the try scorers. In the second game the hosts were trailing 19-8 in Pretoria with 20 minutes to go. In the 63rd minute Habana burst through the tourists' defence to score a memorable try and South Africa went on to win a close encounter, 28-25, to clinch a series victory. He did not play in the final Test, which South Africa lost 28-9 in Johannesburg.

On 5 December 2009, Habana played for the Barbarians against New Zealand and scored three tries as the Barbarians defeated the All Blacks, who had not lost a match in the northern hemisphere in two years, 25-18 at Twickenham. On 26 June 2010, Habana scored a try in the Springboks' 55-11 win over a touring Italy side in East London to draw himself level with Joost van der Westhuizen's Test try-scoring record for the Springboks of 38. At the 2011 Rugby World Cup he scored two tries for the Springboks but the holders of the Webb Ellis Cup were defeated 11-9 by Australia in the quarter-finals. However, it was a landmark moment for Habana, who broke the South African try record during the tournament with his 39th try in a crushing 87-0 win over Namibia.

He won the International Rugby Players' Association Try of the Year in 2012 (and the SuperSport Try of the Year in 2007 and 2012).

At the 2015 Rugby World Cup he scored tries against Samoa and Scotland and a hat-trick versus the USA to equal Lomu's record try haul. South Africa beat Wales 23-19 in the quarter-finals and lost 20-18 to the All Blacks in the semi-finals but Habana failed to score in either match. In the Bronze Final game against the Pumas, he was not among the try scorers in the Springboks' 24-13 win at the Olympic Stadium, London.

In 2016, he was made vice-captain of South Africa and played his 124th (122 starts) and last Test for the Springboks versus Italy at Stadio Artemio Franchi, Florence on 19 November 2016. Fittingly, Habana brought the curtain down on his international career by scoring a try, his 67th Test try, but the touring Springboks lost the game 20-18.

As well as the Golden Lions (2003/04 – 21 games, 17 tries) Habana also played club rugby for Blue Bulls (2005–09 – 14 games, nine tries winning the Currie Cup in 2009), Western Province (2010–13 – eight games, two tries winning the 2012 Currie Cup), Bulls (2005–09 – 61 games, 37 tries winning the Super Rugby Championship in 2007 and 2009), Stormers (Super Rugby 2010–13 – 57 games, 19 tries) and Toulon (2013–18 – 66 games, 23 tries winning the Top 14 French League and the Heineken Cup/European Rugby Champions Cup in 2014 and 2015).

Did You Know That?

Bryan's father was a huge Manchester United Football Club fan and named his son after two of their players who helped the team win the 1983 FA Cup Final, their inspirational captain, Bryan Robson, and their South African goalkeeper, Gary Bailey.

RUGBY WORLD CUP QUOTES

'Actually lifting it was neither a real buzz nor an anti-climax. There was a touch of melancholy. It must be how people feel at the top of Everest. They only have 20 minutes there and won't ever be back. The only way back is down. But that melancholy was overwhelmed by joy. It was all pretty amazing.'

David Kirk after captaining New Zealand to victory over France in the inaugural Rugby World Cup Final in 1987

SEEING RED

Ten countries have seen at least one of their players dismissed at a Rugby World Cup and there have been a total of 17 dismissals – Argentina (1), Australia (1), Canada (3), Fiji (1), Namibia (1), Samoa (2), South Africa (2), Tonga (3), Uruguay (1) and Wales (2). The first player to receive a red card was Huw Richards of Wales in the inaugural tournament in 1987. The Welsh lock punched New Zealand lock, Gary Whetton, during his side's 49-6 quarter-final loss and was handed a one-week suspension for his misdemeanour. He missed Wales's final match of the tournament, their third place play-off versus Australia which they won 22-21. In the latter game, Australian flanker, David Codey, was sent off in the fifth minute, the quickest dismissal in the history of the Rugby World Cup. Codey was given a warning by the referee in the first minute of the game for trampling on an opponent and four minutes later he was given his marching orders after trampling on another Welsh player in a ruck. The last player sent off in a Rugby World Cup at the time of writing was the Uruguayan scrum-half, Agustín Ormaechea, against Fiji on 6 October 2015.

Did You Know That?

Three players were dismissed when Canada played South Africa at the 1995 Rugby World Cup – Canada's captain, Gareth Rees, and teammate Rod Snow along with the Springboks' James Dalton. The trio were sent off in the 70th minute of the game which South Africa won 20-0.

BROTHERS IN ARMS

The first pair of brothers to win the Rugby World Cup playing in the same team were twins, Alan and Gary Whetton. The pair helped New Zealand to glory in the inaugural tournament in 1987, a 29-9 win over France in the final at Eden Park, Auckland, New Zealand. Alan and Gary also played in the same Auckland side. Alan played 65 times for the All Blacks (1984–91, 104 points) whilst Gary appeared 101 times for his country (1981–91, 15 as captain, 36 points).

Did You Know That?

The Whetton brothers enjoy the distinction of being the only twins to have played Test rugby together for the All Blacks.

THE BEST XV AT THE 2015 RUGBY WORLD CUP

On 1 November 2015, *The Independent* newspaper published what it considered to be the Best Team of the 2015 Rugby World Cup. Perhaps not surprisingly, six All Blacks made the side in recognition of their contribution to New Zealand becoming the first ever nation to retain the Webb Ellis Cup.

1. Marcos Ayerza (Argentina)
2. Shota Horie (Japan)
3. W. P. Nel (Scotland)
4. Brodie Retallick (New Zealand)
5. Leone Nakarawa (Fiji)
6. Scott Fardy (Australia)
7. Richie McCaw (New Zealand) – Captain
8. David Pocock (Australia)
9. Greig Laidlaw (Scotland)
10. Dan Carter (New Zealand)

11. D. T. H. Van der Merwe (Canada)
12. Ma'a Nonu (New Zealand)
13. Conrad Smith (New Zealand)
14. Santiago Cordero (Argentina)
15. Ben Smith (New Zealand)

Did You Know That?

W. P. Nel was born in Loeriesfontein, a small town in the Northern Cape of South Africa.

RUGBY WORLD CUP WINNERS

Year	Winners	Host Nation(s)
1987	New Zealand	Australia/New Zealand
1991	Australia	England, France, Ireland, Scotland, Wales
1995	South Africa	South Africa
1999	Australia	Wales
2003	England	Australia
2007	South Africa	France
2011	New Zealand	New Zealand
2015	New Zealand	England

Did You Know That?

Japan is one of only three Tier Two countries to have participated in every Rugby World Cup, with the others being Canada and Romania. Of the three, Canada has gone the furthest in the competition, making it to one quarter-final in 1991.

TALKINGRUGBYUNION.COM'S TEAM OF THE 2011 RUGBY WORLD CUP

Backs

15. **Israel Dagg** (New Zealand) – he was impressive in the group stages, but many questioned whether he could perform to the same level come the big pressure matches and the answer was yes. A superb runner who always beats the first man, unflinching under the high ball, an all-round brilliant player. His offload for the Nonu try in the semi-finals was a moment of class.

   Honourable Mention – **Kurtley Beale** (Australia) & **Leigh Halfpenny** (Wales)

14. **Vincent Clerc** (France) – the tournament's joint top scorer was superb in a stuttering French side. Scored a crucial try in the defeat

to Tonga and popped up with a brilliant score against England in the quarter-finals.

Honourable Mention – **Chris Ashton** (England) & **Cory Jane** (New Zealand)

13. **Conrad Smith** (New Zealand) – unquestionably the best 13 in world rugby and in this tournament he was just a class above the rest. The brains in the All Blacks' backline in the absence of Dan Carter, runs silky lines and rarely misses a tackle. Outstanding.

Honourable Mention – **Manu Tuilagi** (England) & **Aurelien Rougerie** (France)

Did You Know That?

Mamuka Gorgodze is nicknamed 'Gorgodzilla' by his former Montpellier teammates, and 'Gulliver' by Georgian fans. Both nicknames reflect his imposing size (6ft 5in, 118kg) and rampaging style of play.

---

12. **Jamie Roberts** (Wales) – the giant centre really returned to the form that made him the star of the 2009 British and Irish Lions tour. When he is going at full tilt he is a very tough man to stop, but he is also a brilliant decoy runner sucking in defences. It's great to see him back to his best after a tough couple of years.

Honourable Mention – **Ma'a Nonu** (New Zealand) & **Francois Steyn** (South Africa)

11. **James O'Connor** (Australia) – a class act on the wing. His intelligent play is really something to behold, when he has the ball he always looks threatening and under the high ball he rarely makes a mistake. His penalty to win the game against South Africa was brilliant.

Honourable Mention – **Richard Kahui** (New Zealand), **Digby Ioane** (Australia) & **George North** (Wales)

10. **Rhys Priestland** (Wales) – it's amazing to think that the young Scarlet only got the 10 jersey after Stephen Jones got injured before the first warm-up game. His game control and composure was incredible for such a young man. His absence in the semi-finals was very noticeable; Wales weren't the same without him.

Honourable Mention – **Dan Carter** (New Zealand) & **Morne Steyn** (South Africa)

9. **Will Genia** (Australia) – the best nine in world rugby. Despite his fly-half having a rough time Genia never looked flustered and gave

his side some direction. His kicking game has really developed and his distribution is second to none.

Honourable Mention – **Mike Phillips** (Wales) & **Dimitri Yachvili** (France)

Forwards

1. **Tony Woodcock** (New Zealand) – brilliant in the loose and solid in the tight. Was a crucial part of the win over Australia, and was the unlikely hero scoring the only try in the final. He has had a brilliant tournament and the All Blacks aren't the same without him.

   Honourable Mention – **Cian Healy** (Ireland) & **Gethin Jenkins** (Wales)

2. **William Servat** (France) – the experienced Frenchman is a master of the line-out and scrum. He was shaky at times in the group stages, but like most of the French side he came alive in the knockouts.

   Honourable Mention – **Bismarck Du Plessis** (South Africa) & **Keven Mealamu** (New Zealand)

3. **Nicolas Mas** (France) – missed some of the group games, and it is no shock that his return coincided with France's return to form. A world class scrummager who destroyed England, and in the final he got the better of Woodcock on more than one occasion.

   Honourable Mention – **Owen Franks** (New Zealand) & **Martin Castrogiovanni** (Italy)

4. **Brad Thorn** (New Zealand) – the veteran lock could not have asked for a better way to bow out of international rugby. He was man of the match in the semi-final, disrupts every ruck and tackles his heart out. A proper old-fashioned lock.

5. **Luke Charteris** (Wales) – the most improved player this year. His work around the ruck is incredible, smashing anything in his way. At the line-out he rarely puts a foot wrong and like Thorn he tackles like a demon. Another great Welsh performer.

   Honourable Mention – **Danie Rossouw** (South Africa), **James Horwill** (Australia) & **Victor Matfield** (South Africa)

6. **Thierry Dusautoir** (France) – the newly crowned IRB Player of the Year was heroic in the final. Not much more can be said about this man, he tackles everything that is unfortunate enough to cross his path. An inspirational leader, he almost carried his side to the biggest shock in World Cup history.

   Honourable Mention – **Jerome Kaino** (New Zealand) & **Stephen Ferris** (Ireland)

7. **Richie McCaw** (New Zealand) – when Carter was injured New Zealand found a way to cope, but without McCaw they would never have won the World Cup. In the semi-final he got the better of David Pocock; whenever a turnover needs to be won you can guarantee McCaw will win it. Carried his side up the mountain even though he was injured; still the king of the breakdown.

   Honourable Mention – **Sam Warburton** (Wales), **David Pocock** (Australia), **Sean O'Brien** (Ireland) & **Mamuka Gorgodze** (Georgia)

8. **Imanol Harinordoquy** (France) – didn't really get a game in the groups but when he was recalled for the England game, he was colossal. King of the line-out for *Les Bleus* and in contact he is a ferocious ball carrier. Against the Kiwis he produced one of the games of his life, and his efforts were almost rewarded with a winners' medal.

   Honourable Mention – **Kieran Read** (New Zealand) & **Toby Faletau** (Wales)

RAINBOW NATION

The term 'Rainbow Nation' was first heard a year before South Africa hosted the Rugby World Cup finals in 1995. In 1994, the African National Congress won South Africa's first free democratic election by a landslide margin. Archbishop Desmond Tutu coined the phrase 'Rainbow People of God', to describe the population of South Africa shortly after the 1994 election. Tutu was the Archbishop of Cape Town (1986–96) at the time, the first indigenous black African to hold the position, and he regularly referred to 'the Rainbow People of God' during his sermons. The word rainbow alludes to the Book of Genesis and the Biblical story of Noah's flood, God's decision to return the Earth to its watery pre-creation state and then remake it in a reversal of creation, an ensuing rainbow of peace. The word has significant meaning in the African Xhosa culture where 'umnayama' means hope and a bright future. In political terms, the word symbolises the coming together as one of the South Africa people, a unity of many diverse cultures.

   Within weeks of becoming the President of South Africa (10 May 1994–14 June 1999), President Nelson Mandela used the term in a speech to the nation: 'Each of us is as intimately attached to the soil of this beautiful country as are the famous jacaranda trees of Pretoria and the mimosa trees of the bushveld – a rainbow nation at peace with itself and the world.'

THE WINNING CAPTAINS

Year	Winners	Captain
1987	New Zealand	David Kirk
1991	Australia	Nick Farr-Jones
1995	South Africa	Francois Pienaar
1999	Australia	John Eales
2003	England	Martin Johnson
2007	South Africa	John Smit
2011	New Zealand	Richie McCaw
2015	New Zealand	Richie McCaw

SCORING BY THE NUMBERS

At the 2011 Rugby World Cup finals in New Zealand, a total of 2,245 points were scored in the 48 matches played, giving an average of 47 points per game; 181 converted tries (1,267 points), 81 unconverted tries (405 points), 171 penalties (513 points) and 20 drop goals (60 points).

These scoring statistics show that 58% of the total points came from tries in comparison to the tries scored in the previous tournaments: 1987 – 55%, 1991 – 51%, 1995 – 53%, 1999 – 59%, 2003 – 59% and 2007 – 52%. The average points per game in 2011 was 47 in comparison to 1987 – 58, 1991 – 42, 1995 – 54, 1999 – 60, 2003 – 59 and 2007 – 52. However, there were fewer tries and fewer penalty goals per game at the 2011 Rugby World Cup finals than in any of the previous six editions.

INDELIBLE MARK

England World Cup winner Phil Vickery sports an oriental tattoo which means 'I'll fight you to the death'.

IN HIS OWN WORDS

'Greatness is a lot of small things done well every day.'

Jason Robinson, Rugby World Cup winner with England in 2003

WORLD CUP FEVER

In the mid-20th century, nearly every major sport, and many minor ones, launched world championships. Even those with a regular place in the Olympics found such an event profitable both in financial and public relations terms. The Football World Cup began in 1930, the Handball World Championships in 1938, the Rugby League World Cup in 1954, the Orienteering World Championships in 1966, Men's Field Hockey World Cup in 1971 and Cricket (limited-overs) World Cup in 1975. Yet into the 1980s, the International Rugby Football Board (IRFB) refused to even think about a Rugby World Cup. Such a tournament would inevitably bring money into the game, with unknown consequences, and the fact that rugby's professional rival, league, now had a world cup was another reason the IRFB opposed the idea.

With rugby league having shown it could be done, though, whispers of a Rugby World Cup were heard occasionally. In the 1960s the former Australian Test player Harold Tolhurst and Manly club stalwart Jock Kellaher, suggested finding a world champion by holding a month-long tournament in Australia. Great Britain, France, South Africa and New Zealand would fight it out with the home side. The IRFB was not amused. In 1968, the IRFB reiterated its opposition to anything resembling the football World Cup. Even competitions to find national club or regional champions were seen as contrary to the spirit of the game. Only France among rugby powers had a National Championships until 1968, when South Africa's Currie Cup became an annual event. New Zealand launched its Provincial Championships in 1976, but clubs in the British Isles still only played friendlies.

In 1979, Bill McLaughlin, the president of the Australian Rugby Union, asked the IRFB for permission to host a Rugby World Cup to mark Australia's bicentennial celebrations in 1988. The IRFB refused and went further by informing all eight of its member unions not to plan or attend any such competition. Not only did the sport's governing body believe that the underlying amateur principle of rugby would be affected but they were also opposed to a Rugby World Cup being organised by commercial interests.

By the early 1980s winds of change were threatening to blow in the house of cards of amateur rugby. The debacle of the 1981 Springbok tour of New Zealand, the simultaneous FIFA Football World Cup qualifying success of New Zealand's All Whites and the continuing loss of Australia's top union players to league were all signs that rugby was vulnerable even in its southern hemisphere strongholds.

In 1982, the South African Rugby Board (SARB), now effectively isolated from world rugby as a result of that country's apartheid policies, threatened to launch a professional circuit. The same year, nine Australian players refused to tour New Zealand because the daily allowance they were offered was so small. In 1983, Australian David Lord hatched a plan to pay more than 200 top players to play in a travelling eight-nation competition, but it didn't get off the ground. This was an attempt to emulate his countryman Kerry Packer's World Series Cricket, which had revolutionised another staid English-dominated game. Lord had no backer with deep pockets, and pay-per-view television did not yet exist in several of the key markets. In response, both the Australian Rugby Union and the New Zealand Rugby Union wrote separately to the IRFB in 1983 seeking their authority to plan and host a Rugby World Cup – New Zealand aiming to host a tournament in 1987 and Australia the following year. Again the IRFB was steadfast in refusing. In 1984, the Fédération Française de Rugby (FFR) submitted another proposal to the IRFB to host a Rugby World Cup. Forced to do *something*, the IRFB asked Australia and New Zealand to come up with a feasibility study. With 1987 the only southern winter free of major sports events for the rest of the decade, there was no time to waste. If a Rugby World Cup was not approved at the IRFB's March 1985 meeting, the concept would go on the back burner for years.

On 1 December 1984, Australia and New Zealand embarked on a joint feasibility study. On 20 March 1985, the findings were presented at the French railways headquarters in Paris at the annual board meeting of the IRFB. Each one of the eight IRFB member nations had a single vote and the motion to stage a Rugby World Cup was sanctioned by six votes in favour (Australia, England, France, New Zealand, South Africa, Wales) to two votes against (Ireland and Scotland). Even though they voted in favour, South Africa would not be permitted to participate in the tournament due to their ongoing political situation and apartheid regime. Ireland and Scotland voted against the proposal claiming that it threatened the sport's amateur status. Danie Craven, the president of the South African Rugby Board (1956–93), and an IRFB delegate, thought ahead. He realised that favours given at no real cost now might well pay off later. His decision to support the proposal in effect guaranteed that South Africa would later host a similar tournament – if the first one succeeded and apartheid was relaxed. The wily former Springbok captain (16 Tests, 1931–38) thus set the stage for the 1995 Rugby World Cup (won by South Africa at home), which cemented the place of rugby, until then a symbol of Afrikaner supremacy, in the multicultural nation.

The FFR president Albert Ferrasse decided to vote for a Rugby World Cup provided non-IRFB countries were included. Consequently, a body with no paid staff, or even any money to call its own, had just two years to organise rugby's first global tournament. Argentina were offered South Africa's place and duly accepted whilst invitations were issued to Canada, Fiji, Italy, Japan, Romania, Tonga, USA and Zimbabwe, who all accepted. It was agreed that the inaugural tournament comprising 16 teams would be staged jointly by Australia and New Zealand from 22 May to 20 June 1987. The IRFB decided upon 1987 so the inaugural tournament did not coincide with the 1988 Summer Olympic Games which was being hosted by Seoul, South Korea or the 1990 FIFA World Football Cup which was taking place in Italy.

New Zealand and Australia staged a successful tournament, largely thanks to a host of volunteers. The timing was fortunate. Volunteerism would soon decline in the sporting sector, as elsewhere, in response to the same economic forces that were promoting professional rugby. The crowds for pool matches were larger than many expected. Hundreds of millions watched on television around the world, and the tournament made a profit. In the end the IRFB had conceded ground on several issues that might have blighted the Rugby World Cup. The players' daily allowance was increased. A complaint that the All Black captain had been paid to appear in a television advertisement was quietly shelved after the advertisement was pulled from the air. Now the IRFB was accepting large sums of money from sponsors, it seemed hypocritical to insist that players receive no payment for rugby-related activities either on or off the field. Rugby had established itself as a commercial market, and the financial viability of the Rugby World Cup concept was assured. Some purists now argued that holding a regular Rugby

World Cup – the second one would be held in the northern hemisphere in 1991 – would help stave off professional rugby. How wrong they were would become clear in 1995.

Therefore, from tentative beginnings in 1987, the Rugby World Cup has become established as one of the world's major international sporting events. World Cups have since also been held for women's rugby and at age-group level. The first women's event was staged in Wales in 1991 in defiance of the patriarchs of the IRFB who did not recognise it. The USA defeated England 19-6 in the final at the Cardiff RFC grounds in front of 3,000 fans.

Did You Know That?

The Rugby World Cup is now firmly regarded as the eighth-biggest sporting event in the world: 1. Olympic Games, 2. FIFA World Cup, 3. UEFA Champions League, 4. Formula 1, 5. Super Bowl, 6. Wimbledon, 7. Tour de France, 8. Rugby World Cup, 9. Cricket World Cup, 10. NBA.

THE HAKA

Ask any sports fan what they consider to be sport's greatest and most iconic pre-match ritual and most will respond 'the Haka'. New Zealand perform their ceremonial Haka before every international and it is feared and respected by opponents and loved by fans of all rugby nations. However, the Haka is not just a rugby war dance; it is any form of Maori ceremonial dancing which includes a celebration or a welcome to guests. It is a ritual which is embedded in Maori culture and mythology and is believed to have originated from Tane-rore, the son of the Sun God, Tama-nui-te-ra, and his second wife, Hine-raumati, the Summer maid. The trembling hand action performed during the Haka is a physical representation of the shimmering air referred to in *Te haka a Tanerore*. The Maoris believe that when the land is very hot the air shimmers. The newest Haka, *Kapa o Pango*, (meaning 'Team in Black') was specifically written in 2005 for the All Blacks and its composer pointed out that it has nothing whatsoever to do with war.

'It's ceremonial. It's about building your physical, spiritual and intellectual capacity prior to doing something very important. This is not a war dance. It's about building the confidence inwardly. It's a preparation,' said its composer Professor Derek Lardelli, who is an expert in Maori customs and cultural advisor to the national team. Lardelli's Haka includes references to the symbol of New Zealand rugby, the Silver Fern, and calls on the players to dominate and show their supremacy.

The Haka was first witnessed in rugby in Australia in 1884 and came to prominence four years later when a team of Maori players toured England, Ireland, Wales, Australia and New Zealand in 1888/89. However, it was not always a feature of All Blacks rugby over the following 130 years, particularly when the team did not contain several Maori players. In 1905, it was performed before most games played outside New Zealand but was not a constant until 1987 when it became a pre-match ritual in New Zealand. When the All Blacks toured the United Kingdom and Ireland in 1974, the Haka was only performed once in the 26 games they played. The Haka is usually led by a player with Maori heritage but this is not always the case. The *Kapa o Pango* was led in 2005 by Tana Umaga, who was born in New Zealand and is of Samoan descent, and more recently by TJ Perenara who was born in New Zealand. Graham Henry, the coach of the All Blacks from 2004–11, said the *Kapa o Pango* represented modern New Zealand with its Maori, Pacific nations (Fiji, Samoa and Tonga) and European heritage, saying: 'We felt it was a great representation of the unity of the group.'

The most famous Haka is called the *Ka Mate* and was written circa 1820 by the head of the Ngati Toa Rangatira tribe and was first performed before an All Blacks game in 1906. Over the next 99 years it was the most-used Haka, although other versions were composed for particular tours.

New Zealand is not the only nation to perform a ceremonial dance before a match. Fiji first performed their own dance, the *Cibi*, on a tour to New Zealand in 1939. In 2012, Fiji adopted a new war cry, the *Bole*. Meanwhile, Samoa perform the *Siva Tau*, and Tonga perform the *Sipi Tau*.

Did You Know That?

Many players do not like having to watch the Haka or are intimidated by the All Blacks performing it. England's Richard Cockerill had to be pulled away by his captain, Lawrence Dallaglio, in 1997 when he squared up to Norm Hewitt during the Haka. In 2008, Wales refused to turn away at the end of the Haka to start the game at the Millennium Stadium, Cardiff. The All Blacks usually wait for their opponents to turn away first but the Welsh players stood their ground. Prior to the 2011 Rugby World Cup Final France were fined £2,500 for advancing towards the All Blacks and crossing over the halfway line.

BIG NUMBERS DOWN UNDER

During the 2003 Rugby World Cup finals, hosted by Australia, the total stadium attendance was 1,837,547 whilst the television viewing figures for the final, in which England defeated Australia 20-17 after extra time, was 300 million.

IN HIS OWN WORDS

'I think Brian Moore's gnashers are the kind you get in a DIY shop and hammer in yourself. He's the only player we have who looks like a Frenchman!'

Paul Rendall,
England Rugby World Cup squad 1987 and 1991

FIRST BABY-FACED AWARD WINNER

In the week before the 2015 Rugby World Cup Final, World Rugby announced the shortlist for the inaugural Breakthrough Player of the Year award, with the winner set to be revealed at the World Rugby Awards dinner at Battersea Evolution, London, on 1 November.

In order to be eligible for the award, players must have played less than one year of senior international rugby. The nominees were selected by an independent panel, comprising former Wallaby scrum-half George Gregan, former Argentina captain Felipe Contepomi and journalists Stephen Jones, Sarah Mockford and Jim Kayes.

With some of the world's exciting young players leaving their mark on the 2015 tournament, the three nominees for this prestigious award were Scotland centre Mark Bennett, Georgia scrum-half Vasil Lobzhanidze and New Zealand winger Nehe Milner-Skudder.

Mark Bennett (Scotland) – the highly-rated centre made his Test debut in the win over Argentina in November 2014, having previously represented Scotland at age grade level and sevens. One of only five players to start every Six Nations match in 2015, Bennett recovered from a shoulder injury to make the Scotland squad for the 2015 tournament and again proved a danger in the Scottish midfield, scoring twice in the win over Japan and once against Australia in Scotland's controversial 35-34 quarter-final defeat. The 22-year-old started all 13 of his Tests in a young Scottish backline.

Vasil Lobzhanidze (Georgia) – the diminutive scrum-half made his Test debut against Germany in the European Nations Cup on 7 February 2015 and quickly established himself as his country's number one. He wrote his name into the Rugby World Cup history books when he started Georgia's opening win over Tonga, becoming the youngest player in the tournament's history at 18 years and 340 days. Lobzhanidze also played against New Zealand and Namibia to help Georgia secure qualification for the 2019 Rugby World Cup finals, all only four months after he inspired his country to a first World Rugby Under-20 Trophy title.

Nehe Milner-Skudder – a stand-out for the Hurricanes in his debut Super Rugby season in 2015, earning comparisons with his childhood idol Christian Cullen. The full-back cum winger forced himself into the mind of All Blacks selectors as a result and made the most of his chance, scoring twice on his debut against Australia in the Rugby Championship. The 24-year-old started five matches in the 2015 World Cup and continued his penchant for try-scoring doubles, crossing twice against both Namibia and Tonga in Pool C and then once in the quarter-final win against France. Milner-Skudder scored New Zealand's first try in their 34-17 win over the Wallabies in the 2015 Rugby World Cup Final, going over in the far right corner just before half-time, and was named the World Rugby Breakthrough Player of the Year.

Gregan, a Rugby World Cup winner with Australia in 1999, said: 'All three nominees have been outstanding in their own individual performance and shown consistency which has seen them contribute in a huge way to how their teams have performed this year. They are all worthy candidates for this award but unfortunately there can only be one winner. I'm sure all three players have a bright future not only for their teams and the countries they play for but for world rugby in general. I really look forward to watching their careers.'

Did You Know That?

During the 2015 World Rugby Awards ceremony, Japan's final try (scored by Karne Hesketh in the last minute of the game) and their 34-32 victory against South Africa were named the World Cup Best Match Moment, while Rugby World Cup sponsors, Société Générale, named their Dream Team of the Tournament, which included Milner-Skudder at No.14, right wing.

2007 TRY OF THE YEAR

At the 2007 Rugby World Cup finals, Takudzwa Ngwenya's try for the USA in their 64-15 Pool A loss to South Africa at Stade de la Mosson, Montpellier, France, which he scored from his own half after side-stepping Bryan Habana, was named the Try of the Year in international rugby by the International Rugby Players' Association.

Did You Know That?

Ngwenya was born in Harare, Zimbabwe.

BILLY WILLIAMS' CABBAGE PATCH

In 1906, all-round sportsman and property entrepreneur, William Williams, was charged by the Rugby Football Union to find a home ground for the England game. Williams purchased a 10.25 acre (four hectare) market garden in Twickenham in 1907 for £5,500 12s 6d. His choice of site was immediately dubbed 'Billy Williams' Cabbage Patch'. Despite huge difficulties, two covered stands were eventually built east and west of the pitch and the ground was opened on Saturday, 9 October 1909 to less than 2,000 spectators who turned out to see the new ground's tenants, Harlequins, beat Richmond 14-10. The stadium's architect was John Bradley.

The first international match to be played at Twickenham took place on 15 January 1910 when England beat Wales for the first time since 2 April 1898 (a 14-7 win at Rectory Field, London in the 1898 Home Nations Championship), ending a 12-year losing streak. The home side won 11-6 in what was the first Five Nations Championship. The England side quickly found success in its new home and went on to win the 1910 Five Nations Championship, clinching the title by a single point from runners-up, Wales. England then shared the title with Ireland in 1912, and won the Triple Crown twice (1913 and 1914) before the outbreak of World War One in 1914. When the hostilities in Europe commenced on 28 July 1914, the RFU suspended play for the duration of the war and mothballed the stadium.

The first Varsity match was played in December 1921 with Oxford defeating Cambridge. By this time the popularity of Twickenham had soared. Extra accommodation was found in a North Stand built in 1925 by the legendary football stadium architect, Archibald Leitch. By 1931, the famous 'Twickenham Look' had come about. This comprised a huge slab of concrete forming the South Terrace, Leitch's North Stand, and two great double-decker East and West Stands that spoilt the view from Richmond Hill. At the outbreak of World War Two, Twickenham Stadium became a Civil Defence Depot, with special responsibilities as a decontamination centre in the event of a chemical attack on London. The closest the stadium got to being hit by enemy action was in July 1944 when a V1 flying bomb fell in the front garden of a house opposite the West Gate, injuring 16 people.

After the war, and for the next three decades, Twickenham Stadium lagged behind other large grounds in all areas of development. In 1981, a South Stand was built, followed in the 1990s by new North, East and West stands. The 'concrete horseshoe' was completed in 1995 exactly 100 years after the issue of amateurism split the Rugby Football Union in two and almost destroyed the English game. In 2005, the Rugby Football Union celebrated the centenary of the idea to build England's national stadium, which was realised in Twickenham.

PLAY THE GAME

Jonah Lomu Rugby was a video game which was developed by Rage Software and published by Codemasters. It was released in 1997. Commentary for the game was supplied by Bill McLaren and Bill Beaumont.

A NEW DAWN FOR SOUTH AFRICAN SPORT

The 1995 Rugby World Cup finals was the first major sporting event to be held in South Africa following the end of apartheid. It was also the first time South Africa competed in the tournament. Due to the political problems in the country at the time, the 1995 Rugby World Cup was a test for South Africa's new president, Nelson Mandela, to try and unite his divided nation. With South Africa seemingly on the brink of civil war, Mandela asked his people to come together to support the Springboks.

The final between New Zealand and South Africa saw the best attack come up against the best defence. The All Blacks went into the showpiece having scored 315 points in the tournament, with the home nation only conceding 55. Without a try scored in the opening 80 minutes, they went into extra time locked at 9-9. Both sides scored penalties during the first half of extra time but it was Joel Stransky's drop goal which secured South Africa the Rugby World Cup in front of a sell-out crowd at Ellis Park, Johannesburg. The image of Mandela wearing a No.6 Springbok jersey and baseball cap, handing over the Webb Ellis Cup to the South Africa captain, Francois Pienaar, is still one of the most memorable in sporting history.

HOME ADVANTAGE

Only two nations have won the Rugby World Cup on their home soil, New Zealand in 1987 and again in 2011 and South Africa in 1995. England (1991) and Australia (2003) finished runners-up on home soil.

> ### *Did You Know That?*
> Wales (1991) and England (2015) share the record for the worst performance as hosts/co-hosts, exiting at the group stage.

WOLVES WITHOUT ANY BITE

Portugal, nicknamed *Los Lobos* (the Wolves), have only qualified for the Rugby World Cup once, in 2007 when they played in Pool C along with Italy, New Zealand, Romania and Scotland (lost all four games). Portugal were the surprise winners of the 2013/14 European Nations Cup which also featured Czech Republic, Georgia, Romania, Russia and Spain. The 2013/14 European Nations Cup was the fourth edition of the newly reformed European Championship for Tier Two and Three rugby union nations.

> ### *Did You Know That?*
> In 2016, the European Nations Cup changed its name to the Rugby Europe International Championships.

M'LORD

The former England lock, Ben Kay, was nicknamed 'M'Lord' because his late father, Sir John Kay, was a Lord Justice of Appeal in the United Kingdom's Appeals Court.

ENGLAND CLEAN UP

England completed a clean sweep of trophies in 2003, winning the Calcutta Cup, Millennium Trophy, Triple Crown, Six Nations (Grand Slam) and the Rugby World Cup. At the 2003 World Rugby Awards ceremony, England were named IRB International Team of the Year,

Clive Woodward won the IRB International Coach of the Year award and Jonny Wilkinson was named the IRB International Player of the Year.

SAMBA BEAT

Argentina and Uruguay are the only South American countries to have played in a Rugby World Cup. Argentina have been ever present, including qualification for the 2019 edition, whilst Uruguay participated in 1999 and 2003 and also qualified for the 2019 edition.

EVER PRESENT

Since the inaugural Rugby World Cup in 1987, only 12 countries will have contested every tournament including the 2019 Rugby World Cup: Argentina, Australia, Canada, England, France, Ireland, Italy, Japan, New Zealand, Romania, Scotland and Wales. The 1987 Rugby World Cup was contested by 16 countries including Fiji, Tonga and Zimbabwe. A total of 25 nations have qualified for at least one Rugby World Cup finals tournament. From 1987 until 2011, each tournament featured at least one debuting country, but 2015 was the first time no new nation made its debut.

Did You Know That?

The first game of rugby played in Canada took place in 1865 when British soldiers of the Victoria Regiment played students from McGill University in Montreal.

IN HIS OWN WORDS

'Firstly, I have to listen to my body. I've always maintained that when my body tells me it's time to retire, I would. I also want to give the opportunity to other players to develop and play their best for Samoa. Most importantly, I want to spend time with my family. Being a professional rugby player is a very demanding job. Most of the time I'm separated from my wife and my children and I'm always travelling. But I'm at that stage now where I want to focus on other things in life outside rugby.'

Brian Lima after announcing his international retirement, Samoa 1991–2007

BBC SPORT'S TEAM OF THE 2003 RUGBY WORLD CUP

15. Mils Muliaina (New Zealand)
14. Rupeni Caucaunibuca (Fiji)
13. Stirling Mortlock (Australia)
12. Tony Marsh (France)

11. Lote Tuqiri (Australia)
10. Jonny Wilkinson (England)
 9. Fabien Galthie (France)
 1. Bill Young (Australia)
 2. Keith Wood (Ireland)
 3. Phil Vickery (England)
 4. Martin Johnson (England)
 5. Paul O'Connell (Ireland)
 6. George Smith (Australia)
 7. Joe van Niekerk (South Africa)
 8. Lawrence Dallaglio (England)

THE 1991 RUGBY WORLD CUP FINALS

The second Rugby World Cup finals was co-hosted by five countries – England, France, Ireland, Scotland and Wales – and once again 16 teams participated. Unlike the inaugural tournament in Australia and New Zealand in 1987, the International Rugby Board (IRB) invited all member unions to enter qualifying rounds. The eight quarter-finalists in 1987 (Australia, England, Fiji, France, Ireland, New Zealand, Scotland and Wales) were automatically guaranteed berths. The remaining eight slots were contested by 25 countries, with South Africa still banned from the tournament because of its apartheid system. Four regional qualifying competitions were held which resulted in the following eight nations progressing to the 1991 Rugby World Cup finals: Africa – Zimbabwe; Americas – Argentina, Canada and United States; Asia & Oceania – Japan and Western Samoa; Europe – Italy and Romania. This meant that 15 of the 16 teams which competed in 1987 also competed in 1991 along with Western Samoa, who qualified ahead of Tonga.

The All Blacks won Pool 1 with England runners-up whilst Scotland and Ireland dominated Pool 2. Newcomers Western Samoa finished runners-up to Australia in Pool 3 with impressive victories against Wales and Argentina. Fiji had a disappointing tournament, finishing bottom of Pool 4 after losing all three of their games: Canada 13-3 (pool runners-up), France 33-9 (pool winners) and Romania 17-15.

The quarter-finals did not produce any shocks with all four favoured teams reaching the semi-finals: England 19-10 France (Parc des Princes, Paris, France), Scotland 28-6 Western Samoa (Murrayfield Stadium, Edinburgh, Scotland), Australia 19-18 Ireland (Lansdowne Road, Dublin, Ireland) and New Zealand 29-13 Canada (Stadium Lille-Métropole, Villeneuve-d'Ascq, France). The semi-finals paired the two northern hemisphere teams together and the two southern hemisphere teams together. England beat Scotland 9-6 in a scrappy affair at Murrayfield whilst the Wallabies defeated the defending world champions, the All Blacks, 16-6 at Lansdowne Road. A new name would be inscribed on the Webb Ellis Cup.

Four days before the final, New Zealand beat Scotland 13-6 in the third place play-off at Cardiff Arms Park. The final took place at Twickenham Stadium on 2 November 1991 with the home nation hoping to see off the power of Australia. Throughout the tournament England had relied on their forwards and the reliable boot of Jonathan Webb (four conversions, seven penalties and a try in the pool games; one conversion and three penalties in the quarter-final and two penalties in the semi-final). The Wallabies' David Campese, who won the Player of the Tournament award, criticised England's style of play in the press. When it came to the final, England altered their game plan and decided to run at the Wallabies' defence. It backfired and Australia won the game 12-6 thanks to a try scored by Tony Daly and converted by Michael Lynagh, who also kicked two penalties. Webb scored two penalties for England and the Webb Ellis Cup was presented to the Australian captain, Nick Farr-Jones.

After the final whistle, some of the players were asked for their views of the game.

'For some reason we definitely allowed ourselves to be conned a little bit again by the Aussie psychology. Bob Dwyer did a job on us in terms of, "It'll be terrible for the game (of rugby) if England were to win the World Cup: they're boring; they'll take the game back 20 years." Will (Carling) and I have disagreed on this for a number of years; we did change our tactics, we got it wrong,' said Rob Andrew, England's fly-half.

'Anyone who has played rugby will realise if a little back decides to change tactics and the forwards don't agree with you, there's no way you're changing tactics. We didn't want to get into a tactical kicking game and the thinking was let's actually try and play with ball in hand a little bit more,' said Will Carling, the England captain.

'You can't change your style of tactic overnight – you've either got it or you haven't,' said David Campese, the Australia wing.

Final – 2 November 1991
Twickenham Stadium, London, England
Australia 12-6 England
Australia: Marty Roebuck; Bob Egerton, Jason Little, Tim Horan, David Campese; Michael Lynagh, Nick Farr-Jones (c); Tony Daly, Phil Kearns, Ewen McKenzie, John Eales, Rod McCall, Willie Ofahengaue, Simon Poidevin, Troy Coker.
England: Jonathan Webb; Simon Halliday, Jerry Guscott, Will Carling (c), Rory Underwood; Rob Andrew, Richard Hill; Jason Leonard, Brian Moore, Jeff Probyn, Paul Ackford, Wade Dooley, Mickey Skinner, Peter Winterbottom, Mike Teague.

Australia	England
Try Daly	Pens Webb 2
Con Lynagh	
Pens Lynagh 2	

Referee: Derek Bevan (Wales)
Attendance: 56,208

GEORGIA ON MY MIND

Georgia have played in four Rugby World Cups (2003, 2007, 2011 and 2015) and qualified for the 2019 edition. Their best ever finish was 12th in 2015 and they recorded their first ever World Cup win in 2007 when they defeated Namibia 30-0. To date there have been 16 editions of the European Nations Cup (2000–16)/Rugby Europe International Championships (2016 to date) and Georgia have won the tournament a record ten times (Romania five wins, Portugal one win).

TOP OF THE POPS 1991

When Australia won the second Rugby World Cup Final on 2 November 1991, the No.1 song in the UK pop charts was *The Fly* by U2. It was the Irish band's second UK No.1 and was taken from their album *Achtung Baby*. The song only occupied the top slot for a single week before being ousted by Vic Reeves and the Wonder Stuff with *Dizzy*.

A FALL FROM GRACE

Brendan Venter won a Rugby World Cup winners' medal with South Africa when he came on as replacement for James Small in the 1995 final played at Ellis Park, Johannesburg, South Africa. However, four years later at the 1999 Rugby World Cup finals he was sent off against Uruguay in a pool match at Hampden Park, Glasgow, Scotland for stamping and was replaced by Pieter Muller for the rest of the tournament.

> ### Did You Know That?
> After the 1995 Rugby World Cup Final the sport turned professional but Venter continued to practise as a doctor.

NO SOUTHERN HEMISPHERE DOUBLE

No team has won the Rugby World Cup and the Tri-Nations/Rugby Championship in the same year. The Tri-Nations was a southern hemisphere tournament which ran from 1996–2011 and was contested by Australia, New Zealand and South Africa. New Zealand won the inaugural Tri-Nations with Australia claiming the last edition of the tournament. In 2012, Argentina were invited to participate and it changed its name to the Rugby Championship with New Zealand its first ever champions.

Australia won the 1999 Rugby World Cup but were runners-up to the All Blacks in the Tri-Nations; South Africa lifted the Rugby World Cup in 2007 but only managed the wooden spoon in the Tri-Nations; the All Blacks won the Rugby World Cup in 2011 and in 2015 but were runners-up to the Wallabies in the 2011 Tri-Nations and in the 2015 Rugby Championship. New Zealand won 10 Tri-Nations (two wooden spoons), Australia three (four wooden spoons) and South Africa three (ten wooden spoons). In 2018, the All Blacks won their sixth Rugby Championship whilst Australia are the only other winners of it (2015). In the first seven editions of the Rugby Championship, 2012-18, Argentina have won the wooden spoon on six occasions with the Springboks being handed it in 2015.

> ### Did You Know That?
> When it was known as the Tri-Nations, three other trophies were up for grabs: the Bledisloe Cup (Australia v New Zealand), the Nelson Mandela Challenge Plate (Australia v South Africa) and the Freedom Cup (New Zealand v South Africa). From 2012, the Puma Trophy was included which was first contested by Argentina and Australia in 2000.

EDEN PARK, AUCKLAND, NEW ZEALAND

The inaugural IRFB Rugby World Cup Final was played on 20 June 1987 at Eden Park, Auckland, New Zealand. On 23 October 2011, Eden Park became the first ground to host two Rugby World Cup Finals.

In 1902, Harry Ryan, a young, passionate cricketer, stood on Kingsland Road and looked out over a rough paddock. It was strewn with stones, rocky outcrops and cowpats with a low-lying swamp at the bottom. He saw a cricket ground. This was to become Eden Park. Ryan and friends initially leased the land and the Eden Cricket Club was formed. In 1910 the Park became the home of Auckland Cricket and then Auckland Rugby Union leased the Park in 1914, officially making Eden Park its home in 1925. A trust was set up in 1926 providing a group of trustees to manage Eden Park primarily for the benefit of Auckland Cricket and Auckland Rugby. Eden Park Trust manages the Park today. The vision of the founders of Eden Park and the unflinching dedication, sacrifice and personal commitment of those who have followed in their footsteps has resulted in a state-of-the-art international stadium of which Auckland and all New Zealand can be proud. In the successful bid for the 2011 Rugby World Cup, Eden Park received its first public funding grant to redevelop the Southern and Eastern Stands.

Significant events that have occurred at the Park
2015: Cricket World Cup
2014: Wellington Phoenix hosted West Ham United (EPL football)
2014: Inaugural Dick Smith NRL Auckland Nines
2011: Rugby World Cup Final
2002: Visit by the Dalai Lama
1988: Rugby League World Cup Final
1983: Visit by the Prince and Princess of Wales
1974: Russian Olympic gymnastic display
1970: The public welcome to the royal family
1966: Visit by the Queen Mother
1964: New Zealand v India hockey
1963: International Athletics Sports Meeting
1962: New Zealand Secondary School athletics
1961-63: Agfa International Athletic Meetings
1957: New Zealand v Austria soccer 1935: New Zealand v India hockey
1950: British Empire (now Commonwealth) Games
1947: Auckland Schools' Champion of Champions
New Zealand v South Africa soccer
1935: New Zealand v India hockey

Did You Know That?

The final game of the 1981 Springbok tour was played at Eden Park on 12 September 1981. A low-flying Cessna 172 piloted by Marx Jones and Grant Cole dropped flour bombs on to the field as part of widespread protests against the tour and apartheid.

ALWAYS THERE

The winners of the Five or Six Nations have never failed to reach at least the quarter-final stages of the Rugby World Cup in the same year.

Year	Five/Six Nations Winners	Rugby World Cup finish
1987	France	Runners-up
1991	England	Runners-up
1995	England	Semi-finals
1999	Scotland	Quarter-finals
2003	England	Winners
2007	France	Semi-finals
2011	England	Quarter-finals
2015	Ireland	Quarter-finals

Ireland is the only host nation (co-hosts in 1991) which has not reached the semi-finals of the Rugby World Cup. Scotland lost the bronze medal match against New Zealand in 1991 when they were co-hosts whilst Wales, co-hosts in 1991 and host nation in 1999, won the bronze medal in 1991 and lost the bronze medal match in 2011. South Africa and New Zealand (twice) have both won the Webb Ellis Cup on home soil, whilst France, hosts in 2007, lost the bronze medal match to Argentina that year.

Did You Know That?

England hosted the 2015 Rugby World Cup but didn't make it out of their pool.

RUGBY WORLD CUP QUOTES

'Jeez, I would have loved to have won a World Cup, more than anything. But I think, in all honesty, they were a better side.'

England captain, Will Carling, after Australia defeated England 12-6 in the 1991 Rugby World Cup Final played at Twickenham Stadium, London

VISITORS TO MIDDLE-EARTH

On 22 November 2011, a month on from the All Blacks lifting the Webb Ellis Cup for a third time, Statistics NZ reported that 133,000 visitors to the country had ticked a box on their arrival cards to say they were visiting New Zealand to attend a 2011 Rugby World Cup game. Pre-tournament predictions estimated 95,000 rugby fans would travel to the 'Home of Middle-earth'. An estimated NZ$269 million (£142,321,893) was received from ticket sales, NZ$188 million (£99,463,513) of it from Kiwis. Meanwhile, the NZ$81 million spent by visitors on match tickets clawed back just 54% of the NZ$150 million (£79,361,334) hosting fee which the New Zealand Rugby Union had to pay the International Rugby Board. It was claimed that the tournament organisers would be left with a net deficit of NZ$39 million (£20,632,376). Approximately NZ$1.2 billion (£634,800,951) in investments went into projects that contributed to the country's hosting of the 2011 Rugby World Cup, including NZ$555 million (£293,555,614) in stadium upgrades and more than NZ$200 million (£105,785,474) in local government expenses.

Did You Know That?

New Zealand's dramatic scenery is the setting for the mythical world of Middle-earth in the movies *The Lord of the Rings* and *The Hobbit Trilogy*. More than 150 locations throughout the country were used to film each movie.

SOVIET BOYCOTT

A total of 16 nations competed in the inaugural Rugby World Cup in 1987. Seven of the 16 places were automatic choices as they were all members of the International Rugby Football Board (IRFB) – Australia, England, France, Ireland, New Zealand, Scotland and Wales. The remaining nine slots were offered to Argentina, Canada, Fiji, Italy, Japan, Romania, Tonga, USA and Zimbabwe. The Soviet Union declined an invitation to participate in the inaugural Rugby World Cup on political grounds, allegedly due to the continued IRFB membership of South Africa. At the time Georgia and Russia were part of the Soviet Union and both of these nations qualified for the 2019 tournament. Argentina, Canada, Fiji, Italy, Japan, Romania, Tonga, USA and Zimbabwe were all made IRFB members post the 1987 tournament.

Did You Know That?

The most popular sports in Georgia are basketball, football, judo, rugby union, weightlifting and wrestling.

LIKE UNCLE, LIKE NEPHEW

England's Ben Cohen's uncle, George, won a FIFA World Cup winners' medal with England in 1966. Ben was a member of England's 2003 Rugby World Cup winning side.

IN HIS OWN WORDS

'Back 15 years, so I could relive my career again.'

Gethin Jenkins (Rugby World Cup prop for Wales 2003, 2007, 2011 and 2015) during his testimonial year in 2016, when he was asked in his brochure where he would go if he had a time machine, and why

A NEW DAWN FOR THE 2023 RUGBY WORLD CUP

On 15 November 2018, World Rugby and the France 2023 organising committee unveiled the logo and visual identity for the 2023 Rugby World Cup at a special event in Paris. It was exactly one year to the day since France were awarded the hosting rights to the 2023 Rugby World Cup. The brand conveys the vision, passion and ambition of a tournament that will inspire and unite a nation, a sport and the globe in rugby and friendship.

The France 2023 logo is a new take on the blue-white-red of the French tricolour flag, a balance between the authenticity and modernity that are characteristic of France.

A total of ten host cities from Lille in the north to Toulouse in the south will play host to the 20 teams who will compete across the 48 matches that comprise France 2023, the tenth edition of the Rugby World Cup.

Speaking from Paris, World Rugby chief executive Brett Gosper said: 'This is a very exciting milestone on the road to hosting the tenth Rugby World Cup. The distinctive Rugby World Cup 2023 logo symbolises the unity between World Rugby and the organising committee and embodies the vision, passion and unity of a tournament that brings France and the world together through rugby and its character-building values. In a year that will mark 200 years since the birth of rugby, France 2023 will be the perfect celebration of that milestone – a record-breaking celebration of rugby on and off the field that will further the reach and growth of rugby around the world.'

France 2023 CEO Claude Atcher added: 'It will be a pleasure to celebrate 200 years of rugby at France 2023, the tenth Rugby World Cup. It will be a celebration of rugby's heritage and rugby's future. From William Webb Ellis's desire to break from convention at Rugby School, to the diversity, unity and growth of the modern, global game. Our goal is to evoke this spirit and inspire a generation through shared values with strong teamwork showing the best of rugby to France and the best of France to rugby, opening new horizons. Today we deliver a positive message to the world – we are rugby, we are 2023.'

World Rugby chairman Bill Beaumont never played in a Rugby World Cup as he retired from the sport in 1982. He won 34 caps for England and captained his country 21 times including captaining England to an unexpected Grand Slam win in 1980, their first Grand Slam for 23 years. He captained the British and Irish Lions on their 1980 tour of South Africa, playing in ten of the 18 matches. He was the first English captain of the Lions since Doug Prentice in 1930.

IN HIS OWN WORDS

'My teeth came first and the body second.'

Wayne Shelford, New Zealand captain 1987–90, explaining why he was given the nickname 'Buck'

A TALE OF TWO NATIONS

Western Samoa missed out on the inaugural Rugby World Cup but have qualified for every tournament since including the 2019 edition. Western Samoa became Samoa in 1997.

SEA EAGLES SOARING HIGH

Tonga qualified for the 2019 Rugby World Cup and since the inaugural competition they have only missed out on qualification once, in 1991. The Tonga national rugby union team is nicknamed *Ikale Tahi* (Sea Eagles).

I GUESS THAT'S WHY THEY CALL IT THE BLUES

France fly-half Frederic Michalak announced his retirement from international rugby following *Les Bleus'* humiliating 2015 Rugby World Cup quarter-final defeat at the hands of New Zealand. The 33-year-old, who played for Top 14 side Toulon, lasted just 11 minutes of the contest at the Millennium Stadium, Cardiff, Wales, before heading off down the tunnel injured. An eventual 62-13 loss to the defending world champions merely added to his woes, with Michalak admitting afterwards his body could no longer cope with the demands of the international game.

'I had thought I would end my international career on a better note but my body can no longer respond. It's very difficult to perform constantly to a very high level. For me this is the end, for sure,' said Michalak on the French Rugby Federation website. Michalak made 77 appearances for *Les Bleus* (2001–15, 436 points) and played at three Rugby World Cup finals tournaments – 2003, 2007 and 2015.

Did You Know That?

On 22 August 2015, Michalak scored 17 points to help France beat England 25-20 at Stade de France, Paris, in a Rugby World Cup finals warm-up match and surpassed Christophe Lamaison (37 caps, 1996–2001, 380 points) as his nation's all-time leading points scorer. During France's 41-18 win over Canada on 1 October 2015 in a Pool D game at the Rugby World Cup finals, he became France's all-time leading Rugby World Cup points scorer. Michalak scored 14 points in the victory over Canada.

APARTHEID BAN

Apart from New Zealand, who won the inaugural Rugby World Cup in 1987, South Africa are the only other nation to win the first Rugby World Cup they contested when they hosted the 1995 edition. South Africa did not compete in 1987 and 1991 due to an international sporting boycott in opposition to the country's apartheid regime.

Did You Know That?

The side representing Cote d'Ivoire is recognised as Ivory Coast by the International Rugby Board. Ivory Coast has only competed in one Rugby World Cup, finishing 16th from 16 in 1995.

THE WOODEN SPOON WINNERS

Year	Winners	Position
1987	Zimbabwe	16th
1991	Zimbabwe	16th
1995	Japan	20th
1999	Italy	20th
2003	Namibia	20th
2007	Namibia	20th
2011	Namibia	20th
2015	Uruguay	20th

Did You Know That?

Zimbabwe have not qualified for a Rugby World Cup since finishing last in 1991.

PUT IT IN WRITING

Bob Dwyer, Australia's coach when they won the Rugby World Cup in 1991, has written two autobiographies: *The Winning Way* (1992) and *Full Time: A Coach's Memoirs* (2004).

FROM A FRIENDLY RIVALRY TO A GLOBAL WAR
The Home Nations Championship

The first regular international rugby was the annual England versus Scotland match that kicked off in 1871. The other home countries – Ireland and Wales – soon joined in. The first round-robin among all four teams took place in 1883, referred to as the Home Nations Championship, and was won by England. Two years later the British unions appointed themselves as the International Rugby Football Board (IRFB). These were men on a mission to keep 'their' game amateur and middle-class. Professionalism had taken over association football in July 1885 when the Football Association (FA) formally legalised it in England, which had captured the British masses. This, the IRFB declared, must not be allowed to happen to rugby – any form of payment for playing the game would destroy it. Less than ten years later, though, a northern union broke away from the (English) Rugby Union. This new body let working men be compensated for the time they took off work to play the game. A rival code, rugby league, had been born. Traditional rugby men were bitter. Players who 'went north' and converted to rugby league were barred for life from any further contact with the union game.

In the late 19th century rugby caught on across the English Channel. Its biggest advocate was Pierre de Frédy, Baron de Coubertin. The French educator and historian was keen to perk up the nation's manhood in the aftermath of the disastrous Franco-Prussian War (19 July 1870–10 May 1871). The war saw a coalition of German states led by Prussia defeat France (the Second French Empire and later the Third French Empire). The war marked the end of French cultural, economic, ideological and social influence in continental Europe and resulted in the creation of a unified Germany. Rewarding intelligence yet requiring brutality, rugby was seen as perfect training for the anticipated military rematch.

Rugby at the Olympic Games

In 1900, Baron de Coubertin gratified two of his obsessions at once by getting rugby into the modern Olympic Games. France won the first tournament, played in Paris. Rugby survived in the Olympics while Baron de Coubertin remained president of the International

Olympic Committee (IOC), serving from 1896–1925. Only two or three countries, sometimes represented by regional teams, entered each of the four Olympic Games at which it was played (1900, 1908, 1920 and 1924). The current Olympic Rugby (15-a-side) champions are the United States, whose 1924 team was dominated by players from California's elite Stanford University. Attempts to return rugby to the Olympics began in the 1980s. They finally succeeded in 2009 when Rugby Sevens for both men and women was added to the programme for the 2016 Summer Olympics.

The Five Nations Championship

When the Olympic champions, France, played the touring All Black Originals on New Year's Day 1906, they were soundly beaten 38-8. It is claimed that the New Zealand captain, Dave Gallaher, told his team to let the French score a couple of tries. On 22 March 1906, England and France met for the first time with England running out 35-8 winners at Parc des Princes, Paris and the other home unions (Wales who won 36-4 in Cardiff on 2 March 1908; Ireland who won 19-8 in Dublin on 20 March 1909; and Scotland who won 27-0 in Edinburgh on 22 January 1910) followed suit. France joined an expanded Five Nations tournament in 1910 (today known as the Six Nations Championship, following the admission of Italy in 2000) which was won by England. This tournament was played annually except during the two World Wars (no tournament from 1915–19 or from 1940–46). Like the earlier tournament among the home unions, officially it did not exist. These matches were, in theory, unrelated, friendly fixtures, and a champion was crowned only by the press.

France, for whom winning was everything, were banned from top-level rugby for most of the 1930s. Shortly after the 1931 Five Nations Championship, which was won by Wales, France were expelled from the competition. There were two main reasons: revulsion at especially thuggish play in one Test against Wales, and the widespread French practice, dubbed 'shamateurism', of giving star club players highly paid jobs with few actual duties (rugby union was officially an amateur sport until 1995). In response to the ban, the French fostered rugby elsewhere in Europe. Their main opponent in the 1930s was Germany. Ominously for adherents of Baron de Coubertin, the Germans improved rapidly, winning a match in 1938 (a 3-0 victory in Frankfurt, Germany on 27 March 1938). France remained expelled through the 1939 tournament, shared between England, Ireland and Wales, but following the tournament they were readmitted. However, the outbreak of World War Two (1 September 1939–2 September 1945) halted international rugby until 1947.

New Zealand and South Africa

Beyond the Five Nations tournament, international rugby was a network of bilateral rivalries. The game had spread with British settlers in the late 19th century. New Zealand's rapid progress was clearly demonstrated during northern hemisphere tours by a Native side in 1888/89, the All Black Originals in 1905/06 and the Invincibles in 1924/25. South Africa's Afrikaners also took to rugby with a passion after the Anglo-Boer War, a war fought by Britain and her Empire against the Boers. The Boers were comprised of the combined forces of the South African Republic and the Republic of the Orange Free State. The Boer Republics declared war on 11 October 1899 and the conflict ended on 31 May 1902.

For most of the 20th century, world rugby's 'heavyweight' championship was contested roughly once a decade between New Zealand and white South Africa. They first met at Carisbrook, Dunedin, New Zealand on 13 August 1921, the home side triumphing 13-5. Both southern hemisphere nations were convinced of their superiority over the 'hidebound' British and 'erratic' French, but these claims were hard to prove on the basis of irregular one-off tours for which the home side made all the arrangements, including providing the referees.

Rugby at the Commonwealth Games

Many rugby fans thought that such an essentially British sport should be played at the Empire (later Commonwealth) Games which were first hosted by Hamilton, Canada in 1930. The counter-argument was that adding more team sports would make the games too unwieldy. A solution was at last found with the admission in 1998 (hosts, Malaysia) of Rugby Sevens, a fast-paced offspring of the 15-a-side game with wide spectator appeal. New Zealand won the first four Commonwealth Games titles.

RECORD-BREAKING ATTENDANCES

The 2015 Rugby World Cup in England witnessed a record-breaking 2.47 million tickets sold for the tournament. World Rugby anticipate 1.8 million tickets will be sold for the 48 matches to be played at the 2019 Rugby World Cup in Japan.

RAIDING THE PIGGY BANK

Mathew Vaea, the manager of Samoa during the 2011 Rugby World Cup finals, was ordered by the council leaders of his home village in Leauva, Samoa to pay a fine of 100 pigs for misbehaving during the 2011 tournament and thereby for tarnishing his chiefly title of *tuala* by drinking regularly and treating the campaign in New Zealand like a holiday. Vaea was dismissed as manager after the tournament. The Chief of Leauva, Vaifale Iose, said Vaea's actions had brought his position into disrepute and was the reason why Samoa failed to reach the quarter-final stages (they finished third in Pool 3 behind winners South Africa and runners-up Wales).

In an interview with the *Samoa Observer* newspaper the Chief of Leauva said: 'The title of *tuala* received bad publicity in the media because *tuala* Mathew failed to perform some of his duties as the manager for the Manu Samoa.' Revelations of Vaea's conduct were made by his team captain, Mahonri Schwalger, in a post-tournament report which was presented to Prime Minister Tuilaepa Sa'ilele Malielegaoi. Schwalger said Vaea 'did not want to be there' and would disappear for days at a time and claimed that he would drink regularly and treated the tournament like a holiday. Schwalger was supported by other Samoan players who claimed they were let down by the conduct of their manager and some Samoan Rugby Union officials which affected their ability to play well. Samoa had gone into the 2011 Rugby World Cup finals on a high note after defeating Australia 32-23 in a warm-up match at ANZ Stadium, Sydney, Australia on 17 July 2011.

Rather than have to hand over 100 pigs to the village, Vaea paid a monetary fine of 2,000 Samoan tala (£535) and had to make a formal apology to the village elders. The people of Samoa raised more than £1.9 million to fund the team's 2011 Rugby World Cup campaign although the players only received a weekly allowance of £630 which was significantly less than other Pacific teams. One witty journalist joked that Vaea had been hit with a 'swine fine for failing to save Samoa's bacon'. Vaea played eight times at scrum-half for Western Samoa between 1991 and 1995 (including four games at the 1991 Rugby World Cup finals) and scored 25 points.

DUAL INTERNATIONAL WITH BAT & BALL

Rudie van Vuuren is the only man to have appeared in both the Cricket and Rugby Union World Cups. In 1999, he played for Namibia in the Rugby World Cup in Wales, when the team lost all three of their Pool C games against Canada, Fiji and France. In 2003, he represented Namibia in the Cricket World Cup which was co-hosted by Kenya, South Africa and Zimbabwe. Namibia lost all six of their Pool A games to Australia, England, India, Netherlands, Pakistan and Zimbabwe. Later in 2003, he played for his nation in the Rugby World Cup which was hosted by Australia and Namibia finished bottom of Pool A losing all four of their games versus the hosts, Argentina, Ireland and Romania. He is the only Namibian cricketer to have taken five wickets in a one-day international – versus England at St George's Park, Port Elizabeth, South Africa in the 2003 Cricket World Cup.

'Sometimes you can take the passion and aggression of rugby on to the cricket field. I don't think I'm that talented at cricket but sometimes that gives me the edge. And it is the same in rugby. I take the calmness of cricket on to the rugby field,' said van Vuuren after his five-wicket haul.

IN HIS OWN WORDS

'I was captain of Wales, and the shock that happened down there was tremendous. If I'd have failed, I would never, ever have been able to go back. If I'd failed, I couldn't go anywhere – I couldn't go home. I'd have just had to get a normal job and give my rugby up.'

Jonathan Davies, Wales Rugby World Cup squad 1987, speaking on 7 January 2019 about his switch from rugby union to rugby league 30 years earlier on 7 January 1989

MINTED

The 1999 Rugby World Cup design is the 17th rarest £2 coin in circulation and collectors of coins pay as much as £2.73 to own one.

Japan will issue gold and silver coins to commemorate the country's hosting of the 2019 Rugby World Cup. The gold coin, featuring the World Cup trophy on one side and the 2019 tournament's logo and cherry blossoms on the other, will be made with 15.6 grams of 24 carat gold and put on sale for ¥120,000 (around £885). The silver coin will depict a player tackling an opponent and the names of the 12 host Japanese cities, it will be made with 31.1 grams of fine silver and sold for ¥9,500 (£70). The Japanese Finance Ministry said 10,000 of the gold coins and 50,000 silver coins will be made.

Coin Year	Entered Circulation	Active Circulation
1999	4,993,000	1,335,993

Did You Know That?
The rarest £2 coin is the 2002 XVII Commonwealth Games (Northern Ireland) and is worth between £31 and £32.

IN HIS OWN WORDS
'It doesn't matter whether it's cricket, rugby union, rugby league – we all hate England. It's time to get square and knock them off in Marseille.'

ARU chief executive John O'Neill certainly gave England a motivational boost before their quarter-final game versus the Wallabies at the 2007 Rugby World Cup finals – England won 12-10

Did You Know That?
When a London sports news agency received *The Express and Echo's* match report of New Zealand's 55-4 victory, a sub-editor did not believe it and was of the opinion that an error had occurred in transmission. He then reversed the score, claiming that Devon had beaten New Zealand 55-4.

SOUTH AFRICA'S FAMOUS SCOT
George Moir Christie, better known as Kitch Christie, who coached South Africa to victory at the 1995 Rugby World Cup, was born in Johannesburg on 31 January 1940 to a Scottish father and an English mother. He was educated at Leith Academy in Edinburgh and it was during his schooldays that his classmates named him Kitch after the legendary South African soccer striker, Don Kitchenbrand, who played for Glasgow Rangers in the 1950s. From October 1994 to March 1996, when ill health forced him to withdraw from rugby, Christie steered the Springboks to 14 wins in 14 Tests, including the famous win over

the All Blacks in the 1995 Rugby World Cup Final. This winning streak equalled the world record at the time for coaching the most consecutive Test victories with Fred Allen, who coached the All Blacks between 1966 and 1968. Like Christie, Allen also died of leukaemia, sadly passing away on 28 April 2012.

Did You Know That?

Like George Moir Christie, his predecessor as head coach of South Africa, Ian McIntosh, and his successor, Andre Margraff, never won a Test cap for the Springboks.

THE RING MASTER

Mark Ring was described as a player who had more tricks in his pocket than a circus entertainer. The fly-half was capped 32 times by Wales from 1983–91 (34 points) and was an integral part of the Wales team which finished in third place at the inaugural Rugby World Cup finals in 1987. Sadly, injuries during his career restricted his appearances for his country, missing out on the British and Irish Lions tour of Australia in 1989 because of a serious knee injury, although he did go to the 1991 Rugby World Cup finals.

Noted for having a sharp rugby brain and capable of also playing at centre, he played in and won three Welsh Cup finals and played for Cardiff when they defeated a touring Australia side in 1984. He was selected for two World XV touring squads, one to celebrate the Western Province Centenary in 1983 and the other to celebrate the South African Rugby Board's Centenary in 1989. Ring captained Wales on two occasions when they toured Namibia in 1991 but neither match was a Test match. In 1985, Ring was the Welsh Rugby Writers' Player of the Year.

Did You Know That?

In 1850, Reverend Rowan Williams started rugby at Lampeter College in Wales.

WEBB ELLIS CUP GOES ON TOUR

In the summer of 2018, the replica of the Webb Ellis Cup went on tour around the New Zealand provinces along with the Dave Gallaher Trophy (New Zealand winners in 2018), Bledisloe Cup (New Zealand winners in 2018), Hillary Shield (New Zealand winners in 2018), Women's World Cup (New Zealand winners in 2017), Rugby Sevens World Series (South Africa winners in 2017–18) and the Junior World Cup (France winners in 2018) trophies.

DOWN UNDER

In the latter stages of his playing career, Clive Woodward, who coached England to Rugby World Cup glory in 2003, played for the Australian side, Manly.

Did You Know That?

In 1864, Sydney University became Australia's first rugby club.

RUGBY GOLD MEDAL WINNERS AT THE OLYMPIC GAMES

Rugby (15-a-side) was one of the sports which was included in four of the Olympic Games which were held between 1900 and 1924. France were Olympic champions in 1900 (Paris, France), Australasia in 1908 (London, England), USA in 1920 (Antwerp, Belgium) and USA in 1924 (Paris, France).

Did You Know That?

Rugby was reintroduced to the Olympic Games schedule at Rio de Janeiro, Brazil in 2016 but in sevens format. Fiji won the gold medal, Great Britain took the silver medal and South Africa claimed the bronze medal.

HEY BIG SPENDERS!

On 3 January 2018, the *Gazette Review* published a list of the ten highest-paid rugby players in the world.

1. Dan Carter (Racing 92 & New Zealand) – £1.4 million
2. Matt Giteau (Toulon) – £900,000
3. Leigh Halfpenny (Toulon & Wales) – £600,000
4. Sam Burgess (South Sydney – Rugby League) – £500,000
5. Johnny Sexton (Leinster & Ireland) – £494,000
6. Bryan Habana (Toulon) – £474,600 – (retired at the end of the 2018 French Top 14 season)
7. Morgan Parra (Clermont Auvergne & France) – £436,000
8. Thierry Dusautoir (Toulouse) – £408,120
9. Bakkies Botha (Toulon) – £389,000
10. Jamie Roberts (Harlequins & Wales) – £380,000 – (he signed for Bath in March 2018)

THE KING DOWN UNDER

George Musarurwa Gregan was born on 19 April 1973 in Lusaka, Zambia to a Zimbabwean mother and an Australian father. When he was two years old his family moved to Canberra, Australia where he attended St Edmund's College and graduated from the University of

Canberra with a Bachelor of Education (Physical Education). He began his rugby career in 1996 when the Brumbies were founded to compete in the inaugural season of Super Rugby and he remained with them until 2007 when he moved to Europe to sign for Toulon.

Gregan helped the Canberra-based club to two championship-winning seasons in 2001 and 2004 and helped Toulon win promotion back to the Top 14 after securing the Rugby Pro Division Two title. After just one season in France, Gregan moved to Japan and played for Suntory Sungoliath in the Top League, helping the Tokyo-based club to the 2010/11 All-Japan Rugby Football Championship.

After representing Australia at Under-19 and Under-21 level, he was handed his first Test cap on 18 June 1994. The Wallabies beat Italy 23-20 at Ballymore Stadium, Brisbane and he scored his first try in his third Test match, a 73-3 trouncing of Samoa at Sydney Football Stadium, Sydney on 6 August 1994. Eleven days later all of Australia knew his name when he appeared from nowhere to make a spectacular try-saving tackle on New Zealand's Jeff Wilson at Sydney Football Stadium. His perfectly timed tackle helped the Wallabies defeat the All Blacks 20-16 to win the Bledisloe Cup. It remains one of the greatest moments in the history of the Australia versus New Zealand rivalry. He went on to win five more Bledisloe Cups (1998, 1999, 2000, 2001 and 2002).

In 1995, Gregan played in the first of his four Rugby World Cup finals. The Wallabies were the defending champions in 1995 but lost 25-12 to England in the quarter-finals in Cape Town, South Africa. Four year later he helped the Wallabies lift the Webb Ellis Cup in 1999 following a 35-12 victory against France in the final at the Millennium Stadium, Cardiff, Wales. In 2001, as vice-captain, he helped the Wallabies to a 2-1 Test series victory over the touring British and Irish Lions. When John Eales retired from the international game at the end of Australia's successful 2001 Tri-Nations series, Gregan was the automatic selection for the captaincy of the Wallabies.

Australia hosted the 2003 Rugby World Cup but the Wallabies lost the final 20-17 after extra time to England at the Telstra Stadium,

Sydney. Gregan was appointed to the Order of Australia in 2004 and on 31 July 2004, he led the Wallabies out at the Subiaco Oval, Perth for his 100th Test match. Gregan celebrated his centenary match by guiding the Wallabies to a 30-26 win over the Springboks in the Tri-Nations. The scrum-half became only the fourth player to reach the century mark and joined his fellow Wallaby, David Campese (101 caps), to become only the second Australian player to reach 100 Tests. (England's Jason Leonard and France's Philippe Sella had also already passed the century mark.)

'As much as I tried to treat it as just another game, when you are flooded by telegrams and messages you know it's a very special match,' said Gregan at the time.

At the 2007 Rugby World Cup England once again knocked Australia out of the tournament, a 12-10 loss in the quarter-finals. When Gregan captained Australia to a 20-18 Tri-Nations victory against South Africa on 5 August 2006 at Sydney Olympic Park, he not only extended his world record of caps to 124, he also overtook John Eales's Australian record of 55 Tests as captain. On 6 October 2007, Gregan played in his 139th and last Test match for Australia in a 12-10 loss to England at Stade Velodrome, Marseilles, France in the quarter-finals of the 2007 Rugby World Cup. At the end of the 2010/11 season, he took the decision to bring the curtain down on his epic career and took up a position as a consultant with the Brumbies. He also served on the Australian Rugby Union (ARU) board from 2012. Gregan, a player who straddled the end of amateur and beginning of professional rugby, remains the most capped Australian captain of all time, 59 Tests, and is his nation's most capped player with an astonishing 139 caps (1994–2007; 133 starts, six substitute appearances, 18 tries, three drop goals, 99 points, won 99 games, lost 44 games, 71% winning record). He was inducted into the Sport Australia Hall of Fame in 2006 and into the World Rugby Hall of Fame in 2013.

Did You Know That?

Only two players have won more Test caps than Gregan: Brian O'Driscoll 141 (Ireland 1999-2014) and Richie McCaw 148 (New Zealand 2001-15).

WORLD WAR ONE'S RUGBY WORLD CUP

The Armistice of 11 November 1918 brought World War One, fought on land, sea and air between the Allies and Germany, to an end (28 July 1914–11 November 1918). Troops from Australia, Canada, New Zealand and South Africa were all stationed in Britain when the hostilities ceased but there were subsequent delays in getting ships to take them home. To keep up the fitness and the morale of the soldiers, and appease the general public, who wanted to see competitive rugby matches played again, the War Office decided to host an 'Army Rugby World Cup'. This competition would see the British Army (under the name of the 'Mother Country' rather than allow separate teams from England, Ireland, Scotland and Wales) and the RAF also compete in a round robin competition. The Royal Navy were also invited to compete but declined as they did not think they could field a competitive side. On 8 February 1919, representatives from all five nations met at the Junior United Services Club, London to plan matches and identify venues. The competition was originally going to be called the Inter-Services and Dominions Rugby Championship, but when His Majesty King George V offered to sponsor a cup in his name for the winners, the name was changed to the King's Cup. After the round robin stage, the two teams with the most wins would face each other in the final to be played at Twickenham Stadium, London, England. In their first game, the New Zealand Army A team beat the RAF 22-3 in Swansea, Wales; they then defeated the Canadian Forces in Portsmouth, England and followed that with a victory, two weeks later, over the South African Forces at Twickenham. New Zealand then faced the Mother Country in Edinburgh, Scotland and won a close encounter 6-3. Having won their opening four games, New Zealand had already secured their place in the final before losing their final game versus the Australia Forces in Bradford, England. The final was played on 16 April 1919 at Twickenham between the Mother Country and New Zealand. James Ryan led his team to a 9-3 victory over the British Army side and was presented with the King's Cup by King George V. The War Office did not issue an invitation to the French to play in the round robin tournament, claiming that it was organised to cement the links of the British Empire. However, three days later the French allies were invited over to play the winners, but fared no better, losing 20-3 to New Zealand. A return match in Paris was also played to placate the French forces and was won 16-10 by New Zealand.

ALWAYS AT THE PARTY

Country	First Rugby World Cup	No. of Participations
Argentina	1987	8
Australia	1987	8
Canada	1987	8
England	1987	8
France	1987	8
Ireland	1987	8
Italy	1987	8

Country	First Rugby World Cup	No. of Participations
Japan	1987	8
New Zealand	1987	8
Romania	1987	8
Scotland	1987	8
Wales	1987	8
Fiji	1987	7
Tonga	1987	7
USA	1987	7
Zimbabwe	1987	2
Samoa	1991	7
Ivory Coast	1995	1
South Africa	1995	6
Namibia	1999	5
Spain	1999	1
Uruguay	1999	3
Georgia	2003	4
Portugal	2007	1
Russia	2007	1

Did You Know That?

Fiji failed to qualify for the 1995 tournament; Tonga failed to qualify for the 1991 tournament; USA failed to qualify for the 1995 tournament and Samoa were not invited to the inaugural Rugby World Cup in 1987.

IN SAFE HANDS

The London workshops of Thomas Lyte Silver are responsible for the care and restoration of the Webb Ellis Cup. The company also designs and makes trophies for several prestigious sporting tournaments including the FA Cup, the RBS Six Nations trophy, the Barclays ATP World Tour trophy and the European Champions and Challenge Cup. In January 2015, Her Majesty the Queen appointed a Royal Warrant to Thomas Lyte as goldsmith and silversmith to the Royal Household.

Did You Know That?

The engraving on the King's Cup shows Charles Brown as the captain of New Zealand and not James Ryan.

THE 1995 RUGBY WORLD CUP FINALS

The eight quarter-finalists from the 1991 Rugby World Cup finals all received automatic entry for the 1995 tournament along with the host nation, South Africa: Australia, Canada, England, France, Ireland, New Zealand, Scotland and Western Samoa. The remaining seven slots went to the winners of the regional qualifying competitions: Argentina (the Americas), Cote d'Ivoire (Africa), Japan (Asia), Tonga (Oceania) and the three European qualifiers, Italy, Romania and the nation which finished third at the inaugural Rugby World Cup finals in 1987, Wales.

This was the first Rugby World Cup to be hosted by one nation and the last before the professional era. A total of nine stadiums were used, with the majority being given upgrades prior to the tournament to ensure they were up to the required standard. The largest four, Loftus Versfeld, Newlands, Kings Park Stadium and Ellis Park, were used for the knockout games. There were games originally scheduled to have been played in Brakpan, Germiston, Pietermaritzburg and Witbank, but these games were reallocated to other venues. The organisers said the changes made had to do with facilities for both the press and spectators, as well as for security reasons.

Venues were paired:
- Pool 1: Cape Town, Port Elizabeth and Stellenbosch
- Pool 2: Durban and East London
- Pool 3: Johannesburg and Bloemfontein
- Pool 4: Pretoria and Rustenburg

Pool A was won by South Africa with the defending world champions Australia taking the runners-up position. The opening game brought these sides together with the Springboks defeating the Wallabies 27-18 at Newlands, Cape Town. England won Pool B which saw Western Samoa pip Italy (third) and Argentina (fourth) to a quarter-finals place. New Zealand claimed top spot in Pool C which was the most difficult pool whilst Ireland finished second ahead of Wales and Japan. Pool D was won by France with Scotland also qualifying for the quarter-finals. South Africa had the easiest route to the semi-finals after being draw to play Western Samoa who they beat 42-14 at Ellis Park, Johannesburg. France beat Ireland 36-12 at Kings Park Stadium, Durban, England won a tight match against Australia (25-22 at Newlands) and the All Blacks eased into the semi-finals with a 48-30 win over Scotland at Loftus Versfeld, Pretoria. South Africa found it tough going against a powerful France side in the semi-finals but progressed to a home final with a 19-15 victory at Kings Park Stadium. The All Blacks prevented

England from becoming the first country to play in back-to-back finals when they defeated them 45-29 at Newlands. France, runners-up in the inaugural tournament in 1987, won the third-place play-off match against England, 19-9 at Loftus Versfeld.

The Final
24 June 1995
Ellis Park, Johannesburg

The final between New Zealand and South Africa saw the best attack come up against the best defence. The All Blacks went into the showpiece game having scored 315 points in the tournament, with the home nation only conceding 55. Without a try scored in the opening 80 minutes they went into extra time locked at 9 each. Both sides scored penalties during the first half of extra time but it was Joel Stransky's drop goal which secured South Africa the Rugby World Cup in front of a sell-out fanatical crowd at Ellis Park. When the final whistle was blown the entire crowd stood to its feet as all of South Africa celebrated as one. Two skydivers flew into the stadium with signs which read 'Congratulations South Africa' and 'See You In Wales 1999'. An emotional South Africa captain, Francois Pienaar, who inspired his team on the field and his country off it, gathered his teammates together in a huddle and went down on one knee saying a prayer. This game showed that in times like this the pain is so great for one and the ecstasy is so great for the other. Plenty of games had been played without a try being scored and been dull but this one was a thriller. The image of President Nelson Mandela wearing a No.6 Springbok jersey and baseball cap, handing over the Webb Ellis Cup to the South Africa captain, Pienaar, is still one of the most memorable in sporting history. Madiba raised his fists in celebration, as the crowd chanted his name. The Rainbow Nation had triumphed.

In a post-match TV interview Pienaar was asked what it was like to have 62,000 fans supporting his team. Pienaar responded: 'There were not 62,000 people supporting us today. There were 43 million.' And when he was asked what it was like to receive the Webb Ellis Cup from President Nelson Mandela, a smiling Pienaar said: 'What happened was Nelson Mandela said, "Thank you very much for what you've done for South Africa" but I said, "Thank you for what you've done." I almost felt like hugging him but it wasn't appropriate, I guess. Then I lifted the trophy which was unbelievable. I can't describe the feeling as I wouldn't do it justice.'

South Africa: Andre Joubert; Chester Williams, Japie Mulder, Hennie le Roux, James Small; Joel Stransky, Joost van der Westhuizen; Os du

Randt, Chris Rossouw, Balie Swart, Hannes Strydom, Kobus Wiese, Ruben Kruger, Francois Pienaar (captain), Mark Andrews.

New Zealand: Glen Osborne; Jeff Wilson, Walter Little, Frank Bunce, Jonah Lomu; Andrew Mehrtens, Graeme Bachop; Olo Brown, Sean Fitzpatrick (captain), Craig Dowd, Robin Brooke, Ian Jones, Mike Brewer, Josh Kronfeld, Zinzan Brooke.

South Africa (9) 15   **New Zealand (6) 12 – after extra time**
Pens: Stransky (3)   Pens: Mehrtens (3)
Drop Goals: Stransky (2)   Drop Goals: Mehrtens (1)

Attendance: 62,000
Referee: Ed Morrison (England)

Did You Know That?

The South African Mint issued a one-ounce gold proof Protea coin with a total mintage of 406 pieces to commemorate the 1995 Rugby World Cup finals being hosted by South Africa.

RUGBY WORLD CUP QUOTES

'That was probably the worst I ever felt as a Wales player.'
Ieuan Evans, captain of Wales at the 1991 Rugby World Cup, after they lost their opening Pool 3 game of the tournament 16-13 to Western Samoa at Cardiff Arms Park, Cardiff, Wales

A SOLITARY CAP

Benjamin Alo Charles Atiga (New Zealand) was named the 2003 International Rugby Board Under-21 Player of the Year. He only played one Test for the All Blacks when he was called into the squad as an injury replacement for Ben Blair to play Tonga in the 2003 Rugby World Cup. The All Blacks won the game 91-7 at the Suncorp Stadium, Brisbane. Atiga was the 50th All Black which Auckland Grammar School produced and he helped New Zealand win world titles at Under-19 level in 2001 and 2002 and at Under-21 level in 2003 and as captain of his country in 2004.

Did You Know That?

Niue Rugby Football Union was founded in 1952 and was admitted to the International Rugby Board (now known as World Rugby) in 1999. Frank Bunce (55 caps for New Zealand and four caps for Western Samoa) is the great nephew of Sir Robert Rex, the first Premier of the Pacific island state of Niue.

TOP 10 REGISTERED RUGBY PLAYERS PER 100 POPULATION

1. Tonga – 21.2
2. Niue Island 13.9
3. Fiji 13.6
4. Cook Islands 10.9
5. Samoa 6.2
6. New Zealand 3.2
7. Wales 2.7
8. Solomon Islands 1.7
9. St Vincent & the Grenadines 1.6
10. Ireland 1.5

A TRULY GLOBAL EVENT

An estimated global TV audience of 120 million watched the 2015 Rugby World Cup Final. The England versus Wales Pool A game on 26 September 2015 attracted an audience of 11.6 million viewers on ITV, the largest rugby audience in the United Kingdom (UK) since the 2007 Rugby World Cup Final (South Africa beat England 15-6) and the highest peak audience for a sporting event in the UK since the 2014 FIFA Football World Cup Final. On 3 October 2015, a record TV audience was set in Japan when 25 million fans tuned in to watch Japan defeat Samoa 26-5 in a Pool B game. The 2015 tournament was the most digitally engaged to date with social media activity exceeding the whole of New Zealand's Rugby World Cup 2011 during the 2015 Pool stages. The tag #RWC2015 was used twice a second for the duration of the tournament and over 5 million times in total. More than 270 million video views were seen on all social media channels, the World Rugby website attracted 25 million users and the official app was downloaded 2.8 million times in 204 countries. The chairman of World Rugby, Bernard Lapasset, said: 'Rugby World Cup 2015 will be remembered as the biggest tournament to date, but I also believe that it will be remembered as the best. England 2015 has been the most competitive, best-attended, most-watched, most socially engaged, most commercially successful Rugby World Cup. But this special Rugby World Cup has been about much more than numbers, it has been about the amazing atmosphere in full and vibrant stadia, the excitement around the host nation and in Cardiff, the unforgettable moments played out by the world's best players and the friendships that have been created along the way – the very best of our sport has been on display. I am a believer that great people make great events and I would like to thank the organisers England Rugby 2015, the host union the Rugby Football Union, Rugby World Cup Limited, the host cities and venues for delivering a special tournament that has had the teams and fans at heart, but above all, I would like to pay tribute to the volunteers and fans who got behind all 20 teams and who have made this such a special event, the best to date.'

Did You Know That?

The Japanese TV audience of 25 million meant that nearly one in five people in the country (population 127 million) watched the game versus Samoa. In contrast Samoa has a population of 195,100 which is less than the number of fans who attended the 2015 Rugby World Cup semi-finals (80,090 New Zealand v South Africa and 80,025 Argentina v Australia) and the final when 80,125 fans packed into Twickenham Stadium, London to see New Zealand defeat South Africa 34-17.

OLYMPIC CHAMPIONS

The USA qualified for the 2019 Rugby World Cup and have only failed to play in one edition of the tournament, in 1995. Up until sevens made its debut at the 2016 Olympic Games in Rio de Janeiro, Brazil, the United States were the reigning Olympic champions in rugby, having won gold at the 1920 and 1924 Summer Games. In 1920 the USA defeated France 8-0 in Antwerp, Belgium and they retained their gold medal four years later after defeating France 17-3 in Paris. At the end of the 1924 final the crowd invaded the pitch and the French players and police had to protect the USA players from being attacked. The pitch invasion gave rugby a bad name and this, together with the problems of attracting a sufficient number of teams to make it a viable sport, added to the Olympic Committee's desire to include more individual and women's events, spelled the death knell for rugby at the Olympic Games.

Did You Know That?

Fiji won the inaugural Rugby Sevens event at the 2016 Olympic Games with Great Britain claiming the silver medal and South Africa the bronze.

THE MAGNIFICENT 20

Prior to the 2015 Rugby World Cup Final only six players were members of an exclusive club of two-times Webb Ellis Cup winners. Five of the dual winners were members of the dominant Australian sides of 1991 and 1999, namely Dan Crowley, John Eales (captain in 1999), Tim Horan, Phil Kearns and Jason Little. The remaining member of this famous six pack was South Africa's loosehead prop, Jacobus Petrus 'Os' du Randt, who lifted the famous trophy in 1995 and 2007 and who retired as the Springboks' most capped player with 80 caps after the 2007 final victory over England.

However, after the 2015 final this exclusive club had 14 new members following New Zealand's 34-17 victory over Australia at Twickenham, England. Four years previously the All Blacks triumphed 8-7 over France in the 2011 final played at Eden Park, Auckland, New Zealand. A total of 14 players won back-to-back tournaments in 2011 and 2015: Dan Carter, Ben Franks, Owen Franks, Jerome Kaino, Ma'a Nonu, Keven Mealamu, Kieran Read, Colin Slade, Conrad Smith, Victor Vito, Sam Whitelock, Sonny Bill Williams, Tony Woodcock and the only player to captain two Webb Ellis Cup-winning sides, Richie McCaw.

Did You Know That?

The 2015 final marked the end of the international careers of Dan Carter and Ma'a Nonu who moved to France to ply their trade whilst Richie McCaw, Keven Mealamu and Tony Woodcock decided to retire from the game.

A COSTLY TACKLE

Wales met France in the semi-final of the 2011 Rugby World Cup at Eden Park, Auckland, New Zealand. Wales were favourites to beat France based on their form in the tournament: Wales won three of their four Pool D games, losing 17-16 to pool winners South Africa (scored 180 points and conceded 34) and had seen off Ireland in the quarter-finals with a 22-10 victory. In contrast, France had laboured their way to the semi-finals: they finished second to New Zealand in Pool A, losing 37-17 to the All Blacks and 19-14 to Tonga (scored 124 points and conceded 96) and defeated England 19-12 in the quarter-finals. Wales led 3-0 after 17 minutes from a James Hook penalty and looked in control of the game until the referee, Alain Rolland, found himself at the centre of controversy. After France won a line-out in their opponent's half, Vincent Clerc charged through the middle but was upended by Sam Warburton who turned the winger in the air and brought him down on his back. Whilst there was no question that the tackle was illegal, many felt it was a clumsy tackle which did not deserve the red card Rolland showed the Welsh captain. Wales played the remainder of the game with 14 men and lost the match 9-8.

MORE THAN JUST A COACH

Clive Woodward, who was England's coach when they won the 2003 Rugby World Cup, won 21 caps for England from 1980–84, scoring 16 points, and won two Test caps as a player on the British and Irish

Lions' 1980 tour to South Africa (lost 3-1) and their 1983 tour to New Zealand (lost 4-0, only the second time in history they had been whitewashed with the previous whitewash occurring in 1966, again to the All Blacks). In 1981, he was a member of the Barbarians side which beat Australia 12-10 in the final of the Hong Kong Sevens. During his tenure as England coach, 1997–2004, England played 83 Tests, winning 59, drawing two and losing 22. His greatest number of victories came against Wales (eight), the most losses were versus New Zealand (six) and the two draws came against the All Blacks and Australia.

Did You Know That?

On 6 March 2008, Sir Clive Woodward had the privilege of being one of the Olympic torch bearers while running through Russell Square, London.

RUGBY WORLD CUP QUOTES

'I'm delighted with the result. It's important for our country and I think everyone back home is rejoicing. They were a bit unlucky not to get a try – we showed a bit of attitude on the line. What more can I say? I'm over the moon, it's a massive win for us as a group.'

Jake White, head coach of South Africa after the Springboks beat England 15-6 in the 2007 Rugby World Cup Final

REN & G

The 2019 Rugby World Cup in Japan will feature two mascots called 'Ren' and 'G'. They are mythical, lion-like creatures that are said to chase away evil and bring happiness in ancient Japanese culture. Their role is to 'spread the rugby spirit from Japan to Asia and to the rest of the world'. They will appear in the 12 host cities and team camp locations and provide tourist information about Japan to international visitors. 'Ren' is the parent of 'G' and both are genderless.

RUGBY WORLD CUP QUOTES

'It hasn't sunk in. It will take a few days to sink in – it is fantastic for all the players, the management and the whole of England.'

Martin Johnson, England captain, after England beat Australia 20-17 after extra time to win the 2003 Rugby World Cup Final

WINNING HEARTS AND MINDS

Georgia, alongside Japan, captured the hearts of rugby fans all over the world with their exploits during the 2015 Rugby World Cup finals in England. Out of the blocks quickly, Georgia beat Tonga (17-10), frustrated giants New Zealand (lost 43-10), Argentina (lost 54-9) and ground out a scrappy 17-16 win over Namibia to finish third in Pool C behind the All Blacks and the Pumas. This was a great feat for the Europeans which saw them qualify for the 2019 Rugby World Cup finals. Talk was rife about including the side in the Six Nations with nothing but praise for the Georgians and their New Zealand-born coach, Milton Haig.

Japan also finished third in their pool but sent shockwaves throughout the sport by defeating South Africa 34-32 in their opening game. The Brave Blossoms then lost 45-10 to Scotland, beat Samoa 26-5 and defeated the USA 28-18 (South Africa won Pool B with the Scots finishing as runners-up).

In a post-tournament interview with *Talking Rugby Union*, Haig said: 'It was a very well organised tournament that showcased to the world how the gap has closed between the tier 1 teams and the "minnows". Japan's defeat of South Africa showed this clearly. Hopefully we showed that Georgian rugby (along with Japan) has improved and that we are worthy of more matches against tier 1 opposition. We also hope that we gained more fans around the world that will follow Georgian rugby in the future.'

Did You Know That?

Haig took charge of Georgia in 2011 and coached the *Lelos* to European Nations Cup/Rugby Europe Championships success in 2012, 2013, 2014, 2015, 2016 and 2018. The European Nations Cup/Rugby Europe Championships is contested annually by Belgium, Georgia, Germany, Romania, Russia and Spain. In 2012, 2013, 2014, 2015, 2016 and 2018, Georgia also won the Antim Cup which is contested between Georgia and Romania each time the teams meet in a senior international match other than World Cup matches or qualifiers. The trophy is named in honour of the Romanian Orthodox Metropolitan Anthim the Iberian who was born in the Kingdom of Kartli, Georgia in 1650.

THE FASTEST PROP IN WORLD RUGBY

Scott Gibbs was one of the most destructive tacklers to pull on a Welsh jersey and a one-man wrecking ball in attack. He made 53 appearances for Wales from 1991-2001 and scored 10 tries (50 points). During his playing career he was dubbed the 'fastest prop in world rugby' despite actually being a centre, because his build (5ft 9in and 15st 7lb) made him look more like a front-rower. Gibbs went on three tours with the British and Irish Lions (1993, 1997 and 2001), scoring one try. He played rugby union for Bridgend RFC (1990-91), Neath RFC (1991/92), Swansea RFC (1992–94 and 1996–2003) and Ospreys

(2003–04). In 1994, he switched codes and signed for St Helens where he remained for two seasons, playing 48 games and scoring 23 tries for the Lancashire outfit who he helped win the Challenge Cup and the inaugural Super Cup in 1996. During his sojourn in rugby league he also made two appearances for the Wales national rugby league side (both games during the 1995 Rugby League World Cup).

Gibbs will always be remembered by rugby union fans for two standout moments. In their last game of the 1999 Five Nations Championship, Wales played England at Wembley Stadium, London. It was a 'home' game for the Welsh as the Millennium Stadium was under construction. An English victory would see them claim the last ever Five Nations Championship with Italy joining the four home nations and France the following year. When the game entered injury time, Wales trailed by six points (31-25) and a win for England looked inevitable. But the Welsh marched up the pitch and after winning a crucial line-out, the ball was passed to Gibbs who left England players lying all over the pitch after vain attempts to stop him. He scored to narrow the score to 31-30 and Neil Jenkins's conversion gave Wales a famous 32-31 win, which handed the championship to Scotland.

Gibbs played three games for his country at the 1991 Rugby World Cup finals and four games during the 1999 tournament.

In 1997, the British and Irish Lions toured South Africa, the reigning Rugby World Cup holders, and in the first of their three Tests versus the Springboks they won 25-16 at Newlands, Cape Town. The second Test was played at King's Park, Durban and wearing the famous red jersey of the touring side, Gibbs produced a moment that will live forever in the memories of rugby fans. Carrying the ball he thundered towards South Africa's Os du Randt, and Gibbs, nicknamed 'Car-Crash' by his teammates, smashed the 20 stone Springboks' prop, nicknamed 'the Ox', to the deck and simply ran over him.

'Some things just happen on a Lions tour. It happened to me in South Africa. But the biggest factor in that Test series wasn't my run but that somebody called Neil Jenkins kicked the Boks out of the game. He, more than anybody else, was the totem of that tour and won that Test series. I certainly didn't with one run or a couple of tackles,' said Gibbs in 2013 when asked about his bone-shuddering charge. The Lions won the Test 18-15 with a Jeremy Guscott dropped goal to clinch a series victory (won 2-1) whilst Gibbs' thundering run remains part of British and Irish Lions folklore. Gibbs was named the Player of the Series and returned to Wales with his status as a Lions legend guaranteed. In 1997, he was voted BBC Wales Sports Personality of the Year.

MAKING THE CHANGES

The 1999 Rugby World Cup finals, hosted by Wales (with some games played in England, France, Ireland and Scotland), was the fourth edition of the elite tournament. This was the first Rugby World Cup to be held in the sport's new professional era and only four automatic qualification places were available; Wales qualified automatically as the host nation whilst the other three places went to the top three teams from the 1995 Rugby World Cup (champions South Africa, runners-up New Zealand and the winners of the third place play-off match, France). For the first time the tournament was expanded from 16 nations to 20 with qualification for the final 16 places contested between 63 other nations.

The 1999 Rugby World Cup saw the introduction of a repechage, in other words a second bite at the cherry for those nations that had finished runners-up in each qualifying zone. Argentina, Australia, Canada, England, Fiji, Ireland, Italy, Japan, Namibia, Romania, Samoa, Scotland, Spain and the USA all qualified from their qualifying zones whilst Tonga and Uruguay became the first nations to profit from the repechage. Repechage 1 comprised Georgia, Netherlands, South Korea and Tonga which saw Tonga defeat South Korea in the final, 58-26 in Nuku'alofa, Tonga and 82-15 in Seoul, South Korea. Repechage 2 saw Portugal and Uruguay face one another with the winner, Uruguay, meeting Morocco in the final. The first leg of the final was played in Montevideo, Uruguay which the home side won 18-3. In the second leg, played in Casablanca, Morocco won the game 21-18 which meant Uruguay qualified for the finals with an aggregate victory of 36-24.

South Korea, recognised as Korea by World Rugby, has never qualified for a Rugby World Cup finals. They reached the repechage round of qualification for the 1999, 2003 and 2007 tournaments but were eliminated by Tonga each time. Morocco, nicknamed 'the Atlas Lions', have never qualified for a Rugby World Cup finals. Although the majority of matches at the 1999 finals were played outside Wales, the opening ceremony, the first match and the final were held in Cardiff in the recently constructed Millennium Stadium. The tournament was divided into five pools of four teams which meant a quarter-finals play-off round involving the five runners-up and best third-placed team to decide who would join the pool winners in the last eight. The overall attendance for the tournament was 1.75 million.

Did You Know That?

Australia beat France 35-12 in the 1999 Rugby World Cup Final, thereby becoming the first nation to win the Webb Ellis Cup twice and also the only team ever to win the tournament after having to qualify for it.

THE TERMINATOR

Jerry Collins was born on 4 November 1980 in Apia, Samoa, but made his international debut for New Zealand in a 67-19 win over Argentina in Christchurch, New Zealand on 23 June 2001. He was named the Player of the Tournament at the 1999 World Junior Championships (Under-19) which New Zealand won, before going on to become the first player from that team to be called up to the All Blacks, in 2001. Collins played his provincial rugby in New Zealand for Wellington and graduated in to the Hurricanes side in Super Rugby. The 6ft 3in, 17-stone flanker/No. 8 was nicknamed 'the Terminator' for his ferocious tackling. However, he did not win his second All Blacks Test cap until 14 June 2003, a 15-13 loss against England in Wellington, New Zealand.

Collins was selected for New Zealand's 2003 Rugby World Cup finals squad in Australia where they finished third (beat France 40-13) and he played in all three Tests versus the British and Irish Lions in 2005 (the All Blacks won the series 3-0) before helping the All Blacks to the 2005 Tri-Nations title. Collins played in his second Rugby World Cup finals in France in 2007 (he captained his country in two of their four Pool C games; a 108-13 thrashing of Portugal and an 85-8 win over Romania, standing in for Richie McCaw) and was one of New Zealand's best performers in what proved to be a disappointing tournament (they lost 20-18 to France in the quarter-finals). After the tournament he retired from Test rugby with 48 caps (42 starts, six as substitute), having won 42 games and lost six, for a winning ratio of 87.5%. He scored 25 points for the All Blacks.

Collins then moved to France to play for Toulon in the Top 14, and subsequently joined the Celtic League side Ospreys in 2009 and won the inaugural Celtic League Grand Final (known as the Magners League) with them, defeating Leinster 17-12 in the final in Dublin, Ireland. From 2011–13, he played for Yamaha Júbilo in Japan and in January 2015 he signed for the French club, Racing Club de Narbonne Méditerannée. On 5 June 2015, Collins and his partner Alana Madill tragically lost their lives when their car lost control on the A9 autoroute near Beziers in southern France and collided with a bus. He was only 34 years old.

BABY FACE

At the 2007 Rugby World Cup finals, Thretton Palamo became the youngest player ever to appear in one of the showpiece tournaments, when he played for the USA in their 64-15 Pool A loss to South Africa on 30 September 2007 at Stade de la Mosson, Montpellier, France. He was 19 years and nine days old when he came on as a replacement in the 75th minute of the game. The previous record was held by Argentina's Federico Méndez who played in the 1991 Rugby World Cup finals aged 19 years 63 days (a 32-19 loss in Pool 3 to Australia on 4 October 1991 at Stradey Park, Llanelli, Wales). Méndez went on to play for the Pumas in the 1995 and 2003 Rugby World Cup finals and won a total of 74 caps for his country between 1990 and 2004 (scored 70 points).

SWING LOW SWEET CHARIOT

It is believed that the song 'Swing Low, Sweet Chariot' may date back to 1865 when a slave called Wallace Willis may have been inspired by the Red River and the story of the Prophet Elijah being taken to heaven by a chariot. There are several theories behind the meaning of the song, including one which claims there is a coded message in it to slaves encouraging them to escape from their owners. It is also believed that slaves sang the song longing to be set free. The earliest known recording of the song was in 1909 by students from Fisk University. The Fisk Jubilee Singers, as they were known, popularised the song during a tour of the US and Europe. Joan Baez sang it during the Woodstock festival in 1969. It is believed to have been adopted by England fans during the 1988 Five Nations Championship. On 19 March, England played Ireland at Twickenham Stadium having lost 15 of their previous 23 games in the competition whilst the home crowd had not seen a try scored at the ground in over two and a half years. England scored six tries in the second half of their 35-3 rout of the Irish and every time a try was scored a section of the crowd sang the song.

Did You Know That?

England's plane home after they won the 2003 Rugby World Cup was named *Sweet Chariot*.

Did You Know That?

Although the plane arrived back at 5am, more than 8,000 fans were waiting at Heathrow airport to greet the England team. They then went on an open top bus tour of London with an estimated 750,000 fans lining the streets of the capital.

RUGBY'S GREATEST EVER ACT OF GENEROSITY

Sonny Bill Williams is a rugby legend having won the Rugby World Cup twice with the All Blacks in 2011 and again in 2015. However, he did one thing off the field of play which will immortalise his name in the hearts of not only All Black fans but all rugby fans and one young English schoolboy in particular. On 31 October 2015, the All Blacks centre collected his second Rugby World Cup winners' medal after helping his nation defeat Australia 34-17. After the medal ceremony Williams walked around the side of the Twickenham pitch on a lap of honour with his teammates. Suddenly a young boy, 14-year-old Charlie Line, ran on to the pitch to congratulate his hero, Sonny Bill. However, before he could reach his hero, a steward tackled young Charlie to the turf and almost flattened him. Williams picked Charlie up, pushed the steward to one side and gave Charlie a hug before leading him back to his family in the stands. And then quite remarkably Sonny Bill took the gold medal from around his neck and placed it around Charlie's neck.

'A young fella snuck on the field somehow but when he was coming up to give me a hug, he got smoked by a security guard, full-on tackled him. He could have been eight or seven and the other fella was a full-on man, so it looked like he would break his ribs or something. The moment probably just got the better of him but he was just so excited to get on the field with the All Blacks. I thought I'd make it a night to remember for him, rather than my medal being hanging up at home or something like that. It will be hanging around that young guy's neck and he can tell that story for years to come. The way he got round the security guard he could be a future All Black in the making. The bonds that we have as brothers in the changing room are the most important thing. The medal represents the win, but going in and seeing the smiles on the boys' faces, knowing that we've accomplished something no other All Blacks team has done, is pretty special,' said the All Black legend when asked if he would regret parting with his medal. And when the British media reported that Charlie offered to return the medal, Williams insisted that Charlie hold on to it and then posted a message on his Instagram page: 'Only takes one thing to change someone's life. Enjoy it Charlie bro.'

The day after the final World Rugby gave Sonny Bill a replacement medal during the 2015 World Rugby Awards. Williams received a standing ovation from all those in attendance in recognition of his act of generosity. 'World Rugby would like every winner to go home with a medal and they have found the final one,' announced the master of ceremonies as he invited Sonny Bill to come forward and receive his medal. Williams' kind gesture to young Charlie came a week after he offered two tickets to the All Blacks' semi-final victory over South Africa to Syrian refugees.

TIMID LIONS

Spain, nicknamed *Los Leones* (the Lions), has only ever qualified for one Rugby World Cup, in 1999. Although rugby union in Spain dates back to 1901, Spain did not play its first international until 20 May 1929, beating Italy 9-0 in Barcelona.

Did You Know That?

Spain's record win is 90-8 against the Czech Republic in Madrid, Spain on 2 April 1995. Their record loss was a 92-10 defeat to Australia in Madrid on 1 November 2001.

CONSISTENCY COUNTS

In the lead-up to the 2007 Rugby World Cup the eventual winners, New Zealand, won 38 of their previous 43 Tests whilst four years earlier, England won 35 of their previous 40 Tests before lifting the Webb Ellis Cup in 2003.

DYNAMITE DICK

Richard Moriarty famously captained the Welsh side which finished third in the inaugural Rugby World Cup in 1987. During his playing career he played 472 times for Swansea RFC (1976–98, scored 32 tries) and is the club's all-time record appearance maker. Nicknamed 'Dynamite Dick', he took no prisoners on the pitch and captained Swansea RFC from 1986-89 before going on to coach the side and serve on their board of directors. He was capped 22 times by his country (1981–87), eight times as captain (never lost a game), and scored two tries. He made a try-scoring international debut versus Australia on 5 December 1981 in an 18–13 victory at the National Stadium, Cardiff, Wales. Moriarty brought the curtain down on his career in the third-place match at the inaugural Rugby World Cup finals, a 22-21 win over the Wallabies at Rotorua International Stadium, Rotorua, New Zealand on 18 June 1987.

Did You Know That?

Richard Moriarty is the elder brother of fellow Swansea RFC and Wales rugby union and Wales rugby league player, Paul Moriarty. His nephew, Ross, has won more than 30 Wales caps and played for the Dragons for the 2018/19 Pro14 campaign.

THE OLYMPIC LOOPHOLE

Tim Nanai-Williams was born in Auckland, New Zealand to Samoan parents. He played age-group rugby representing New Zealand in the under-17s and schoolboys and also played for Counties Manukau's under-20 team. He was a member of the New Zealand and Counties Manukau sevens teams from 2008 to 2009 and has also represented New Zealand and Samoa in sevens rugby. From 2000–15, World Rugby's strict eligibility rules said that a player could only play senior rugby for one country ever, regardless of which version of the game he played (15s or sevens). Therefore, unlike footballers, rugby players holding more than one passport could not change their national affiliations. However, under the Olympic Games Charter, competitors who have represented one country may switch to another if they hold a passport for the new country and have not represented the former country for three years. World Rugby adopted the Olympic Games Charter rules for sevens rugby. The change in the eligibility rules opened the Olympic loophole, so players who make the switch in sevens rugby will also be eligible to play for that country's 15-a-side national team as well. In 2015, Nanai-Williams became the first player to change his international allegiance through the Olympic loophole (players still cannot switch directly from one national 15s team to another). Having previously played for the Samoan sevens teams, he made his international rugby union debut at full-back for Samoa in the historic Test match against the All Blacks in Apia on 8 July 2015. New Zealand had never visited Samoa before but left the Pacific Islands with a 25-16 victory. The All Blacks side included several players with Samoan heritage; Jerome Kaino, Nepo Laulala, Keven Mealamu, George Moala, Charles Piutau, and Sonny Bill Williams. Ma'a Nonu and Julian Savea would have also played for the All Blacks had they not appeared for their club side, the Hurricanes, in the Super Rugby final four days earlier. Nanai-Williams played for Samoa at the 2015 Rugby World Cup and scored one try for his country in their 25-16 win over the United States. He is a cousin of New Zealand's two-times Rugby World Cup winner, Sonny Bill Williams.

Did You Know That?

Samoa became independent from New Zealand in 1962 but since then have provided the All Blacks with some of their greatest ever players including Frank Bunce, Jerry Collins, Mills Muliaina, Rodney So'oialo, Va'aiga Tuigamala, Tana Umaga and Bryan Williams.

STRENGTH OF A BULL, TOUCH OF A PIANO PLAYER

Philippe Sella was born on 14 February 1962 in Tonneins, France and commenced his rugby career as a junior rugby league player for Tonneins XIII before switching codes to rugby union when he signed for Sporting Union Agen Lot-et-Garonne (commonly referred to as Agen) in 1982. Whilst playing for Agen he worked as a physical education teacher and when the sport became professional in 1995, he left France and moved to England, where he played for Saracens from 1996–98. When he joined Saracens he teamed-up with fellow new recruits Kyran Bracken (England 1993–2003), Michael Lynagh (Australia 1984–95) and Francois Pienaar (South Africa 1993–96).

Sella had already helped Agen clinch the French National Championship in 1982 and 1988 and in 1998, he was a member of the Saracens side which lifted the Tetley's Bitter Cup.

He made his Test debut as a winger for France on 31 October 1982 versus Romania in a 13-9 loss at Dinamo Stadion, Bucharest, Romania. However, it wasn't long before the French national coach, Jacques Fouroux (1981–90), recognised the young Sella's unique talents and switched him inside (six of his first seven Tests were on the wing) where he would go on to become perhaps the greatest centre the sport has ever seen. Fouroux once said of Sella: 'He has the strength of a bull but the touch of a piano player.' Apt words indeed for such a talented player who mesmerised defences across the globe. In the 1980s, Philippe Sella was the world's best centre and personified the best of French rugby with his combination of strength, pure class and remarkable skill as a player and as a human being. During his international career, 1982–95, he formed some outstanding centre partnerships, firstly with Didier Codorniou, followed by Denis Charvet, then Marc Andrieu, Franck Mesnel and finally, Thierry Lacroix. Sella's accurate passing, his pace and swerve which enabled him to evade the clutch of opponents with consummate ease and his rock solid defending was the perfect marriage to his partners in the centre of the French side who possessed different attributes which complemented Sella's outstanding qualities and mesmerising performances.

On 3 July 1994, he became the first rugby player to be capped 100 times by his country when *Les Bleus* defeated the All Blacks 23-20 at Eden Park, Auckland, New Zealand. When he played his 111th and final Test for France on 22 June 1995, a 19-9 win over the old enemy, England, in the third place match at the 1995 Rugby World Cup finals (played at Loftus Versfeld, Pretoria, South Africa), he became the world's most capped player. In his 13-year international career with *Les Bleus* he helped his nation win three Five Nations Championship titles (1987, 1989 and 1993) and share the title in three other tournaments (1983 with Ireland, 1986 with Scotland and 1988 with Wales). He scored 125 points and played in three Rugby World Cup finals tournaments: 1987, France finished runners-up; 1991, reached the quarter-finals; and 1995, when they finished in third place. Rugby fans will always remember Sella for his Gallic flair and his sublime running style as he charged towards the opposition from midfield. In 1999, he was inducted into the International Rugby Hall of Fame and in 2008, he was inducted into the IRB Hall of Fame.

Did You Know That?
Sella scored a try in all four of France's 1986 Five Nations Championship matches, a feat previously only achieved by Patrick Esteve (France), Howard Catcheside (England), Arthur Wallace (Scotland) and since by Gregor Townsend (Scotland).

A LEAKY DEFENCE
Japan are the only nation to have conceded more than 1,000 points at the Rugby World Cup. From the inaugural edition in 1987 until the most recent in 2015, Japan have conceded 1,259 points (Played 28, Won 4, Drawn 2, Lost 22, Points For 526).

TOP 10 MOST POINTS CONCEDED AT A RUGBY WORLD CUP

Team	Year	Mat	Won	Lost	Draw	For	Aga	Diff
Namibia	2003	4	0	4	0	28	310	-282
Namibia	2011	4	0	4	0	44	266	-222
Uruguay	2003	4	1	3	0	56	255	-199
Japan	1995	3	0	3	0	55	252	-197
Uruguay	2015	4	0	4	0	30	226	-196
Namibia	2007	4	0	4	0	30	212	-182
Japan	2007	4	0	3	1	64	210	-146
Portugal	2007	4	0	4	0	38	209	-171
Georgia	2003	4	0	4	0	46	200	-154
Italy	1999	3	0	3	0	35	196	-161

Did You Know That?

Before Namibia gained its independence from South Africa in 1990, they competed in the Currie Cup, South Africa's domestic cup competition, as South West Africa. They achieved their best result in 1988 when they finished third.

IRELAND'S FIRST RUGBY WORLD CUP COACH

Mick Doyle was the head coach of Ireland at the inaugural Rugby World Cup in 1987. However, prior to Ireland's opening game against Wales, Doyle suffered a heart attack at the tournament's opening dinner. During his playing career, he won 20 caps as a flanker for Ireland between 1965 and 1968 and toured South Africa with the British and Irish Lions in 1968. He coached Leinster to Interprovincial Championship glory in five consecutive years from 1979 to 1983. He was Ireland's head coach from 1984–87 and in 1985 he guided them to a Triple Crown and Five Nations Championship success. His last game for Ireland was against Australia on 26 October 1968, a 10-3 victory at Lansdowne Road, Dublin when he lined out alongside his brother Tommy.

IN HIS OWN WORDS

'I always remember I was digging a trench in Pontypridd Park when I had the call to say I'd been selected for Wales. I can tell you I stepped out of that trench pretty quick!'

Garin Jenkins, 58 caps for Wales 1991–2002 (10 points), a former coalminer

RUGBY's TEN COMMANDMENTS FOR SUCCESS

Prior to the 2007 Rugby World Cup, Sir Clive Woodward, who guided England to glory in the 2003 tournament, gave an interview to *The Times* in which he gave his 'Ten Commandments' on how to win the Rugby World Cup. **1.** You need the whole game behind you. **2.** Try to arrive as favourites. **3.** Experience. **4.** Playing in your own hemisphere and particularly your own country. **5.** A settled team. **6.** A tried and trusted way of playing. **7.** Leadership. **8.** The need for world class people in support of the players. **9.** Deal with the energy sappers and the termites. **10.** Totally understand your opposition.

Did You Know That?

In 1854, Trinity College at Dublin University founded Old Rugbeians, the first rugby club in Ireland.

RUGBY WORLD CUP QUOTES

'When [coach] Clive Rowlands told me I was going to be captain, quite simply it was absolutely amazing, the feeling was one of such elation. You talk of milestones and peaks in your career and to be named as captain for the World Cup squad was icing on cake.'

Richard Moriarty, captain of Wales at the 1987 Rugby World Cup

31 PUMAS

Every member of Argentina's 31-man squad at the 2015 Rugby World Cup was born in Argentina, meaning they were the only nation without a foreign-born player. No fewer than 13 members of the Samoan squad were born outside the Pacific Island, meaning they had the most foreign-born players at the tournament. The 13 were all born in New Zealand to Samoan parents whilst Tonga had 12 players who were not born in the Polynesian kingdom. The remaining squads all had at least one foreign-born representative; France 10, Australia 9, Italy 9, Japan 9, Scotland 9, Wales 9, USA 9, Canada 5, Ireland 5, New Zealand 5, Romania 4, England 3, Fiji 3, Namibia 2, Georgia 1 (Merab Sharikadze, born in Moscow to Georgian parents), South Africa 1 (Tendai 'The Beast' Mtawarira, born in Zimbabwe was the only Springbok from outside the Rainbow Nation) and Uruguay 1 (Alejo Corral born in Argentina qualifies on residency). A total of 20 countries participated at the 2015 Rugby World Cup from a qualifying pool of 96. The 20 countries included players from 13 other countries who did not qualify in their own right: Africa had World Cup players born in Algeria, Burkina Faso, Cote d'Ivoire, Democratic Republic of the Congo, Nigeria and Zimbabwe while other nations included players born in Belgium, Israel, Netherlands, Papua New Guinea, Russia, Saudi Arabia and Spain.

TOP OF THE POPS 1995

When South Africa won the third Rugby World Cup Final on 24 June 1995, the No.1 song in the UK pop charts was *Unchained Melody* by Robson Greene and Jerome Flynn. It was the debut single for the acting duo who starred in the TV series *Soldier, Soldier*. The pair specialised in remaking former hits. This was actually the third time at the top for the song, having previously topped the charts in 1955 and 1990. It occupied the top slot for seven weeks before being ousted by the Outhere Brothers with *Boom Boom Boom*.

SUPER KAINO

Jerome Kaino made his Test debut for the All Blacks in a 34-23 victory over Ireland at Hamilton, New Zealand on 10 June 2006. Kaino, who was born in Faga'alu, American Samoa, moved to Auckland, New Zealand with his family when he was a child. He played at centre and full-back as a teenager before developing into one of New Zealand's most promising young loose forwards. In his first year with the Blues in 2004 he was named the IRB Under-21 Player of the Year and was Player of the Tournament at the 2004 IRB Under-21 World Championship and New Zealand Age Grade Player of the Year the same year. Kaino helped the All Blacks to back-to-back Rugby World Cup Final wins in 2011 and 2015 and in 2011 he was named the New Zealand Rugby Player of the Year, finishing ahead of Richie McCaw and Ma'a Nonu in the voting. When he decided to join Toulouse for the 2018 season it meant the end of his All Blacks career; 81 caps and 60 Test points, from 12 tries. Kaino scored a try in his All Blacks debut against the Barbarians (non-Test cap) at Twickenham in December 2004.

IRELAND'S CLEAN SWEEP OF WORLD RUGBY AWARDS

Ireland ended 2018 by sweeping the board at the annual World Rugby Awards which were held in Monaco on 25 November 2018. The Six Nations Grand Slam winners were named Team of the Year, Joe Schmidt was named Coach of the Year and Johnny Sexton was crowned Men's Player of the Year, the first time in seven years this prestigious individual award had not been awarded to a New Zealand player (Thierry Dusautoir in 2011). In his five years in charge of Ireland, Schmidt has guided Ireland from being ranked the eighth best nation in the world to the second best. Sexton, the captain of Leinster, saw off stiff challenges from the other nominees: Rieko Ioane (New Zealand), Faf de Klerk (South Africa), Malcolm Marx (South Africa) and the All Blacks' Beauden Barrett, who was looking to claim a hat-trick of consecutive individual awards. It was the first time Ireland had claimed the treble of awards which were introduced by World Rugby in 2001. Ireland suffered just one defeat in 2018, an 18-9 loss in their first Test against Australia in Brisbane in June, a game Sexton was rested for. Sexton returned for the next two Tests and helped Ireland to a first series win in Australia for 39 years. 'If a number 10 wins an award like this it is due to the team around him. We have some of the best coaches in the world and are led superbly,' said the 33-year-old Sexton.

RUGBY WORLD CUP QUOTES

'I recalled childhood memories of FA Cup captains at Wembley.'
Australia captain, Nick Farr-Jones, after lifting the Webb Ellis Cup at Twickenham Stadium in 1991

A ROYAL WELCOME

On 12 October 2015, the Queen hosted an event at Buckingham Palace to welcome the Rugby World Cup to England. A total of 400 guests, including the captains of all 20 nations participating, were received by

Her Majesty, who was accompanied by her husband Prince Philip, her daughter Princess Anne and her grandson Prince Harry. The Queen was presented with a specially commissioned World Cup participation medal by the director of World Rugby, Bernard Lapasset. Prince Harry was seen talking to his grandmother as the pair wistfully stared at the Webb Ellis Cup. However, that was the closest an Englishman got to the famous trophy as Australia had knocked the host nation out of the competition nine days earlier by beating them 33-13 at Twickenham Stadium, London. Prince Harry served as the honorary president of England 2015. The Queen was the patron of the Rugby Football Union for 64 years until Harry took over the role in 2016 (Harry had been vice patron of the RFU since 2010). Princess Anne is the patron of the Scottish Rugby Union whilst Harry's brother, William, is the vice patron of the Welsh Rugby Union.

WORLD'S TOP 10

In November 2012, Kyle from the *terrific-top10.com* website published its list of what it considered to be the Top 10 Best Rugby Players in the World.

1. Jonah Lomu (New Zealand)
2. Martin Johnson (England)
3. Dan Carter (New Zealand)
4. David Campese (Australia)
5. Richie McCaw (New Zealand)
6. Jonny Wilkinson (England)
7. Brian O'Driscoll (Ireland)
8. Percy Montgomery (South Africa)
9. Naas Botha (South Africa)
10. Shane Williams (Wales)

Did You Know That?

Despite playing during the time when South Africa was almost completely banned from international rugby due to apartheid, Naas Botha scored 312 points in his 28 Tests for the Springboks. He was famous for his ability to score drop goals under pressure.

World Rugby Team of the Year Award Winners

2018 – Ireland
2017 – New Zealand
2016 – New Zealand
2015 – New Zealand
2014 – New Zealand
2013 – New Zealand

2012 – New Zealand
2011 – New Zealand
2010 – New Zealand
2009 – South Africa
2008 – New Zealand
2007 – South Africa
2006 – New Zealand
2005 – New Zealand
2004 – South Africa
2003 – England
2002 – France
2001 – Australia

Did You Know That?

Bernard Laporte, the coach of France in 2002, was renowned for his commitment to improving discipline in the national side. On one occasion he suspended the player he made captain of France, Fabien Pelous, for foul play. Laporte saw discipline as a key factor for team morale and for promoting the game of rugby.

RUGBY WORLD CUP QUOTES

'Well, straight after the game I turned to anyone who was there just to celebrate and go crazy. And then I realised I was going to get the trophy from the Queen. I thought "better make sure you don't swear" and after that was just really excited to represent the team and Australian rugby. I was filled with an immense satisfaction that we had achieved what we wanted to do – goals which had been set by some of us four years ago.'

John Eales, captain of Australia, after being asked how he felt after winning the 1999 Rugby World Cup Final

TOP OF THE POPS 1999

When Australia won the fourth Rugby World Cup Final on 6 November 1999, the second time they lifted the Webb Ellis Cup (1991), the No.1 song in the UK pop charts was *Keep On Movin'* by Five. It was the first UK No.1 for the UK boy band who had six Top 10 hits, including three successive No.2s prior to this success. The song only spent one week in the top slot before being ousted by the former Spice Girl, Geri Halliwell, with *Lift Me Up*.

WESTERN SAMOA SHOCK WALES

'Thank heavens Wales weren't playing the whole of Samoa,' was a famous quip after rugby minnows, Western Samoa, defeated one of the sport's powerhouses, Wales, 16-13 in the two sides' opening Pool 3 game at the 1991 Rugby World Cup finals. It was the first time one of the sport's leading nations had come unstuck against one of the unfancied teams. The superb kicking of Mathew Vaea (scored one conversion and one penalty) made the difference at Cardiff Arms Park, Cardiff, Wales on 6 October 1991. The result was not only one of Welsh rugby union's darkest hours but it also resulted in one of the five co-host nations of the tournament (the other co-hosts were England, France, Ireland and Scotland) failing to make the quarter-final stages after finishing third in Pool 3 behind the winners Australia and Rugby World Cup debutants, Western Samoa. Wales had finished in third place in the inaugural Rugby World Cup finals in 1987. The result remains one of the biggest shocks in Rugby World Cup history.

Did You Know That?

At the 1999 Rugby World Cup finals, Samoa repeated their shock win from eight years earlier by defeating Wales 38-31 at the Millennium Stadium, Cardiff, Wales in a Pool D game on 14 October 1999. The islanders became the first visiting team to win at Wales's new home ground (opened on 26 June 1999).

ALMOST A HERO

François Trinh-Duc was born in Montpellier, France on 11 November 1986. He began playing rugby aged just four at the Pic-Saint-Loup rugby school near his home. In 2004, he signed for Montpellier where he remained until joining Toulon in 2016. He won his first Test cap when he was picked by the France head coach, Marc Lievremont, for *Les Bleus'* 2008 Six Nations Championships squad. On 3 February 2008, he made his debut versus Scotland in a 27-6 win at Murrayfield, Edinburgh, Scotland and went on to play in the remaining four games (won two, lost two). At the 2011 Rugby World Cup finals, he scored a drop goal which helped France defeat England 19-12 in the quarter-finals. In the 2011 Rugby World Cup Final he came on for the injured Morgan Parra in the 23rd minute of the game. In the seventh minute of the second half he started the move which led to his captain, Thierry Dusautoir, scoring a try and his conversion brought the French to within one point of the host nation, New Zealand, at 8-7. With 15 minutes of the game remaining, and the score still standing at 8-7, *Les Bleus* were awarded a penalty. However, Trinh-Duc missed the 48-metre attempt and the All Blacks held on to win the final 8-7.

IN HIS OWN WORDS

'Remember that rugby is a team game. All 14 of you make sure you pass the ball to Jonah.'

An anonymous fax to the New Zealand rugby team in 1995 before they played England in the semi-finals of the 1995 Rugby World Cup. The All Blacks won the game 45-29 with Jonah Lomu scoring four tries.

Did You Know That?

Trinh-Duc was the first ever rugby player of Vietnamese origin to play for the French national team. His paternal grandfather, Trinh Đúc Nhiên, was born in French Indonesia and immigrated to Agen, Lot-et-Garonne, France during the First Indochina War (19 December 1946–1 August 1954). His paternal grandmother was Italian but his father, Philippe, was born in France.

World Rugby Men's Player of the Year Award Winners

2018 – Johnny Sexton (Ireland)
2017 – Beauden Barrett (New Zealand)
2016 – Beauden Barrett (New Zealand)
2015 – Dan Carter (New Zealand)
2014 – Brodie Retallick (New Zealand)
2013 – Kieran Read (New Zealand)
2012 – Dan Carter (New Zealand)
2011 – Thierry Dusautoir (France)
2010 – Richie McCaw (New Zealand)
2009 – Richie McCaw (New Zealand)
2008 – Shane Williams (Wales)
2007 – Bryan Habana (South Africa)
2006 – Richie McCaw (New Zealand)
2005 – Dan Carter (New Zealand)
2004 – Schalk Burger (South Africa)
2003 – Jonny Wilkinson (England)
2002 – Fabien Galthié (France)
2001 – Keith Wood (Ireland)

Did You Know That?

Thierry Dusautoir was born in Abidjan, Côte d'Ivoire to a French father and an Ivorian mother. Nicknamed 'the Beast', he did not take up rugby until he was 16 with his favourite sport up until then being judo. He is a graduate chemical engineer.

LES BLEUS' BIG SURPRISE

In the minds of many French sports journalists, France went into the 1999 Rugby World Cup finals in Wales without a hope of even making it out of their pool. *Les Bleus* were not in a good place, having finished rock bottom (winners of the wooden spoon) of the 1999 Five Nations Championship with just one win (10-9 v Ireland in Dublin in their opening game) and three consecutive defeats, 34-33 to Wales in Paris, 21-10 to England in London and 36-22 to Scotland at Stade de France. In preparation for the 1999 Rugby World Cup the French went on tour in the hope of trying to recover some renewed self-belief, if not confidence, in their squad. France beat a strong Samoa side 39-22 in Apia, Samoa; lost 20-16 to Tonga in Nuku A'lofa; lost 54-7 to the tournament favourites, the All Blacks, in Wellington, New Zealand and ended their tour with a 34-23 defeat to the 1999 Rugby World Cup hosts, Wales, in Cardiff. But at the 1999 Rugby World Cup the French players not only stirred a nation into a frenzy, they once again earned the respect of the rugby world as a team to be feared. France eased their way through Pool C and won it with victories over Canada 33-20, Namibia 47-13 and Fiji 28-19 to claim a quarter-final tie against Argentina. France beat the Pumas 47-26 at Lansdowne Road, Dublin, Ireland and overpowered the All Blacks 43-31 at Twickenham Stadium, London, in the semi-finals. However, *Les Bleus* were no match for Australia in the final, losing 35-12 at the Millennium Stadium, Cardiff. Much to the surprise of the French players and staff, around 10,000 fans turned out to welcome their heroes on the team's return to Paris.

Did You Know That?

Lansdowne Road took its name from the adjacent street called Lansdowne Road. The old stadium was demolished in 2007 to make way for the construction of the Aviva Stadium, which opened in 2010.

WORLD RUGBY COACH OF THE YEAR

The World Rugby Coach of the Year is awarded annually by World Rugby (from 2004 to 2007, the award was called the International Rugby Board International Coach of the Year).

2018 – Joe Schmidt (Ireland)
2017 – Eddie Jones (England)
2016 – Steve Hansen (New Zealand)
2015 – Michael Cheika (Australia)
2014 – Steve Hansen (New Zealand)
2013 – Steve Hansen (New Zealand)

2012 – Steve Hansen (New Zealand)
2011 – Graham Henry (New Zealand)
2010 – Graham Henry (New Zealand)
2009 – Declan Kidney (Ireland)
2008 – Graham Henry (New Zealand)
2007 – Jake White (South Africa)
2006 – Graham Henry (New Zealand)
2005 – Graham Henry (New Zealand)
2004 – Jake White (South Africa)
2003 – Clive Woodward (England)
2002 – Bernard Laporte (France)
2001 – Rod Macqueen (Australia)

Did You Know That?

Declan Kidney was the head coach of Ireland from 2008-13 and in his first year in charge he guided the Irish to the Triple Crown and Grand Slam in the Six Nations Championship. Rod Macqueen coached Australia from 1997 to 2001 and in 1999, Australia won the World Rugby Cup, thereby becoming the first nation to win the Webb Ellis Cup twice (winners in 1991). In 2000, the Wallabies won the Tri-Nations Series for the first time and the following year his Australian side defeated a highly rated touring British and Irish Lions side.

RUGBY WORLD CUP QUOTES

'We have to play a lot better against New Zealand. If we play badly, they will beat us and the French press will decapitate us like Marie Antoinette.'

Jo Maso, the France general manager, before *Les Blues* beat New Zealand 43-31 in the semi-finals of the 1999 Rugby World Cup

HALF ALL BLACK, HALF WALLABY

David Kirk captained New Zealand to glory in the inaugural Rugby World Cup in 1987. On Australia Day 2009 (26 January) he took up Australian citizenship at a ceremony having lived in Australia for a decade. 'We've lived here as a family for ten years. My children have grown up here, particularly the younger one, and it just seemed like the right time,' said Kirk during an interview with *Television Three News*. But after confirming that he would hold dual citizenship, the All Blacks legend made it clear where his heart lay. 'I grew up in New Zealand. My heart, my emotion, my commitment of course is to New Zealand.' When he was asked about his rugby allegiance, he said: 'Of course I'm an All Blacks supporter. I'm a massive All Blacks supporter and it's the All Blacks all the way.'

NEW ZEALAND RUGBY FOOTBALL UNION FOUNDED

As rugby increased in popularity, it became more important to standardise the administration of rugby in the colony (the Colony of New Zealand was a British colony that existed in New Zealand from 1841 to 1907, created as a Crown colony). Despite some opposition, a New Zealand Rugby Football Union was founded in Wellington on 16 April 1892. During the 1880s there had been many squabbles about fixtures, scoring values, and the interpretation of the laws of the game. A supreme authority along the lines of the (English) Rugby Football Union was needed to give guidance and pass judgement on such matters. Visiting teams also found it awkward to have to deal separately with local unions rather than an overall governing body. Suggestions for a New Zealand union gained little momentum until 1891, when E.D. Hoben, the secretary of the Hawke's Bay union, toured the country promoting the idea. He received enough support to convene a meeting in Wellington in November 1891 at which a constitution was drafted for examination by the unions. Delegates representing the Auckland, Canterbury, Hawke's Bay, Manawatū, Otago, Taranaki, Wairarapa and Wellington unions met again in Wellington on 16 April 1892. Bush, Marlborough, Nelson, Poverty Bay and South Canterbury did not send representatives but offered their support. The powerful Canterbury and Otago unions did not initially join the NZRFU. By 1895, however, they and Southland were all affiliated with the national organisation.

WALLABY TEAM OF THE DECADE

In 2005, the Australian Rugby Union celebrated ten years of professional rugby by naming a Wallaby Team of the Decade. A panel of 30 judges was assembled made up of commentators and journalists to compile a starting XV. The panel decided on six automatic selections (in italics below) with the remaining nine being selected for their respective positions. Not surprisingly, the only five Australian players to have won two Rugby World Cups (1991 and 1999) were all selected: Dan Crowley, John Eales, Tim Horan, Phil Kearns and Jason Little.

1. Richard Harry (loosehead prop)
2. Phil Kearns (hooker)
3. Andrew Blades (tighthead prop)
4. David Giffin (lock)
5. *John Eales (lock & captain)*
6. Owen Finegan (blindside flanker)
7. George Smith (openside flanker)
8. *Toutai Kefu (No. 8)*
9. *George Gregan (scrum-half)*
10. *Stephen Larkham (fly-half)*
11. Joe Roff (left wing)
12. *Tim Horan (inside centre)*
13. Jason Little (outside centre)
14. Ben Turner (right wing)
15. *Matthew Burke (full-back)*

Reserves - 16. Jeremy Paul 17. Dan Crowley 18. Nathan Sharpe 19. Phil Waugh 20. Chris Whitaker 21. Dan Herbert 22. Lote Tuqiri
Coach – Rod Macqueen (1999 Rugby World Cup winning coach)

Did You Know That?

Toutai Kefu won 60 caps for the Wallabies (1997–2003, scored 50 points) and will coach Tonga into the 2019 Rugby World Cup finals in Japan.

AN IMPRESSIVE DEBUT

New Zealand's Luke McAlister was named the 2002 IRB International U19 Player of the Year. He made his debut for the All Blacks on 9 June 2005 in the third Test against the touring British and Irish Lions at Eden Park, Auckland when the 21-year-old replaced an injured Dan Carter at first five (fly-half). His debut was an impressive one, scoring 13 of the All Blacks' points in a 38-19 win. His worst moment for his country came in their narrow 20-18 loss to France in the quarter-finals of the 2007 Rugby World Cup in Cardiff, Wales, when he was sin-binned early in the second half by the English referee, Wayne Barnes, for illegally blocking a French player and preventing a try-scoring opportunity. When he came back on, and with Dan Carter and Nick Evans both injured, he failed to take control of the All Blacks' backline strategy including trying to organise a dropped goal attempt which if scored would have seen the All Blacks proceed to a semi-final encounter against England. New Zealand's defeat to France meant they failed to reach the semi-final stages for the first time in World Cup history. McAlister played 31 times (includes 11 as substitute) for the All Blacks and scored 153 points (seven tries, 26 conversions and 22 penalties).

Did You Know That?
The winner of the inaugural IRB International U19 Player of the Year Award, Gavin Henson of Wales in 2001, never played at a Rugby World Cup.

RUGBY WORLD CUP WINNING COACHES

Year	Winners	Coach
1987	New Zealand	Brian Lochore
1991	Australia	Bob Dwyer
1995	South Africa	Kitch Christie
1999	Australia	Rod Macqueen
2003	England	Clive Woodward
2007	South Africa	Jake White
2011	New Zealand	Graham Henry
2015	New Zealand	Steve Hansen

Did You Know That?
Graham Henry coached Wales at the 1999 Rugby World Cup, guiding them to the quarter-finals as the host nation.

IN HIS OWN WORDS

'I was this guy who'd been racing around down there, on that field in 1999, running straight over people, scoring tries, winning games, having fun. And I ended up so sick I couldn't even run past a little baby.'

Jonah Lomu (New Zealand) speaking about how his kidney condition affected his playing career

BRING BACK BILL

Going into the 1999 Rugby World Cup finals, hosted by Wales, the Australian team dubbed its pursuit of the Webb Ellis Cup, 'Bring back Bill', in honour of the Wallabies' first title which they won in England in 1991 at Twickenham Stadium, London. Australia went on to win the 1999 Rugby World Cup with a 35-12 victory over France at the Millennium Stadium, Cardiff, Wales. An exhausted Wallabies squad arrived in Sydney less than 48 hours after captain, John Eales, held aloft the Webb Ellis Cup, and were greeted at the airport by an expectant crowd who sang *Waltzing Matilda* as their triumphant heroes disembarked the plane.

Did You Know That?

Waltzing Matilda is the unofficial national anthem of Australia. The song title is Australian slang for travelling on foot (waltzing) carrying your belongings in a 'matilda' (a bundle of clothes etc) over your back.

RUGBY WORLD CUP WINNING COACHES – WHERE ARE THEY NOW?

Up to and including the 2015 Rugby World Cup Final, eight men have coached a Rugby World Cup winning side. But what did they do post their success and where are they now?

Brian Lochore
New Zealand 1987

He went on to coach the All Blacks at the 1995 Rugby World Cup and subsequently served as a selector. In 1999, he received a knighthood for his services to rugby and was inducted into the International Rugby Hall of Fame. The Lochore Cup, which is played for in the Heartland Championship (part of New Zealand's domestic competition), is named in his honour. In 2011, he was inducted into the International Rugby Board Hall of Fame and currently chairs the Queen Elizabeth II National Trust. He is also a patron of New Zealand Rugby.

Did You Know That?

Lochore was also a Wairarapa tennis representative from 1957 to 1961 and from 1979 to 1980.

Bob Dwyer
Australia 1991

After guiding the Wallabies to their 12-6 win over England in the final he took charge of the Leicester Tigers when the game turned professional in 1996. He steered the Tigers to the 1997 Heineken Cup Final and in the same year they won the Pilkington Cup. The following year he took charge of recently relegated Bristol whom he guided back to the top flight at the first time of asking. He left Bristol in 2000 and in 2001, went home to Australia to coach the New South Wales Waratahs in Super Rugby (it was known as the Super 12 at the time). He resigned from his role in 2003 but stayed with the New South Wales union as a development officer and the next year he was made a Member of the Order of Australia for services to rugby union. In 2011, he was inducted into the International Rugby Board Hall of Fame and survived a heart attack in 2013. He was nicknamed 'Barbed Wire' by the Leicester Tigers players because of his harsh attitude towards them.

Kitch Christie (George Moir Christie) South Africa 1995

After guiding the Springboks to their 15-12 after-extra-time victory over the All Blacks on home soil in the 1995 final, Christie remained in the post until 1996 including leading the Rainbow Nation to a then record 14 consecutive victories and South Africa were unbeaten during his tenure (1994–96). In 1995, his health deteriorated from leukaemia and he stepped down as head coach in March 2016. However, his treatment went well enough to permit him to fulfil a lifelong dream and he took charge of Northern Transvaal for the 1997 Super 12 season. His ill health returned, resulting in him being unable to travel with the Blue Bulls to Australasia in the early part of the season. Within weeks he was back in hospital and quite sickeningly it was during his stay in hospital that he experienced one of the lowest points in his life when Hentie Serfontein, the president of Northern Transvaal, visited him to tell him his services were no longer required. 'He fired me like a dog,' said Christie in his typically forthright fashion. Following a course of specialist treatment in the USA in late 1997 he returned to the sport as a technical director to the Falcons in 1998. On Easter Sunday 1998 he was hospitalised again and sadly passed away on 22 April 1998 aged 58. In 2011, he was inducted posthumously into the International Rugby Board Hall of Fame. In his autobiography entitled *Rainbow Warrior*, Francois Pienaar recalled how Christie joined the team huddle before a 24-14 win over England at Twickenham Stadium on 18 November 1995, and stood between himself and James Dalton. 'The usual end to such a Springboks huddle is for the players to squeeze each other and shout "Bokke". James and I squeezed the coach and discovered later we'd fractured two of his ribs. He never said a word,' wrote Pienaar, who captained South Africa to Rugby World Cup glory in 1995.

Roderick Ian Macqueen
Australia 1999

Macqueen was appointed the head coach of Australia in September 1997 and just over two years later he coached the Wallabies to a Rugby World Cup Final win when they defeated France 35-12 in the 1999 final. After leading the Wallabies to victory over the touring British and Irish Lions in 2001, he retired. In 2010, he was persuaded out of retirement and was appointed as the first coach and director of rugby to the newly formed Melbourne Rebels but stepped down from his role at the end of the 2011 Super Rugby season. In 2000, he was presented with an Australian Sports Medal and the following year he was inducted into the Sport Australia Hall of Fame. He was made a Member of the Order of Australia in 2003 and in 2004 he was awarded the Joe French Award which recognises outstanding service to the Australian Rugby Union. In 2011, he was inducted into the International Rugby Board Hall of Fame.

> ### Did You Know That?
> In 2000, Macqueen guided Australia to their first ever Tri-Nations success.

Clive Woodward
England 2003

Clive Woodward still had four years left on his contract after England stunned Australia in the 2003 Rugby World Cup Final, winning 20-17 after extra time in Sydney. But within a year he was gone as England's form dipped dramatically and he announced his resignation on 1 September 2004. He was head coach of the British and Irish Lions tour to New Zealand in 2005, a series they lost 3-0. In the summer of 2005, he took up a new role, and in a new sport, when he became the performance director of Southampton Football Club. Woodward was a close friend of the Southampton chairman, Rupert Lowe. When Harry Redknapp left his role as the manager of Southampton in December 2005, there was speculation that Woodward would replace him even though he lacked experience as a football manager. In the end, Southampton appointed George Burley as their new manager and Woodward was given a new role, director of football, to work alongside Burley. However, on 31 August 2006, Southampton issued a statement in which they said that Woodward was no longer working at the club. On 6 September 2006, Woodward was introduced by the British Olympic Association as their new director of elite performance. In 2007, he was appointed to the board of directors at Leicester Tigers.

At the 2008 Summer Olympic Games in Beijing, China he worked as deputy chef de mission and undertook a review of practices at the Games in preparation for London playing host to the 2012 Olympic Games. After the London Olympics he left his post as director of sport at the British Olympic Association. Woodward received a knighthood in 2004 and in 2011, he was inducted into the International Rugby Board Hall of Fame.

> ### *Did You Know That?*
> Woodward is an honorary president of the Wooden Spoon Society, a children's charity that receives the support of the rugby world.

Jake White
South Africa 2007

South Africa's 15-6 win over England in the 2007 Rugby World Cup Final brought to an end New Zealand's 40-month reign as the world's No.1 rugby union nation. However, despite guiding the Springboks to World Cup glory his contract as head coach was not renewed after 31 December 2007. Nine days after he lifted the Webb Ellis Cup, the South African Rugby Union stated that White had not re-applied for the post but White said that his contract did not require him to re-apply and that he had asked for some time to consider his options, which was not afforded to him. From 2008–12 he took on a role working at the International Rugby Board (IRB) assisting with their technical committee. He also held positions in the IRB as a consultant, as well as in the South African Rugby Legends Association's upliftment programmes for underprivileged people. From 2012/13, he coached the Brumbies in Australia and on 18 June 2013 they defeated the touring British and Irish Lions 14-12 at Canberra Stadium, Canberra. It was the Lions' first loss to a non-international side since 2005 when they were defeated 19-13 by the Maori All Blacks at Waikato Stadium, Hamilton on 11 June (the British and Irish Lions drew 13-13 with the Emerging Springboks at Newlands Stadium, Cape Town on 23 June 2009). In 2014, White was appointed the director of rugby at the Sharks in Durban, South Africa and led them to the semi-finals of the 2014 Super Rugby competition. In September 2014 he resigned from his role with the Sharks in pursuit of an international role prior to the 2015 Rugby World Cup. On 13 October 2014, White joined Tonga as a member of the backroom staff, and acted as a technical advisor to their head coach, Mana Otai, for the 2014 tour of Europe. Tonga played three Tests during their tour, defeating Georgia and the United States but losing the third Test to Scotland. White was expected to be kept on by Tonga but on 30 December 2014 he was introduced as the new head coach of Montpellier in France. He stayed with Montpellier for three years before taking up a new position as head coach of Toyota Verblitz, Toyota, Aichi, Japan. In 2011, he was inducted into the International Rugby Board Hall of Fame.

Did You Know That?

White took South Africa from sixth in the IRB World Rankings (2003) to first (2007). He also guided South Africa to Tri-Nations success in 2004, was named the IRB International Coach of the Year in 2004 and 2007 and was in charge when the Springboks achieved their biggest ever victory, a 134-3 demolition of Uruguay in 2005.

Graham Henry
New Zealand 2011

Before he guided New Zealand to victory in the 2011 Rugby World Cup Final (an 8-7 win over France at Eden Park, Auckland, New Zealand), Graham Henry was a school teacher at Auckland Grammar School, where he coached the rugby team from 1973–81. He moved on to coach rugby at Kelston Boys' High School (1982–91), Auckland (1992–96 – they won the National Provincial Championship in 1993, 1994, 1995 and 1996 and the Ranfurly Shield in 1995 and 1996) and the Blues (1996–98 – they won the Super 12 Championship in 1996 and 1997 and lost the 1998 final). When he was overlooked for the position of head coach of the All Blacks, he accepted an invitation from Wales to become their new head coach in the summer of 1998 following a disastrous tour of Africa by the Welsh (beat Zimbabwe 49-11, lost 96-13 to South Africa and lost all four games played against provincial sides). In his first Test as head coach of Wales they lost 28-20 to South Africa at Wembley Stadium, London in an autumn international and then defeated Argentina 43-20 at Stradey Park, Llanelli, Wales. In the 1999 Lloyds TSB Five Nations Championship, Wales beat Italy 60-21, England 32-31 and France 34-33, to record their first win in Paris in over 20 years (a 25-20 victory at Parc des Princes in the 1975 Five Nations Championship) and inflict France's first lost at their new Stade de France home. The win in France instilled a new confidence in the Welsh and they won their next nine Tests with the media labelling Henry 'the Great Redeemer'. Henry was appointed the British and Irish Lions head coach for their 2001 tour of Australia, making him their first head coach who was not from one of the home four nations. They lost the series 2-1. After Ireland racked up their record score, 54-10, against Wales in the 2002 Six Nations Championship, Henry returned to New Zealand to take up a post as the defensive coach of the Blues for the 2002 season, during which they won the Super 12 title. Henry finally landed the job he dreamt of in December 2003 when he replaced John Mitchell as the New Zealand head coach following the All Blacks' 22-10 loss to Australia in the semi-finals of the 2003 Rugby World Cup. His first Test as the All Blacks coach was against the 2003 Rugby World Cup winners, England. Henry's new look All Blacks eased to a comfortable victory, 36-3, in a Test played at Carisbrook, Dunedin, New Zealand. In 2005, he masterminded New Zealand to a 3-0 series whitewash over the touring British and Irish Lions and followed this up with 2005 Tri-Nations success. After coaching the All Blacks to an 8-7 win over France in the 2011 Rugby World Cup final on home soil, he stepped down from his role but the following year he became an assistant coach with Argentina (2012–13), a consultant with Leinster (2016) and in 2018 rejoined Auckland as an assistant coach. During his tenure in charge of his home nation, New Zealand won the IRB World Rugby Team of the Year award five times (2005, 2006, 2008, 2010 and 2011) and in each of those five years he was named IRB World Rugby Coach of the Year. He was in charge of the All Blacks for 103 Tests, winning 88 and losing 15 for an impressive winning ratio of 85.43%. In 2012, he was made a Knight Companion (KNZM), Sir Graham William Henry.

Did You Know That?

Graham Henry played rugby union for Canterbury and cricket as a wicketkeeper for Canterbury (1965/66) and Otago (1967/68) in the Plunket Shield.

Steve Hansen
New Zealand 2015

Steve Hansen is seeking to create rugby history at the 2019 Rugby World Cup in Japan by coaching a nation to two Rugby Union World Cup Final wins. Stephen William Hansen was born on 7 May 1959 in Mosgiel, a suburb of Dunedin in Otago, New Zealand and in 2015, he coached the All Blacks to Rugby World Cup glory when they defeated their old enemy, Australia, 34-17 in the final at Twickenham Stadium, London. Hansen's parents were dairy farmers on the Taieri Plain, south-west of Dunedin, and he attended Taieri High School. He played rugby for High School Old Boys RFC. His senior rugby career as a player was an uneventful one, making just 21 appearances for the Canterbury provincial rugby union team at centre. Hansen embarked on a coaching career in 1996 with Canterbury (1996–2001) and by the time he packed his bags to become the head coach of Wales in 2002, he had guided Canterbury to two National Provincial Championship titles in 1997 and 2001. He was also as assistant coach to Wayne Smith and Robbie Deans at the Canterbury Crusaders from 1999–2001 in Super Rugby. When he arrived in Cardiff to take charge of Wales, the team was no longer the force they used to be with Hansen becoming their ninth national coach in 13 years. Ironically, he succeeded Graham Henry who he would later go on to succeed as the head coach of the All Blacks. Despite the ignominy of winning the wooden spoon in the 2003 RBS Six Nations Championship, Wales performed well at the 2003 Rugby World Cup finals, losing 28-17 in the quarter-finals to England in Brisbane, Australia. In 2004, he decided not to renew his Welsh contract and accepted an invitation from Graham Henry to become an assistant coach under him with New Zealand. When the All Blacks lifted the Webb Ellis Cup in 2011 under Henry's leadership, Hansen played a key part in the team's success. It was the first time since the inaugural tournament in 1987 that the All Blacks were crowned world champions (they beat France 29-9 at Eden Park, Auckland in the 1987 final). Graham Henry's contract expired in December 2011 and on 16 December 2011, Hansen became the All Blacks' new head coach.

His first year in charge was a hugely successful one, defeating a touring Ireland side 3-0 (which included a record defeat for the Irish, 60-0 in Hamilton) and a 22-0 win over the Wallabies in Auckland, the tenth consecutive year the All Blacks won the Bledisloe Cup. Of the 20 games played by the All Blacks in 2012, they won 18, drew one (18-18 v Australia in Brisbane) and lost one (38-21 to England at Twickenham Stadium in their last game of the year). However, the year did end on a high for Hansen when he was named the IRB Coach of the Year and appointed a Companion of the New Zealand Order of Merit in the 2012 Queen's Birthday and Diamond Jubilee Honours for his services to rugby. The following year, 2013, the All Blacks went unbeaten in the Rugby Championship, winning all 14 of their games (including an 11th straight Bledisloe Cup victory), to become the first team to achieve this feat in the professional era. A third successive Rugby Championship was secured in 2014, culminating in Hansen being named World Rugby Coach of the Year for the third year in a row. The All Blacks visited Samoa in 2015 to play them in the first ever official Test match between the two countries, winning the game 25-16, but they lost the Rugby Championship to Australia with the Wallabies claiming their first scalp over New Zealand (27-19) since 2011. But the All Blacks, the host nation, were still favourites to win the 2015 Rugby World Cup.

They topped Pool C with wins over Argentina, (26-16), Namibia (58-14), Georgia (43-10) and Tonga (47-9) and then saw off France 62-13 in the quarter-finals. Their semi-final match-up against South Africa was a bruising affair but they claimed their place in the final with a 20-18 victory. On 31 October 2015, New Zealand made Rugby World Cup history by becoming the first nation to retain the Webb Ellis Cup after beating Australia 34-17 in the final at Twickenham Stadium. It was also the first time the All Blacks lifted the famous trophy on foreign soil, having won it as host nation in 1987 and 2011.

Hansen was reappointed the head coach of the All Blacks on 25 July 2016 and led them to a fourth Rugby Championship in five years, with it becoming the first side in either Rugby Championship or Tri-Nations history to secure their title four rounds in. The All Blacks won all six games easily, Australia 42-8 and 29-9, Argentina 57-22 and 36-17 and South Africa 41-13 and 57-15. The following Bledisloe Cup game versus Australia saw the All Blacks claim a 37-10 win at Eden Park. Their 18 consecutive wins, a new tier one world record, was brought to an end by Ireland at Soldier Field, Chicago, USA on 5 November 2016. The Irish put in a magnificent performance to beat the All Blacks 40-29, to claim their first win over them in 111 years and at the 29th attempt. For the fourth time in five years, Hansen was voted World Rugby Coach of the Year.

The British and Irish Lions toured New Zealand in 2017, their first series versus the All Blacks since 2005, which ended in a draw with one win each (New Zealand's first home defeat since 2009, Hansen's first home loss as head coach) and a draw in the third game. In the 2017 Rugby Championship, the All Blacks won six games from six which included a record defeat for South Africa, 57-0. France toured New Zealand in 2018, and suffered a 3-0 series loss, resulting in the All Blacks retaining the Dave Gallaher Trophy for the fifth consecutive time. Hansen's side won five of their six Rugby Championship matches to claim a sixth title, the only loss coming against South Africa, 36-34, which was the Springboks' first win in New Zealand since 2009 (32-29). In their penultimate Test of the year, the All Blacks were once again beaten by Ireland (16-9) in Dublin on 17 November 2018, Ireland's first home victory over them in their history.

Did You Know That?

Hansen will step down as head coach of the All Blacks after the 2019 Rugby World Cup. Going into their 2019 season, New Zealand had won 84 of his 95 Tests in charge and drawn three. They lost to Australia (twice), Ireland (twice), South Africa (twice), England and the British and Irish Lions.

FANTASY 2011 RUGBY WORLD CUP XV

After New Zealand beat France 8-7 in the 2011 Rugby World Cup Final, many journalists put pen to paper on who they considered to be the best XV at the tournament. Paul Ackford from the *Daily Telegraph* selected the following side.

15. Israel Dagg (New Zealand)
14. George North (Wales)
13. Ma'a Nonu (New Zealand)
12. Jamie Roberts (Wales)
11. Corey Jane (New Zealand)
10. Dan Carter (New Zealand)
9. Mike Phillips (Wales)
8. Imanol Harinordoquy (France)
7. Richie McCaw (New Zealand)
6. Schalk Burger (South Africa)
5. Lionel Nallet (France)
4. Victor Matfield (South Africa)
3. Adam Jones (Wales)
2. Keven Mealamu (New Zealand)
1. Jean-Bapiste Poux (France)

Did You Know That?

Harinordoquy won two Top 14 titles (2005, 2006) and the 2012 Amlin Cup playing for Biarritz. He also lost two Heineken Cup finals with Biarritz in 2006 and 2010. At international level he was capped 82 times for his country (2002–12) and scored 65 points helping the French to five Six Nations Championships (2002, 2004, 2006, 2007 and 2010), which included three Grand Slams (2002, 2004, 2010).

THE 1999 RUGBY WORLD CUP FINALS

6 November 1999
Millennium Stadium, Cardiff, Wales
Australia 35–12 France

On 6 November 1999, Australia faced France in the first professional Rugby World Cup Final at the Millennium Stadium, Cardiff, Wales. Following the 1995 Rugby World Cup Final, hosted and won by South Africa, the International Rugby Board had opened the sport to the professional era.

Australia won all three of their Pool E games, 57-9 versus Romania, 23-3 versus Ireland and a 55-19 win over the USA, scoring 135 points and conceding just 31. Meanwhile France also dominated Pool C, winning all three games, 33-20 versus Canada, 47-13 versus Namibia and a 28-19 victory over Fiji, scoring 108 points whilst conceding 52. The quarter-finals draw pitched the Wallabies against the host nation, Wales (other venues in England, France, Ireland and Scotland were also used), whilst France were drawn to play Argentina. Australia progressed to the semi-finals after defeating Wales 24-9 with France beating the Pumas 47-26. In the semi-finals, the Wallabies won a dramatic and tight encounter against the defending world champions, South Africa, 27-21 after extra time at Twickenham Stadium, London. To reach the final France would have to see off the tournament favourites, New Zealand. This encounter between the northern and southern hemisphere was one of the greatest ever Rugby World Cup finals games. The All Blacks led 24-10 at half-time at Twickenham Stadium but the French fought back in the second half, overturning the 14 points deficit to win the game 43-31 and reach their second Rugby World Cup Final (1987). Australia were too strong for France in the final and became the first nation to win the Webb Ellis Cup twice (1991) after beating *Les Bleus* 35-12.

France let themselves down in the final through their indiscipline which allowed Matt Burke a number of kickable opportunities which the Wallabies full-back punished by kicking seven successful penalties. However, France led 6-3 early in the game, thanks to the reliable kicking of Christophe Lamaison, and almost went further in front, but Abdelatif Benazzi's try was subsequently disallowed because of a knock-on. Burke kicked three more penalties to send the Wallabies in at half-time leading 12-6. In the second half France continued to give away penalties which Burke converted with unerring accuracy to make the score 21-12 after 64 minutes. The French players looked tired as the Wallabies piled immense pressure on their defence. Clearly their heroic efforts against the All Blacks in the semi-finals were beginning to show and undoubtedly resulted in them making so many errors which then resulted in penalties. With 15 minutes remaining Ben Tune crashed over the line virtually unchallenged to score the first try of the game which was converted by Burke, his 23rd point of the final. Then France committed yet another infringement which Burke once again punished with a penalty. Deep into injury time Owen Finegan forced himself over the line to score a try from a rolling forward surge through the exhausted French defence which Burke converted to seal a 35-12 victory for Australia. John Eales, the captain of the Wallabies, collected the famous gold trophy from Queen Elizabeth II. Australia became the first dual winners of the Webb Ellis Cup and Eales along with teammates, Dan Crowley, Tim Horan, Phil Kearns and Jason Little became dual Rugby World Cup winners having also played in the 1991 final when the Wallabies defeated England 12-6 at Twickenham Stadium. Burke's 25 points haul is the most ever by any player in a Rugby World Cup Final. Amazingly, Australia only conceded one try during the tournament, Juan Grobler crossing over the Wallabies' line for the USA.

After the final whistle, Australia's Stephen Larkham said: 'It was a real power struggle throughout most of that game: lots of niggle on and off the ball and a really physical game for everyone. We finally wore them down and scored some good tries in the end.'

A clearly disappointed France captain, Raphael Ibanez, said: 'Looking back it's clear that the title was undoubtedly deserved by Australia. I think that when you're engaged in a match with such intensity, at such a high level, it's like arm-wrestling. We lost that arm-wrestle; we lost it mentally and physically. It was an overwhelming occasion and, yes, we used up a lot of our energy. We didn't have enough strength or stamina to beat Australia on that day.'

Meanwhile, John Eales said: 'In the last three or four minutes of that final, we knew that that game was ours. It was a very different feeling – running around, still doing your work but being able to enjoy the last moments of a World Cup Final. It's funny, but even though the scoreline (35-12) looked one-sided at the end it never felt one-sided out there on the field. You never take it for granted that you're going to come out on top. There was Her Majesty the Queen presenting us with our trophy and our winners' medals. For a kid growing up in Australia, out in the back yard kicking the ball over the washing line and pretending you're a Wallaby, to actually be out there receiving the trophy, it's a big dream. It's a very special moment and it's a hard one to really put into words. It's as much relief as it is elation. It's a sense of brotherhood with these people that you've been on this journey with, it's this sense of sacrifice and knowing that it's special for all of you in your own particular way but also in a collective way.'

Australia: Matthew Burke; Ben Tune, Tim Horan, Daniel Herbert, Joe Roff; Stephen Larkham, George Gregan; Andrew Blades, Michael Foley, Richard Harry, John Eales (captain), David Giffin, Matt Cockbain, David Wilson, Toutai Kefu

France: Xavier Garbajosa; Christophe Dominici, Emile Ntamack, Richard Dourthe, Philippe Bernat-Salles; Christophe Lamaison, Fabien Galthie; Cedric Soulette, Raphael Ibanez (captain), Franck Tournaire, Abdelatif Benazzi, Fabien Pelous, Marc Lievremont, Olivier Magne, Christophe Juillet

Australia	France
Tries Tune, Finegan	Pens Lamaison 4
Cons Burke 2	
Pens Burke 7	

Referee: André Watson (South Africa)
Attendance: 72,500

Did You Know That?

There was a certain irony in Australian captain, John Eales, being presented with the Webb Ellis Cup by the Queen on the very same day Australia had held a referendum on replacing her. The vote was 45.13% in favour with 54.87% against. Incidentally, Australia were coached by Rod Macqueen.

RUGBY WORLD CUP QUOTES

'No, not after coaching the All Blacks. It's okay to coach another country but now I've coached the All Blacks I couldn't coach against them. I couldn't do it. I'd love to coach the All Blacks until the day I die, it's the best job in the world as far as I'm concerned for a rugby coach. But is that right for the team?'

New Zealand coach Steve Hansen after the All Blacks won the 2015 Rugby World Cup, in response to a journalist's question if he would ever accept a position with another nation

THE BIRTH OF THE RUGBY BALL

Richard Lindon (30 June 1816–10 June 1887) is credited with making the first ever rugby ball. Lindon, a boot and shoemaker by trade, lived and worked in Rugby and supplied footwear to the residents of Rugby as well as to the teachers and pupils from the nearby school, Rugby School. In 1849, Lindon was asked by the pupils to make footballs for them and he duly obliged. Back then the balls were more plum-shaped than spherical because they comprised a pig's bladder encased in stitched panels of leather. The balls had to be inflated by mouth using the snapped stem of a clay pipe. Richard's wife, Rebecca, the mother of 17 children, had the job of blowing up the balls. But it was a hazardous task as it was possible to become ill if the pig had died of a disease. Mrs Lindon died from a lung infection after breathing in the air from too many bad bladders. In 1862, Lindon replaced the pig's bladder with the India rubber bladder but it was too difficult to blow up by mouth. After seeing a medical ear syringe, Lindon invented a larger brass version of it to blow up his footballs, which led to the manufacture of the first round ball. However, the balls still had a button at each end to hold the stitching in place and it wasn't until the 1880s that a buttonless ball was manufactured.

Did You Know That?
The distinctive oval Rugby School football, made by William Gilbert, was placed on display at the Great Exhibition which was held at the Crystal Palace in London from May to October 1851.

CALCUTTA CUP USED AS A BALL

Dean Richards (48 caps) played for England at the 1987, 1991 and 1995 Rugby World Cups. In 1988, England beat Scotland 9-6 at Murrayfield in the Five Nations Championship to win the Calcutta Cup. Following the game, it was claimed that Richards, nicknamed 'the Policeman', and Scotland's John Jeffrey (40 caps), nicknamed 'the Great White Shark', played rugby with the Calcutta Cup along Princes Street, Edinburgh. The trophy was severely dented and cost several hundreds of pounds to repair. Scottish Rugby Union handed Jeffrey a five-month ban from playing for the international side for his antics whilst Richards was only given a one-week suspension by the English Rugby Football Union.

However, in 2010, some 22 years after the incident, Jeffrey finally revealed what actually occurred during a radio interview with BBC Radio Scotland. 'It was stupid high jinks gone wrong. But it was certainly not kicked around like a football. It was thrown – but it was dropped. It's a chapter of my life that I am not terribly proud about. There were four Scots in bed before the end of the dinner – I so wish I had been. Dean Richards and I had the cup and we spotted Brian Moore in the corner and said, "Come on, let's go and pour the whisky over him." So we emptied the contents of the cup over his head and ran. It was absolutely schoolchild behaviour. The first door we saw was open, so out we went and we saw a taxi. We jumped in and found ourselves in the middle of Edinburgh with the Calcutta Cup. We visited two or three hostelries and the cup got damaged during that time. I remember looking at it – and I must have sobered up. I thought, "Good Lord, this is a bit of a mess." We took it back to the hotel, handed it in to reception and bolted. I went to bed and waited for the knock on the door, which came at breakfast time the next morning. I got up and said, "Yeah, I took it out with some player" – I didn't name Dean – "and I brought it back and I'll take responsibility for it." I didn't object to the sentence I got. What I did object to was the fact that there were two of us involved, two of us took the rap and one gets five months and one gets one week, which was totally out of kilter. It was very disproportionate,' said Jeffrey.

Rugby was first introduced to India in 1872 and a year later the Calcutta (Rugby) Football Club was founded by past students of Rugby School and in 1874, the newly formed club joined the Rugby Football Union. However, following the departure of a local British army regiment, interest in the sport declined whilst cricket, polo and tennis began to thrive as they were better suited to the hot climate. In 1878, the Calcutta (Rugby) Football Club was disbanded but its members decided to keep the memory of the club alive by having the balance in the club's bank account, 270 silver rupees, melted down to be made into a trophy. The trophy was then presented to the Rugby Football Union (RFU) to be used as 'the best means of doing some lasting good for the cause of Rugby Football'. The cup was first competed for on 10 March 1879 and resulted in a 3-3 draw at Raeburn Place, Edinburgh. The trophy is 18 inches (45 cm) high, sits on a wooden plinth whose plates hold the date of each match played along with the winning country and the names of the two team captains. It is delicately etched and decorated with three king cobras which serve as the handles with an Indian elephant sitting on top of its circular lid.

Did You Know That?

The Rugby Football Union was founded in 1871 and the first international match (20-a-side) took place between Scotland and England at Raeburn Place, Edinburgh on 27 March 1871. Scotland won the game by one goal to none.

RUGBY WORLD CUP QUOTES

'People back home were baying for my blood. They have got it.'

John Hart on announcing his retirement as New Zealand coach following back-to-back losses to France (43-31 in the semi-finals) and South Africa (22-18 in the third place play-off match) at the 1999 Rugby World Cup

RED MIST

Simon Shaw was a member of England's successful 2003 Rugby World Cup-winning team and represented his country at the 2007 and 2011 Rugby World Cup tournaments. Shaw holds the unwanted record of being the first England international player to be shown a red card when he was sent off against New Zealand at Eden Park, New Zealand on 19 June 2004 in a 36-12 defeat. Mike Burton (1975) and Danny Grewcock (1998) had been asked to leave the field before referees first carried an actual red card in 1999. On 26 November 2005, Lewis Moody became the first England player to be sent off at Twickenham Stadium for his part in a brawl during an autumn Test match versus Samoa which England won 40-3. Shaw played in all three of England's warm-up matches ahead of the 2003 Rugby World Cup but was not named in Clive Woodward's 30-man squad for the tournament. However, following an injury to Danny Grewcock he was flown out to Australia but he keeps his 2003 Rugby World Cup winners' medal in a drawer at home because he feels he didn't win it as he didn't play in any of the games.

Did You Know That?

On 26 November 2016, Elliot Daly became only the fifth England player to be sent off when he received his marching orders versus Argentina at Twickenham Stadium. Daly tackled Argentina's No 8, Leonardo Senatore, while he was still in the air after catching the ball. After consulting the TMO the referee had no hesitation in brandishing the red card for what he deemed to be a late, clumsy and dangerous challenge which resulted in Senatore landing on his head. England won the autumn international Test 27-14.

ENGLAND TEAM SNUBS PRINCESS ANNE

Duncan Hodge (26 caps) played for Scotland in the 1999 Rugby World Cup. However, his most memorable performance in the Scotland jersey came in the final game of the 2000 Six Nations Championship, the inaugural Six Nations Championship with the inclusion of Italy. The Scots faced England who had already secured the title but a win over the Scots, the previous year's Five Nations champions, would give England the coveted Grand Slam. Going into the game Scotland lay at the foot of the table following four successive defeats including a 34-20 loss in Rome to Italy. But thanks to a magnificent Man of the Match performance from Hodge versus England at Murrayfield, Scotland ran out 19-13 winners with Hodge converting his own try and kicking four penalties to score all of the points for Scotland. The win meant Scotland had won the Calcutta Cup and avoided finishing bottom of the table (Italy occupied last place). It was the Scots' first win over the old enemy since 1990.

After Princess Anne, patron of the Scottish Rugby Union since 1986-87, presented the victorious Scotland team with the Calcutta Cup, the England team were to be presented with the inaugural Six Nations Championship trophy. However, the England players, clearly in a huff after being prevented from claiming the Grand Slam, snubbed the Princess Royal by remaining in their changing room and refused to go back out on to the Murrayfield pitch to collect the trophy.

Hodge travelled to the 2011 Rugby World Cup in New Zealand as the Scotland squad's kicking coach and four years later he was Scotland's attack coach when the Rugby World Cup was hosted by England in 2015. When he was 19, Hodge was given the choice of touring South Africa and Zimbabwe with Scotland's national cricket team, or playing under-21 national rugby and completing his university exams. He chose the latter option.

Did You Know That?

The Scottish Football Union was formed in 1873 and was originally affiliated to the Rugby Football Union.

RUGBY WORLD CUP QUOTES

'The heart is willing, the head is willing, but the body has had enough.'
An emotional Ireland captain, Keith Wood, after playing his final game in the green shirt, the 43-21 loss to France in the quarter-final of the 2003 Rugby World Cup at Telstra Dome, Melbourne, Australia

TOP 10 ATTENDANCES FOR A RUGBY WORLD CUP FINALS GAME

1. 89,267, Wembley Stadium, London, Ireland 44-10 Romania, 2015 Rugby World Cup finals, Pool D.
2. 89,019, Wembley Stadium, London, New Zealand 26-16 Argentina, 2015 Rugby World Cup finals, Pool C.
3. 82,957, Telstra Stadium, Sydney, England 20-17 Australia, 2003 Rugby World Cup Final.
4. 82,444, Telstra Stadium, Sydney, Australia 22-10 New Zealand, 2003 Rugby World Cup semi-final.
5. 82,346, Telstra Stadium, Sydney, England 24-7 France, 2003 Rugby World Cup semi-final.
6. 81,350, Telstra Stadium, Sydney, Australia 24-8 Argentina, 2003 Rugby World Cup, Pool A.
7. 81,129, Twickenham Stadium, London, Wales 28-25 England, 2015 Rugby World Cup, Pool A.

8. 81,010, Twickenham Stadium, London, Australia 33-13 England, 2015 Rugby World Cup, Pool A.
9. 80,863, Twickenham Stadium, London, Australia 15-6 Wales, 2015 Rugby World Cup, Pool A.
10. 80,430, Stade de France, Paris, South Africa 15-6 England, 2007 Rugby World Cup final.

Did You Know That?

During the 2007 Six Nations Rugby Championships, Ireland played their home games at Croke Park, Dublin (home of the Gaelic Athletic Association) as their Lansdowne Road home was being rebuilt (when finished it was called the Aviva Stadium). Ireland played two home games in the competition: 81,000 fans watched Ireland lose 20-17 to France and a crowd of 83,000 were in attendance when Ireland beat England 43-13.

RUGBY'S LAST COALMINER

Garin Jenkins (58 caps, 10 points, 1991–2002) played for Wales in three Rugby World Cup finals tournaments, 1991, 1995 and 1999 but surprisingly he was never selected for a British and Irish Lions tour. He made his Test debut on 4 September 1991 in a 22-9 loss to a touring French side at the National Stadium, Cardiff, Wales. During his early career, Jenkins worked as a coalminer for four years underground at Lady Windsor Colliery in Ynysybwl, Wales. 'I was always proud to be a miner, but carrying the tag of the last miner to have played for Wales is a big responsibility. When you look down the list of miners who played for Wales there are some incredible names there,' said Jenkins.

On 4 November 1992, he was a member of the Swansea team which famously defeated a touring Australia side 21-6 at St Helen's, Swansea, scoring a try in the victory. When he retired, after a 23-13 loss to South Africa at the Millennium Stadium, Cardiff on 26 November 2000, he was his country's most capped hooker until his record was surpassed by Matthew Rees on 14 June 2014.

IN HIS OWN WORDS

'For me the emotion is very strong at the moment. I would never have thought that something like this could happen when I started to play rugby. For me it was just to play with a rugby ball and to share that rugby ball with teammates, no more.'

Philippe Sella, 111 caps for France 1982–95, after being inducted into the IRB World Rugby Hall of Fame in November 2008

THE CAPTAIN'S LOG – DAVID KIRK MBE

The name of David Kirk will go down in the history of rugby union as the first player to hold aloft the Webb Ellis Cup after captaining his country, New Zealand, to victory in the inaugural Rugby World Cup in 1987. David Edward Kirk was born on 5 October 1960 in Wellington, New Zealand and grew up in Palmerston North. In 1982, he made his debut for Otago but left the Dunedin-based province in 1985 for Auckland. Kirk made his All Blacks debut on 1 June 1985 when England toured New Zealand and the halfback (scrum-half) played his part in an 18-13 win at Lancaster Park, Christchurch. But amazingly he only ran out in 16 more Tests for his country including six in the inaugural Rugby World Cup, before his international career came to an end.

Kirk played in Auckland's 28-23 win over Canterbury in the 1985 Ranfurly Shield. In 1986, he boycotted the rebel Cavaliers tour (the unofficial New Zealand tour to South Africa) along with teammate John Kirwan because of South Africa's apartheid system. That same year, he was appointed captain of the 'Baby All Blacks', a young and inexperienced All Black team selected to play a one-off Test against France and the first Test of a three-Test series against Australia while the Cavaliers were banned.

When the All Blacks went on a tour of France in November 1986, Jock Hobbs was preferred by the selectors as captain. In 1987, Hobbs was ruled out by recurring concussion before the World Cup team was selected, making way for Michael Jones. The veteran hooker and captain of the Cavaliers, Andy Dalton, was selected as the captain of the team. A hamstring injury during a practice session sidelined Dalton for the All Blacks' opening game of the tournament, a 70-6 win over Italy in which Kirk scored two tries. Dalton's position as hooker for the game was handed to a young Sean Fitzpatrick, whose impressive performance in only his fifth Test cemented his starting place in the side for the rest of the tournament, whilst Kirk retained the captaincy. Kirk scored a try in each of the next two Pool 3 games, a 74-13 win over Fiji and a 46-15 victory against Argentina.

After defeating Scotland (30-3) in the quarter-finals and Wales (49-6) in the semi-finals, Kirk led out his nation to face France in the 1987 Rugby World Cup Final. A crowd of 48,000 packed Eden Park, Auckland on 20 June, hoping for an All Black victory on home soil. New Zealand dominated the game from start to finish although it did not produce the running rugby many had expected. Kirk scored a try in New Zealand's 29-9 victory. When he was photographed holding aloft the famous Webb Ellis Cup, the iconic image shows him as bloodied and muddied.

He only played one more Test for the All Blacks, captaining the side to a 30-16 victory over Australia at the Concord Oval, Sydney on 25 July 1987 to win the Bledisloe Cup. In October 1987, at the age of 26, he took up his twice-deferred Rhodes Scholarship at Oxford University where he studied Philosophy, Politics and Economics. He played scrum-half for Oxford University against Cambridge University in the 1987 (lost) and 1988 (won) Varsity matches.

In his 17 Tests (11 as captain), 1985–87, he scored 24 points (won 14, lost three, an 82.35% win ratio). When he completed his studies he worked in London for three years for McKinsey and Co before returning to New Zealand to take up an appointment as first executive assistant and then chief policy advisor to the Prime Minister of New Zealand. He was the Wellington NPC's representative coach in 1993 and 1994. He subsequently worked in business management, becoming the chief executive of major publicly listed Australasian media company Fairfax Media in 2005. In 2011 he co-founded Bailador, a technology investment fund which is now listed on the Australian Stock Exchange.

He is also the chairman of listed New Zealand companies Kathmandu and Trade Me. David Kirk was appointed a Member of the Order of the British Empire in the 1988 New Year's Honours for services to rugby. On 24 October 2011, he was inducted into the IRB Hall of Fame alongside the other six Rugby World Cup-winning captains and the seven head coaches from the tournament's inception in 1987 through to 2007.

Did You Know That?

In 1839, former Rugby School pupil, Arthur Pell, formed a rugby football team at Cambridge University.

THE CAPTAIN'S LOG – NICK FARR-JONES

Nicholas Campbell Farr-Jones was born on 18 April 1962 in Caringbah, New South Wales, Australia. Aged 12 he entered Newington College (1974–79), a day and boarding school in Sydney and then went to St Andrew's College (1980–85), a co-residential college within the University of Sydney, where he studied law. Newington never selected the young scrum-half for a first XV game, but when he attended university he became a regular in their side. When he received a call-up to the national side for Australia's 1984 tour of Europe, he was still studying to be a lawyer, as rugby union was still an amateur sport at the time.

On 3 November 1984, a 22-year-old Farr-Jones pulled on the famous gold jersey of the Wallabies for the first time. He made his international Test debut against England at Twickenham Stadium, London, in a comfortable 19-3 win. He made a good impression and played in the subsequent tour wins against Ireland (16-9), Wales (28-9) and Scotland (37-12, scored his first Test try). In the five Tests he played in 1985, he was on the winning side on four occasions, losing a close game 10-9 to New Zealand in Auckland. After helping the Wallabies to a 2-1 Bledisloe Cup series win over the All Blacks during their tour of New Zealand in 1986, he was an automatic choice for the Australian squad selected to represent their nation in the inaugural Rugby World Cup finals tournament in 1987. The following year he was named the captain of the Wallabies having established himself as part of an Aussie trio famously dubbed the 'Holy Trinity', along with David Campese and Michael Lynagh.

Farr-Jones captained Australia for the first time on 12 June 1988, taking on the role of skipper from Lynagh, in a 28-8 win over a touring England side at the Concord Oval, Sydney (Lynagh scored one try, three conversions and two penalties in the game). Going into the Test, Farr-Jones had a hand in 46 of Campese's world record tally of 64 international tries. But then the Wallabies lost 2-0 (drew one game) to New Zealand in the 1988 Bledisloe Cup, which was followed up by a 2-1 series defeat to the British and Irish Lions during their 1989 tour of Australia. His captaincy was being questioned by many sports journalists and this intensified when Australia lost the 1990 Bledisloe Cup after they lost the first two of three Tests against the All Blacks. They lost 21-6 in Christchurch which was followed by a 27-17 defeat in Auckland. But the Wallabies rallied in the final Test and defeated New Zealand 21-9 in Wellington. An under-pressure Farr-Jones celebrated his side's victory by jumping naked into Wellington Harbour.

The following year, 1991, was Rugby World Cup year and the Wallabies went into the tournament in good form after wins over Wales (63-6 in Brisbane) and England (40-15 in Sydney) and a drawn Bledisloe Cup series (a 21-12 win over the All Blacks in Sydney and a 6-3 defeat in Auckland). They started the World Cup with a 32-19 win over Argentina, then scraped past Western Samoa 9-3, but Farr-Jones had a knee injury and was rested for the Wallabies' final Pool 3 game, a 38-3 win over one of the co-hosts, Wales. In their close quarter-final encounter with Ireland in Dublin, a game they squeezed 19-18, he was substituted in the second half with what was feared at the time to be a serious injury. But a sore knee was not going to stop Farr-Jones from leading his team into battle against their nemesis, New Zealand, in the semi-finals of the World Cup. The Wallabies beat the All Blacks 16-6 in the Irish capital at Lansdowne Road. On 2 November 1991, he led the Australian side out at Twickenham Stadium, London to face another one of the co-hosts, England, in the final. It was a hugely disappointing game, dominated by kickers, with the Wallabies claiming the Webb Ellis Cup thanks to a 12-6 victory. Farr-Jones became only the second player to captain his nation to Rugby World Cup glory.

He captained Australia to a 2-1 Bledisloe Cup series win over New Zealand in 1992 and after beating South Africa 26-3 in Cape Town on 22 August 1992, Farr-Jones decided it was time to retire from the international game. It was his 59th appearance for his country but in July 1993, he was persuaded out of retirement to play four more times for the Wallabies – a 25-10 loss to New Zealand in the Bledisloe Cup (Dunedin, New Zealand), a 19-12 loss to the Springboks in Sydney and he brought the curtain down on his hugely successful Test career by helping the Wallabies defeat the touring Springboks 28-20 (Brisbane) and 19-12 (Sydney). The latter two victories helped cement Australia's position as the best team in the world at the time. Farr-Jones won a total of 63 caps (36 as captain, one as sub) between 1984 and 1993, and scored 37 points. In 1989, he married Angela Benness and they have four children: Jessica, Amy, Benjamin and Joshua.

Did You Know That?

During his international career, Nick Farr-Jones formed a world record half-back partnership with Michael Lynagh, playing in 47 Tests together.

THE CAPTAIN'S LOG – FRANCOIS PIENAAR

Francois Pienaar was born on 2 January 1967 in Vereeniging, Transvaal, South Africa, the eldest of four boys in a working class

Afrikaner family. Despite the fact that he only played three years of international rugby union (1993–96), Francois Pienaar is one of the sport's most iconic figures after uniting a divided and racist nation behind a single dream, a Rainbow Nation (the term Archbishop Desmond Tutu gave the new South Africa under Nelson Mandela's leadership), by captaining South Africa to Rugby World Cup Final glory in 1995. It was the Springboks' first participation in the sport's elite tournament, post the end of the apartheid era which had stagnated the country for decades.

When he left his high school, Hoërskool Patriot, Witbank, Pienaar won an athletic scholarship to Rand Afrikaans University (now the University of Johannesburg) and studied for two law degrees, B Proc and LLB. As a student he was a keen sportsman but rugby was his first love. Aged 20, he made his provincial debut in 1989 as a flanker for Transvaal Province (now the Golden Lions) and under his astute leadership, Transvaal won the inaugural Super 10 title, the Currie Cup, Lion Cup and the Night Series in 1993. Under his captaincy the Lions won 100% of their matches in 1993.

In 1992, the South African Rugby Football Union (SARFU) was formed after the personal intervention from the country's new President, Nelson Mandela. The new organisation was a merger between the South African Rugby Board and the non-racial South African Rugby Union. This ended over eight years (1984–92) of being world rugby outcasts and on 15 August 1992, the Springboks welcomed New Zealand to Ellis Park, Johannesburg for a match dubbed 'the Return Test'. The All Blacks won a tight game 27-24. On 26 June 1993, Pienaar won the first of his 29 Test caps in a 20-20 draw with France at Kings Park Stadium, Durban, South Africa. He was made captain of the Springboks for his first Test, after the international retirement of Naas Botha, and so was the first Springbok player to be named captain on debut. In 1994, he captained Transvaal when they retained the Currie Cup, the Lion Cup and the Yardley Shield and he was voted International Player of the Year by *Rugby World* magazine. Following an 18-18 draw with the All Blacks in Auckland, New Zealand on 6 August 1994, Pienaar skippered the Springboks to 15 consecutive victories including all five of their games at the 1995 Rugby World Cup finals. On 24 June 1995, he was presented with the famous Webb Ellis Cup by the South African President, Nelson Mandela, following their 15-12 final win over New Zealand at Ellis Park, Johannesburg. During a post-match TV interview Pienaar was asked what it was like to have 62,000 fans supporting his team. Pienaar responded: 'There were not 62,000 people supporting us today. There were 43 million.' However, the man who helped unite a divided nation by leading his country to Rugby World Cup glory, won only eight more caps in the famous green and gold jersey (won five, lost three) before being ignominiously dropped by the new Springboks coach, Andre Markgraaff, prior to a 1996 Tri-Nations match versus the All Blacks. It was mooted that Markgraaff was not happy with the key role Pienaar played in rugby union's move from being an amateur sport to professionalism in 1995. So after just 29 Tests, all as captain, in which he scored three tries (15 points), his international career was brought to an abrupt end (won 19, drew two, lost eight).

But this was not the end of his rugby career. In 1997, he moved to England and joined Saracens as a player/coach and, along with his fellow new recruits, Michael Lynagh and Philippe Sella, he helped them win their first trophy in 127 years, the Tetley's Bitter Cup in 1998. Saracens defeated Wasps 48-18 in the final played at Twickenham Stadium, London (they also finished second in the Zurich Premiership).

Francois Pienaar was a players' captain because he gave absolutely everything he had for his team. He inspired and lifted his teammates through his courage, often putting his body on the line to the point of risking serious injury, and his ruthless, combative nature was the embodiment of the side. These attributes were never more evident than in the 1995 Rugby World Cup Final when he stood in the path of a rampaging man mountain, Jonah Lomu, time and time again. Indeed, despite having a severe calf strain, he played the full 20 minutes of extra time in the final. When the opposition had possession of the ball, he was a defensive rock and the first to try and win it back. It was as though every game was his last.

Pienaar retired in 2000, having also scored 17 tries in 100 games for Transvaal (89 as captain, 1989–96, 83 points) and 11 tries in 44 games for Saracens (1997–2000, 55 points). His legacy is one of a man whose actions on the field for the Springboks, in tandem with Nelson Mandela, brought a divided nation together as one, a Rainbow Nation. Together, these two great leaders showed the world how a divided people could set their differences aside by learning to have mutual respect for each other's beliefs and cultures. Their unique friendship helped South Africa find a new identity through sport. The 1995 Rugby World Cup was the first major sporting event to take place in South Africa following the end of apartheid. 'We had no idea whatsoever that it was going to be so big, that our nation would rally behind a sport that was dominated by whites and hated by black people in South Africa,' said Pienaar after the tournament. Pienaar dedicated the team's campaign to President Mandela. In the f`oreword to Francois

Pienaar's autobiography, fittingly titled *Rainbow Warrior*, President Nelson Mandela wrote the following: 'It was under his inspiring leadership that rugby, a sport previously associated with one sector of our population and with a particular brand of politics, became the pride of the entire country.'

Did You Know That?

On the day after South Africa's opening match of the 1995 Rugby World Cup finals, a 27-18 win over the pre-tournament favourites, Australia, at Newlands, Cape Town, Francois Pienaar took his South Africa teammates to Robben Island to see the cell in which Nelson Mandela, Prisoner No. 466/64, had spent 18 of his 27-year incarceration.

THE CAPTAIN'S LOG – JOHN EALES

John Eales was born in Brisbane, Australia on 27 June 1970 and attended St William's Primary School, Grovely in Brisbane and later Marist College, Ashgrove which is situated in a suburb of Brisbane. Eales was a keen cricketer at school and played for the school team which included the future Australian Test cricketer Matthew Hayden. Before taking up a career playing rugby, Eales also played cricket for Queensland University in the Brisbane QCA cricket tournament. He graduated from university in 1991 with a Bachelor of Arts degree with a double major in psychology.

He began his rugby career in 1989 with his local side, Brothers Rugby Club and signed for Queensland Reds in 1990. Eales played lock for Queensland Reds where he was given the nickname 'Nobody', because 'Nobody's perfect'. On 22 July 1991, he was give his Test debut, a 63-6 hammering of Wales in his home city at Ballymore Stadium. He was selected for the Wallabies' 1991 Rugby World Cup finals squad and played in Australia's 12-6 win over England in the final, at Twickenham Stadium, London on 2 November 1991. In 1996, he took over the captaincy of his country from Rod McCall and three years later he skippered the Wallabies to victory in the 1999 Rugby World Cup Final. Eales was presented with the Webb Ellis Cup by Queen Elizabeth II at the Millennium Stadium, Cardiff, Wales on 6 November 1999, after their 35-12 win against France. He went on to win 86 caps (84 from the second row, two at No.8) and captained the Wallabies on 55 occasions, scoring 173 points (two tries, 31 conversions and 34 penalties). Australia won 66, lost 18 and drew two of the games he played in.

Eales was a skilful player with fast hands and could read set pieces extremely well. He was also a super defender with a great engine. In

2001, he captained his country to a 2-1 series victory over the British and Irish Lions and he played his final Test match on 1 September 2001 (a 29-26 win over New Zealand in the Tri-Nations in Sydney). His career ran in parallel with the Wallabies' most successful era. Eales captained Australia to Bledisloe Cup success over New Zealand in 1998, 1999, 2000 and 2001 and two Tri-Nations titles in 2000 and 2001. Australia did not win the Tri-Nations again until 2011. When he retired from international rugby he was the most capped lock in rugby union history, with 84, a record which has subsequently been beaten by a number of players. In 2001, he played his final game for Queensland Reds, making 122 appearances and scoring 402 Super Rugby points. He won successive Super 10 titles with Queensland Reds in 1994 and 1995.

Eales was awarded the Order of Australia in 1999 for services to the community and rugby; the Australian Sports Medal in August 2000 for his contribution to Australian Rugby; in 2001 he was inducted into the Australian Institute of Sport 'Best of the Best'; he was named Queenslander of the Year in 2002; in the same year he gave his name to the John Eales Medal, which is awarded annually to the best Australian rugby union player; he was inducted into the Sport Australia Hall of Fame in 2003; in 2007 he was inducted into the International Rugby Board Hall of Fame; he was appointed to the Australian Rugby Union board following the retirement of Peter Cosgrove in 2010 and in 2011 he was inducted to the Wallaby Hall of Fame.

Did You Know That?

At the 2007 Rugby World Cup finals hosted by France, John Eales acted as a rugby ambassador and he was an athlete liaison officer for the Australian Olympic Committee in the Athens (2004), Beijing (2008) and London (2012) Olympic Games.

THE CAPTAIN'S LOG – MARTIN JOHNSON, OBE, CBE

Martin Osborne Johnson was born on 9 March 1970 in Shirley, Solihull, Warwickshire, England. He was the second of three brothers and when he was seven years old, his family moved to Market Harborough, Leicestershire where he attended Ridgeway Primary School, Welland Park School and Robert Smyth School. He came from a sporting family as his great-grandfather was a wrestler. Before he embarked on his rugby career he played American football for the Leicester Panthers as a defensive end or tight end.

Aged 19, he was invited for a trial with King Country province in New Zealand by the former All Blacks legend, Colin Meads. His trial was a success and Johnson played two seasons for the club. In

1990, he was selected for the New Zealand Under-21 side which toured Australia. On 14 February 1989, Johnson made his debut for Leicester Tigers against the RAF, which was followed by his Courage League debut versus Bath (Tigers won 15-12 to deny Bath a season undefeated). However, he returned to New Zealand and did not play for Leicester again until the following year. On 20 April 1992, he played for the Barbarians against Swansea in a 55-12 victory.

He made his Test debut for England on 16 January 1993 at Twickenham Stadium, London in the Five Nations Championship, when England coach Geoff Cooke called him up as a late replacement for the injured Wade Dooley (England won 16-15). Johnson didn't play again for England until November 1993, but he was selected for the British and Irish Lions tour of New Zealand in June/July 1993. He played in four matches including the second and third Tests and subsequently captained the Lions on their tours to South Africa in 1997 and Australia in 2001, playing a total of 11 games, including eight Tests. In 1995, he won the Five Nations Championship Grand Slam with England and helped his country to a fourth-place finish at the 1995 Rugby World Cup finals in South Africa. He was made the captain of Leicester Tigers in 1997 and in November 1998, Clive Woodward handed the England captaincy to Johnson. However, England only managed to reach the quarter-finals of the 1999 Rugby World Cup finals in Wales (lost 44-21 to South Africa). He led England to glory in the inaugural Six Nations Championship in 2000 and again in 2001.

The pinnacle of Johnson's international career came in 2003 when the inspirational lock led England to the Six Nations Championship Grand Slam and Rugby World Cup glory. On 30 March 2003, England faced Ireland at Lansdowne Road, Dublin, Ireland in a showdown for the Grand Slam as both sides had won their previous four games. Johnson dispensed with the pre-match protocol by lining his side up on the right-hand side of the red carpet before the playing of the national anthems and refused to move his side when requested to do so by Irish match officials. Ireland then had to line-up to the left of England which resulted in the Irish President, Mary McAleese, having to walk on the grass to greet the teams. England beat Ireland 42-6 and the following day, the Irish Rugby Football Union sent a letter of apology to President McAleese for the England team's failure to 'follow established and communicated protocol'. Meanwhile, the Rugby Football Union also wrote to the Irish President offering her a 'full and unreserved apology'. On 22 November 2003, Johnson became the first player outside the southern hemisphere to hold aloft the glittering Webb Ellis Cup when the Australian Prime Minister, John Howard, presented him with it in the Telstra Stadium, Sydney following England's dramatic 20-17 victory after extra time over the host nation. It was, and remains, the greatest ever moment in the history of English rugby and was a fitting swansong to Johnson's international career.

The 2003 Rugby World Cup Final was his 92nd (started 90, won 71, lost 19 and drew two, 78.2% winning ratio) and last appearance in an England jersey and the 39th (won 34, lost five, 87.17% wining ratio) time he led England out. He is joint sixth in the list for most England caps (Jason Leonard leads the way with 114) and only Will Carling (59) and Chris Robshaw (43) have captained England more times. Johnson won five Five/Six Nations Championships (1995, 1996, 2000, 2001 and 2003), with two Grand Slams in 1995 and 2003 and six Triple Crowns in 1995, 1996, 1997, 1998, 2002 and 2003. As a Lion he lost the New Zealand tour in 1993 (2-1), won the South African tour in 1997 as captain (2-1) and lost the tour to Australia as captain in 2001 (2-1). Johnson was the first player to captain two British and Irish Lions touring sides (Sam Warburton was a co-captain with Alun Wyn Jones in 2013 and also a co-captain with Peter O'Mahony in 2017).

At the end of the 2004/05 season, Johnson hung up his boots having made a total of 307 appearances for Leicester Tigers (1989–2005) and during his 16-year career at Welford Road he led them to two Pilkington Cup wins (1993 and 1997), back-to-back Heineken Cup titles in 2001 and 2002 and five Premiership titles including four in a row between 1998/99 and 2001/02 (the other title was in 1994–95). He made his final bow in a 39-14 defeat against London Wasps in the 2005 Premiership Final at Twickenham Stadium, London on 24 May 2005. Johnson's testimonial match was played at Twickenham Stadium on 4 June 2005 (Martin Johnson XV v Jonah Lomu XV) and he returned to England's HQ to play in the 'Help for Heroes' charity match on 20 September 2008 when he was England manager.

On 1 July 2008, and despite having no previous coaching experience he succeeded Rob Andrew as the manager of England and coached his country to Six Nations Championship success in 2011. He left his position as the national team manager on 16 November 2011 one month after losing 19-12 to France in the quarter-finals of the 2011 Rugby World Cup in New Zealand and was succeeded by Stuart Lancaster. Under him, England played 38 Tests, winning 21, drawing one and losing 16 – 55% winning ratio. Martin Johnson was awarded an OBE in 1997 and in 2003 he was honoured with a CBE following England's Rugby World Cup triumph. He has a function room named after him at Twickenham Stadium.

THE CAPTAIN'S LOG – JOHN SMIT

John Smit was born on 3 April 1978 in Polokwane, South Africa. He attended Fields Primary School in Rustenburg and Pretoria Boys' High School after that. He played rugby for his high school's XV from 1994–96 and also went to the University of Natal for one year (1997) and played for their rugby team. In 1997, he joined the Sharks in Durban and played Currie Cup and Super Rugby for them until 2011, with stints in France and London in between. Aged 22, Smit was awarded his first international Test cap by the Springboks' coach, Nick Mallet, versus Canada on 10 June 2000, a game the Springboks won 51-18 at Basil Kenton Stadium, East London, South Africa. Smit had already played and captained South Africa's Under-21 side. He played in a further nine Tests that year and in 2001 he won another 11 caps. On 17 November 2001, he scored his first Test try when South Africa beat Italy 54-26 in Genova, Italy. Smit did not appear again in a green and gold jersey until 11 October 2003 after missing 18 months with a recurring shoulder injury.

South Africa coach, Rudolf Straeuli, included Smit in his squad for the 2003 Rugby World Cup finals and Smit came on as a replacement in the Springboks' opening Pool C match, a 72-6 win over Uruguay in Perth, Australia. When South Africa met Georgia in their third Pool C match, Smit became the 51st player to captain the Springboks. They won the game 46-19 in Sydney, but then exited the tournament at the quarter-final stages, losing 29-9 to New Zealand in Melbourne.

The game versus Uruguay was the beginning of a record run of 46 consecutive Test matches for Smit, taking him up to 16 June 2007 when the Springboks defeated the Wallabies 22-19 in a Tri-Nations encounter in Cape Town, South Africa. Despite this impressive run he was not really an immediate first choice for the side until 2004, when the newly-appointed Springboks' coach, Jake White, made him captain of his country. Smit's record-breaking sequence of appearances came to an end with South Africa's first match of the 2007 Tri-Nations after he suffered an injury in their 22-19 victory over Australia in Cape Town (22 June 2007). However, he was back in the side by September for the 2007 Rugby World Cup finals hosted by France.

The Springboks topped Pool A winning all four of their games; 59-7 versus Samoa, 36-0 versus the reigning world champions, England, 30-25 versus Tonga and 64-15 versus the USA. Smit missed the win over Tonga and was replaced as captain by Bobby Skinstad. But he was back for the quarter-finals and before South Africa's game with Fiji, Smit spoke to his teammates: 'Remember the look in the eyes of the Aussies and the Kiwis yesterday – I don't want to see that here.' (Australia had lost 12-10 to England and New Zealand had lost 20-18 to France in their quarter-final games.) Smit's motivational address worked as the Springboks beat Fiji 37-20 and in the semifinals they defeated the surprise team of the tournament, Argentina, 37-13. They had reached their first Rugby World Cup Final since winning the Webb Ellis Cup on home soil in 1995. The 2007 Rugby World Cup Final was played at Stade de France, Saint-Denis, Paris, France on 20 October 2007. It was a re-run of an earlier Pool A match as the Springboks once again faced England, meaning one of these two nations would win the coveted Webb Ellis Cup for a second time (England were hoping for back-to-back titles). The Springboks ran out 15-6 winners and just like Francois Pienaar 12 years earlier, Smit captained South Africa to Rugby World Cup glory. He was presented with the sport's most famous trophy by the President of France, Nicolas Sarkozy. Smit, a natural born leader, was outstanding in the six games he played, a player with excellent organisational skills, a driving force for the side, calm under extreme pressure and an inspirational captain who spread an infectious winning mentality among his teammates.

'We have had the responsibility of carrying the hopes of a nation on our shoulders and now we have a team that is taking the trophy back home to the nation. I certainly hope that being able to lift this cup and take it back home can create a scenario that everyone binds together and we start forgetting about counting numbers and colours,' said Smit after lifting the famous trophy. Then thinking about the fans, he added: 'This is for all of you. Thank you very much for all your support, even in bad times. I'm sitting here and trying not to cry. It's a feeling you can't put into words.

After the 2007 Rugby World Cup finals, Smit moved to France and signed for Clermont. Following the appointment of Peter de Villiers as the head coach of South Africa, and despite Smit's move to France, the South African Rugby Union announced on 20 February 2008 that he would retain the captaincy of the Springboks. However, he returned to South Africa in 2008 after only one year in Europe and rejoined the Sharks, where he stayed until 2011. On 7 June 2008, Smit reached a landmark occasion when he captained his country for the 50th time, a 43-17 victory against Wales in Bloemfontein. Following another win over the touring Wales side, 37-21 in Pretoria on 14 June 2008, Smit then led out the Springboks for their opening game of the 2008 Tri-Nations tournament (5 July 2008) but he suffered a groin injury at the end of their 19-8 loss to the All Blacks when he was lifted and dumped by New Zealand lock, Brad Thorn, after the final whistle had been blown. The injury ruled him out of the rest of the tournament with the veteran Springboks lock, Victor Matfield, taking over the captain's armband.

The following year, 2009, Smit captained the Springboks to a 2-1 series win over the touring British and Irish Lions (he scored a try after just four minutes in the narrow 26-21 win over the tourists in the first Test in Durban and played in all three matches in the series) and helped South Africa win the 2009 Tri-Nations, winning five of their six games which included an impressive three-game clean sweep over the All Blacks. In the first of the three wins over New Zealand, a 28-19 victory on 25 July 2009 in Bloemfontein, South Africa, he equalled the record of 59 Tests as captain which was jointly held by Australia's George Gregan and Will Carling of England. A week later, 1 August 2009, the Springboks beat the All Blacks 31-19 in Durban and Smit became the most capped Test captain in the history of rugby union. Six Tests later, Smit skippered the Springboks to a 55-11 victory over Italy in East London, South Africa on 26 June 2010, the 50th time he led his country to a victory as captain. On 21 August 2010, he won his 100th cap in a 29-22 loss to New Zealand in Johannesburg, South Africa in a Tri-Nations game. He became the 16th player to reach the century milestone of Test caps and only the second South African to join this exclusive club – Percy Montgomery won 102 caps from 1997–2008.

Smit captained the Springboks at the 2011 Rugby World Cup finals in New Zealand despite fears concerning his performances at both provincial and international level. The defending world champions topped Pool D, winning all four of their games: 17-16 versus Wales, 49-3 versus Fiji, 87-0 versus Namibia and 13-5 versus Samoa. In the quarter-finals South Africa faced Australia in a battle of the southern hemisphere giants but were eliminated from the tournament following an 11-9 loss in Wellington. The defeat also brought the curtain down on Smit's international career after 111 Tests (94 starts, 40 points) which produced 69 wins, two draws and 40 defeats equating to a 63.06% win ratio. He remains one of his country's most successful captains after leading the Springboks to 46 victories in 64 Tests. Smit only lost to six teams during his international career – Australia (P 24, W10, D1, L13), England (P11, W6, L5), France (P9, W3, D1, L5), Ireland (P6, W3, L3), New Zealand (P21, W8, L13) and the British and Irish Lions (P3, W2, L1). He won all ten Tests versus Wales.

At the time of his retirement, Smit was the most capped hooker in the world with 96 Test caps (he also played at prop). Following his international retirement his record for the most Tests as captain was surpassed by Ireland's Brian O'Driscoll in 2012 (133 caps, 1999–2014) and then by the All Blacks' legend, Richie McCaw, who won a world record 148 caps (110 as captain) from 2001–15. After the 2011 Rugby World Cup finals Smit signed for the Aviva Premiership champions, Saracens, and played Premiership Rugby for the London-based club until he hung up his boots in 2013. In addition to winning the Rugby World Cup, Smit also captained South Africa to Tri-Nations glory in 2004 and 2009. Smit was inducted to the World Rugby Hall of Fame in 2011 and was awarded the Order of Ikhamanga (OIS silver medal) by the President of South Africa for excellent achievement in sport.

'When you start out as a Springbok, it's about proving you're good enough to be there. But as you play more Tests, that feeling dissolves and you realise it's not about you, it is about standing up to the responsibility of what this team means to your country.' – John Smit.

Did You Know That?

In 1999, Smit was a nominee for the South Africa Young Player of the Year award, won the Players' Player of the Year award in 2005, and in 2009 he was a nominee for South Africa Player of the Year.

THE CAPTAIN'S LOG – RICHIE McCAW ONZ

Richard Hugh McCaw was born on 31 December 1980 in Oamaru, North Otago, New Zealand. His father was a farmer and his mother was a school teacher in Kurow, Waitaki District. McCaw's great-grandfather immigrated to New Zealand from the Scottish Borders in 1893. He played rugby for his local rugby club in Kurow and when he went to boarding school at Otago Boys' High School in Dunedin aged 14, his interest in the sport increased. In 1998, he came to the attention of national selectors during a draw with Rotorua Boys' High School in the final of the secondary schools cup. But he missed out on being selected for the New Zealand Secondary Schools team. After leaving high school he went to Lincoln University, Christchurch, where he studied agricultural science. In 1999, he was a member of the New Zealand Under-19 side which won the Junior World Championships and the following year he was selected for the New Zealand Under-21 side. A year later, 2001, he quit his studies to embark on a rugby union career and signed for Canterbury, where he remained until he hung up his boots in 2015. On 31 March 2001, McCaw he made his senior rugby debut for Crusaders and that same year he captained the New Zealand Under-21 team.

During his career McCaw played as an openside flanker, a blindside flanker and at No.8. He made his debut for the All Blacks on 17 November 2001 in a 40-29 win over Ireland at Lansdowne Road, Dublin, Ireland. In 2002 and 2003 he played a key role in the All Blacks' Tri-Nations victories which ended Australia's five-year reign as Bledisloe Cup winners. He participated in the first of his four Rugby World Cup finals in 2003 when the All Blacks lost 22-10 in the semi-finals to the Wallabies in Sydney, Australia. New Zealand beat France 40-13 in the third place play-off match. Aged 23, McCaw captained New Zealand for the first time when the All Blacks defeated Wales 26-25 at the Millennium Stadium, Cardiff, Wales on 20 November 2004.

In 2005, he played twice versus the British and Irish Lions, helping the All Blacks to a 3-0 series victory, the first time in 22 years that the tourists lost every Test match on tour. That same year, he helped the All Blacks to the first of four successive Tri-Nations triumphs, with McCaw captaining the side to victory on the latter three occasions. He was named International Rugby Board World Player of the Year in 2006 and won the award again in 2009 and 2010. McCaw led the All Blacks during the 2007 Rugby World Cup finals but they were knocked out of the tournament by the host nation, France, losing 20-18 in the quarter-finals.

In 2008, McCaw made his debut for the Barbarians in an 18-12 defeat to Australia at Wembley Stadium, London, England. On 26 June 2010, he surpassed Sean Fitzpatrick's record of 39 Test wins as the captain of New Zealand when the All Blacks beat Wales 29-10 in Dunedin, New Zealand. He won his 50th cap as captain on 7 August 2010, marking the occasion with a 20-10 win over the Wallabies in Christchurch, New Zealand to retain the Bledisloe Cup. On 7 September 2010, he captained his country for the 52nd time in a 23-22 win over Australia in Sydney to pass Fitzpatrick's record as the most capped Test captain in All Blacks history, scoring a try in the game. That same year McCaw led New Zealand to a fifth Tri-Nations title in six years and finished the year by leading his side to only their fourth Grand Slam tour of the UK and Ireland (the second under McCaw's leadership, after doing the same in 2008). He surpassed Australian George Gregan's record number of Test wins (94) following New

Zealand's 60-0 win over Ireland in Hamilton, New Zealand on 25 June 2012. When he led the All Blacks to a 41-13 victory against Argentina in Auckland on 15 August 2015 he became the most capped player in rugby union history after passing the 141 Test caps Brian O'Driscoll won for Ireland. McCaw skippered the All Blacks to Rugby World Cup finals glory in 2011 with a narrow 8-7 victory over France in the final in Auckland, New Zealand and helped his nation retain the Webb Ellis Cup four years later when they defeated their bitter rivals, Australia 34-17 at Twickenham Stadium. He is the only player to have captained his nation to Rugby World Cup glory on two occasions. The 2015 final was his 148th and last game for the All Blacks (started 141, won 131, drew two, lost 15, scored 135 points). Other records he holds include scoring more Test tries than any other forward (27) and he won more Rugby World Cup finals games (20) than any other player. He is also the most-capped captain in world rugby (110) and won the most Tests as captain (97). In addition to his two Rugby World Cup triumphs, he won seven Tri-Nations/Rugby Championship titles and ten Bledisloe Cup series. He played 145 Super Rugby games for the Crusaders, winning four Super Rugby Championships (2002, 2005, 2006 and 2008), three as captain.

In December 2011, he turned down the offer of a knighthood from the then New Zealand Prime Minister, John Key. 'He made the call that he's still in his playing career and it didn't feel quite right for him, that day where he's no longer on the pitch may be the right time for him,' said Key. In the 2016 New Year's Honours List, McCaw was appointed a member of New Zealand's highest honour, the Order of New Zealand. This honour surpassed the knighthood he turned down because only 20 living New Zealanders can gain membership at any one time.

Did You Know That?

McCaw's other passion is flying and in 2010 he was made an honorary squadron leader in the Royal New Zealand Air Force and six years later, 2016, he was promoted to honorary wing commander.

IN HIS OWN WORDS

'At half-time, both parties (of coaching teams), the French and us, were waiting to go down (to the changing rooms). In the quarter-finals we were able to take a lift; we had a lift each. This time there was no one there and only one lift came. We all had to get in the lift together and it was pretty hard to ignore each other!'

Rod Macqueen, head coach of Australia following his side's 35-12 win over France in the 1999 Rugby World Cup Final

THE 2003 RUGBY WORLD CUP FINALS

Australia went into the 2003 Rugby World Cup finals as the defending world champions, looking to become the first nation to win the Webb Ellis Cup back-to-back and the first nation to lift the trophy three times. The Wallabies also had home advantage as the host nation. The pool stages went according to current form with the Wallabies winning Pool A (runners-up, Ireland), France winning Pool B (runners-up, Scotland), England winning Pool C (runners-up, South Africa) and New Zealand winning Pool D (runners-up, Wales).

The first quarter-final saw two southern hemisphere powers, New Zealand (winners in 1987) and South Africa (winners in 1995) do battle at the Telstra Dome, Melbourne, a game the All Blacks won 29-9. The hosts brushed aside Scotland 33-16 at Suncorp Stadium, Brisbane in the second quarter-final whilst France saw off the challenge of Ireland, winning 43-21 at the Telstra Dome, Melbourne. The last quarter-final brought together two old foes, England and Wales. The pair had last met nine months earlier when England beat Wales 26-9 at the Millennium Stadium, Cardiff, Wales on their way to winning the 2003 Six Nations Grand Slam. Wales ended up with the wooden spoon having lost all five of their matches. England defeated Wales 28-17 at Suncorp Stadium, Brisbane.

The semi-final matches were played at Telstra Stadium, Brisbane. First up were the tournament favourites and world champions in 1987, the All Blacks, versus Australia. The great antipodean rivals had met at this stage before when the Wallabies defeated New Zealand 16-6 in the 1991 semi-finals at Lansdowne Road, Dublin, Ireland. These southern hemisphere rugby giants had been dominant in the tournament since the inaugural Rugby World Cup finals in 1987 – New Zealand winning the first and runners-up in 1995, whilst Australia were crowned world champions in 1991 and 1999. Indeed, only South Africa in 1995 had been able to break their duopoly. New Zealand were favourites to send the partisan fans among the 82,000 in attendance home disappointed, having beaten Australia twice in the 2003 Tri-Nations Series: Australia lost 50-21 at the Telstra Stadium and went down 21-17 at Eden Park, Auckland, New Zealand. The All Blacks had also won both of their games versus the Springboks to win their fifth Tri-Nations Series title. But in the 2003 World Cup semi-final it was the assured kicking of Elton Flatley which helped the Wallabies win the game 22-10 (he converted Stirling Mortlock's try and scored five penalties). England won the battle of the northern hemisphere in the second semi-final, defeating France 24-7. Jonny Wilkinson scored all of England's points: five penalties and three drop goals, a sign of things to come. The All

Blacks regained their form in the third-place play-off, crossing the line six times to win 40-13 at Telstra Stadium.

So 12 years after Australia defeated England 12-6 at Twickenham Stadium, London, England to win the 1991 Rugby World Cup, the two nations met again in the 2003 final. And this time the Wallabies were playing on home soil. In their pool, England had won all four games scoring 255 points and conceding a meagre 47 (they beat South Africa 25-6). The Wallabies had been even more dominant in the pool stages, winning all four games scoring a total of 273 points and allowing just 32 against (Ireland lost 32-16 to the Wallabies and Australia set the Rugby World Cup finals record winning margin, which still stands today, beating Namibia 142-0 at the Adelaide Oval, Adelaide; 22 tries and 16 conversions). After having beaten Australia in four successive Tests – 22-19, 21-15, 32-31 and a 25-14 win in Melbourne just five months earlier – Clive Woodward's side were red-hot favourites to lift the Webb Ellis Cup. However, buoyed by their surprise semi-final win over the All Blacks, the Wallabies had faith in themselves to make rugby history.

The Wallabies started the game strongly when Lote Tuqiri, a Fijian-born Australian dual-code player, out-jumped Jason Robinson to gather a superbly flighted kick by Stephen Larkham to cross over the line with just six minutes on the clock. Elton Flatley's conversion attempt hit the uprights and bounced back. However, three penalties from the trusted boot of Jonny Wilkinson soon silenced the home support as England led 9-5 after 28 minutes. England ended the half strongly when Robinson slid in to score but a rare miss from Wilkinson meant the two sides went in at the interval with England leading 14-5. In the 47th minute, England conceded a penalty from a poor line-out which Flatley punished to bring the Wallabies within a converted try of taking the lead. Fourteen minutes later England's discipline once again let them down when Phil Vickery was penalised for illegally handling the ball in a ruck. Flatley stepped up and made no mistake to make the score Australia 11 England 14.

Despite piling on the pressure, Australia could not find any way past a stubborn England defensive wall. As the game entered the final minute, England looked set to become the first ever northern hemisphere nation to hold aloft the coveted Webb Ellis Cup. However, Australia had a put-in on England's 22-metre line. The scrum collapsed and the South African referee, Andre Watson, blamed England for it and awarded the Wallabies an 80th-minute penalty. Flatley set the ball down on the kicking tee and despite the immense pressure on him to score his fourth penalty of the game to force extra time, coupled with the cacophony of boos from the English fans behind him, he coolly slotted the ball through the uprights to level the score at 14-14. Both sides now faced an energy-sapping two periods of ten minutes' extra-time. Just two minutes into the first period England won a penalty when Justin Harrison pulled his man down in a line-out. Wilkinson placed the ball on the kicking tee, did his usual kicking preparations, and fired the ball over the bar to give his side a 17-14 lead. With three minutes of the allotted 100 minutes remaining, England's line-out was as disastrous as it had been throughout the game with hands flapping in the air to grasp the ball. When Lawrence Dallaglio handled the ball on the ground the South African official was left with no other option but to blow his whistle, and much to the delight of the home crowd, award the Wallabies a kickable penalty. With nerves of steel the Wallabies' ice-man made the scores 17-17 to set up a nail-biting finish for the 82,957 fans inside the stadium and the 300 million watching it on TV across the globe. However, heartbreak was soon to follow for the men in gold when, with the clock showing just 26 seconds to go, Wilkinson moved back into the pocket and received a pass from Matt Dawson. Wilkinson dropped the ball on to his less-favoured right boot and split the posts to win the 2003 Rugby World Cup Final, 20-17. That drop goal has become the defining moment in England's Rugby World Cup history and it was Wilkinson's first success from four attempts in the game. It was a stunning end to a truly breathtaking final. Martin Johnson, England captain, became the first European to hold aloft the Webb Ellis Cup when the Australian Prime Minister, John Howard, presented him with the trophy.

After the game a delighted Johnson said: 'It was a huge effort by the entire squad of players, coaches and backroom staff, everybody. Thanks to the fans, they were incredible. I can't say enough about the team, because we had the lead and we lost it but we came back. And I can't say enough about Wilko at the end. He is a very special player, a very special person. You've got to give credit to Australia, they're a very good team and they made it very difficult for us. I'm just so happy for the players, they've put their heart and soul into it. It couldn't have been any closer and I'm just happy I'm on the right side.'

Clive Woodward, the England coach, said: 'We came very close to blowing it. Every decision seemed to go against them [England], and yet they still won, and that is the sign of a champion team. They are a great bunch of players with a great captain, and I am just very proud and privileged to be in charge of them.' Meanwhile, Wilkinson said: 'It's indescribable. It's something we've wanted, we've worked for so long both individually and as a team.'

Final – 22 November 2003
Telstra Stadium, Sydney, Australia
England 20–17 Australia (after extra time)

England: Josh Lewsey; Jason Robinson, Will Greenwood, Mike Tindall, Ben Cohen; Jonny Wilkinson, Matt Dawson; Trevor Woodman, Steve Thompson, Phil Vickery, Martin Johnson (capt), Ben Kay, Richard Hill, Neil Back, Lawrence Dallaglio. Replacements: Dorian West, Jason Leonard, Martin Corry, Lewis Moody, Kyran Bracken, Mike Catt, Iain Balshaw.

Australia: Mat Rogers; Wendell Sailor, Stirling Mortlock, Elton Flatley, Lote Tuqiri; Stephen Larkham, George Gregan (capt); Bill Young, Brendan Cannon, Al Baxter, Justin Harrison, Nathan Sharpe, George Smith, Phil Waugh, David Lyons. Replacements: Jeremy Paul, Matt Dunning, David Giffin, Matt Cockbain, Chris Whitaker, Matt Giteau, Joe Roff.

England	Australia
Try Robinson	Try Tuqiri
Pens Wilkinson 4	Pens Flatley 4
Drop Goal Wilkinson	

Referee: Andre Watson (South Africa)
Attendance: 82,957

Did You Know That?

During the trophy presentation the flags of St George were out in force with one in particular bearing a message for England's biggest critic, the legendary Australian rugby player, David Campese which read: 'Campese U woman, Iron my Undies!' 'Swing Low, Sweet Chariot' floated across the stadium and after the presentation a number of songs by The Beatles reverberated around the stadium including one which was most appropriate, 'A Hard Day's Night'.

OVERSEAS PLAYERS BAN LIFTED

Michael Cheika, the head coach of Australia, successfully petitioned the Australian Rugby Union to reverse a long-standing policy by allowing him to pick overseas players for his 2015 Rugby World Cup finals squad if they had made 60 or more international appearances despite not playing in the Super Rugby Championship. One player to benefit from this was 33-year-old Matt Giteau who Cheika lured out of his Test exile at Toulon, France where he had been playing superbly since his shock exclusion from the Wallabies' 2011 Rugby World Cup finals squad. His move to Toulon did not take effect until after the 2011 tournament. Giteau celebrated his 100th cap with a man of the match performance in Australia's highly controversial 35-34 victory over Scotland in the quarter-finals of the 2015 Rugby World Cup. He played in the 2015 Rugby World Cup Final, a 34-17 defeat to the Wallabies' arch-rivals, the All Blacks, at Twickenham Stadium, London. Giteau won his 103rd (2002–16, 698 points) and final Test cap on 20 August 2016, a 42-8 loss to New Zealand in Sydney, Australia in the Rugby Championship. Until he was selected for the Wallabies' 2015 Rugby World Cup finals squad, Giteau had planned to earn some money on the after-dinner speaking circuit. 'I never thought I'd be playing in a World Cup semi-final a year ago. I thought I'd be doing a couple of speaking gigs to get a bit of cash. That was the plan but it's just been an amazing ride for me this last six months. We showed a lot of character at the end against Scotland. Personally, I'm just happy we survived another week. The 100th cap was good, but the man of the match award I think should have gone to someone else in our team,' said Giteau ahead of their 29-15 victory against Argentina in the semi-finals.

Did You Know That?

Giteau attended St Edmund's College, Canberra, a school which also produced other Wallabies including George Gregan, Matt Henjak and Ricky Stuart. His dad, Ron, played rugby league, his older sister, Kirsty, is a dual code rugby player and his wife, Bianca Franklin, played netball for the Adelaide Thunderbirds.

MORE THAN JUST A PRESIDENT

On 25 May 1995, the morning of the opening ceremony of the 1995 Rugby World Cup hosted by South Africa, President Nelson Mandela was making a public address before a huge crowd in the black township of Ezakheni. Pointing to the Springbok baseball cap he was wearing, he said: 'This does honour to our boys. I ask you to stand by them because they are our kind.' That same day the front page of the *Sowetan* daily newspaper carried the headline: 'AMABOKOBOKO' (Zulu for 'Our Springboks'). Mandela's first meeting with the South African squad was at a Bok training session in Cape Town before the opening game and it was at this meeting when Hennie le Roux presented him with the Springbok baseball cap. When President Mandela walked out on to the pitch at Ellis Park, Johannesburg 30 days later, 24 June 1995, to present the trophy to the Springboks captain, Francois Pienaar after South Africa had beaten New Zealand 15-12 after extra time, he was still wearing the baseball cap and one of Pienaar's No.6 jerseys. 'When

I saw the President walking towards me carrying the William Webb Ellis Cup and wearing my No 6 Springbok jersey – the one I had given him after we'd beaten the Australians (their opening game) – I knew this was a victory far, far more important than anything we'd ever achieve on the rugby pitch. Other presidents would probably have worn their best silk suit. When Mr Mandela chose to wear my Springbok shirt, it symbolised change, the coming together of a nation. The new South Africa was actually born then. I was only the third captain to experience winning the World Cup, but I don't think any of the others could have experienced it the way I did. The emotion of beating the New Zealand All Blacks in the final on South African soil so soon after the political revolution was a fairy tale. I know it is a cliché, but that's what it was for me. A fairy tale. As a boy I'd never dared dream I'd ever be a Springbok. So to be captain of a Springbok team which beat the best in the world – watched by a black president – was totally beyond my wildest imaginings,' recalled Pienaar during a charity dinner in 2008. On the morning of the final versus the All Blacks, one of Mandela's bodyguards telephoned the Springbok training camp to request a shirt for the president to wear during the game. Each Springbok player was given two jerseys per game, one to wear and one to swap with an opposing player, and Pienaar gave his spare jersey to Mandela.

Did You Know That?

Mandela and Pienaar became very close friends. President Mandela attended Francois's wedding to his fiancée, Nerine, and gave them a set of crystal glasses and a crystal decanter. When Nerine gave birth to their first son, Jean, the Pienaars were awoken at 4am one morning by a telephone call. Francois recalled the incident. 'Nerine picked up the phone – at first I thought it might be a nuisance call – and said: "You had better take this, it's Nelson Mandela." He started chatting to me as if it was a completely normal situation. Then he congratulated me on my son and asked if he could be a godfather. I thought about it – for a split second – and yelled, "YES!"'

THE DRAGONS

According to historical newspaper reports, the Hong Kong national rugby union team dates back to the late 1870s which would make it Asia's oldest rugby union playing nation. Hong Kong has never qualified for a Rugby World Cup finals. It is claimed that when British colonists arrived in Hong Kong towards the end of the 19th century they brought the sport with them. The Hong Kong Rugby Union was formed in 1952 but many games took place in the colony prior to its formation. The first president of rugby in Hong Kong was W. E. Stoker with R. A. De Rome the first chairman. In 1924, the first match was played as an inter-port game between Hong Kong, nicknamed 'The Dragons', and Shanghai. The teams were predominantly made up from British sailors, army/navy men, local policemen, British expatriates living in the port cities and merchants from both ports. Between 1924 and 1942 the two teams competed for the Saker Cup which was donated by Richard Maxwell Saker, who made his debut for Hong Kong in December 1904 and became the fourth president of the Hong Kong Rugby Union in 1935. The inaugural Saker Cup match took place on 2 January 1924 in Hong Kong which Shanghai won 1-0. During the Second World War, the Saker Cup was presumably stolen during the Japanese occupation of Hong Kong (Hong Kong were the holders of the trophy). On 10 February 1948, the first post-war match between the two teams was played in Shanghai. A new trophy was required and so Sir Arthur Morse, the new chairman of HSBC, donated an impressive rose bowl trophy to the inaugural winners, Shanghai. In 1934, a Hong Kong team played an Australia Universities team and won the game 11-5. In 1988, Hong Kong Rugby Union was affiliated to the International Rugby Board. Hong Kong participated in the repechage of the 2015 Rugby World Cup but lost 24-3 to Uruguay. They also took part in the 2019 repechage but failed to qualify for the 2019 Rugby World Cup finals which will be hosted by Japan.

> ### *Did You Know That?*
> In 1976, the first ever edition of the Hong Kong Sevens was held which helped establish the sport in Hong Kong and helped put Asia on the global rugby map.

AUSSIE COACHES HANDED A GAGGING ORDER

World Rugby officials denied Michael Cheika and his coaching staff their request to stand on the field with the players when the national anthems were being played prior to their 2015 Rugby World Cup Final encounter versus New Zealand at Twickenham Stadium, London. Cheika wanted every man standing side by side but the sport's governing body maintained its strict stance on its policies for the entire tournament before, during and after games. 'We were probably a little bit disappointed tonight because we (the coaches) wanted to go out and sing the national anthem with our team. But World Rugby wouldn't let us. We were probably disappointed about that. But it's neither here nor there if that's the way it is. We've really enjoyed it, we've tried to improve over the whole tournament. It came pretty quick for us as a group and we tried to make the best of it as we could,' said a disappointed Cheika following his side's 34-17 defeat.

SPY GAMES

Less than 24 hours before Australia played New Zealand in the 2015 Rugby World Cup Final, the Wallabies discovered that a photographer had taken some snaps of their game plan which were subsequently published in the *Daily Mail*. Notes carried by coach Michael Cheika and assistant Mario Ledesma were photographed at Twickenham Stadium. The notes encouraged Australian players to 'expose' the All Blacks wing duo of Nehe Milner-Skudder and Julian Savea under the high ball or in the backfield. The notes also advised the Wallabies to counter New Zealand's excellent kicking game with the words 'own the air space, catch everything, chase everything, escort wingers!!!' But this was not the first time a 'Spying Bombshell' had come to light in rugby: Sir Clive Woodward, England's 2003 Rugby World Cup winning coach, had changing rooms and team hotel rooms swept for bugs. In 2005, All Blacks coaches Graham Henry and Wayne Smith could not believe their eyes when they saw men dressed in camouflage attire in the bushes filming their training in west London. In 2008, Steve Hansen, head coach of the All Blacks, expressed his concerns in Brisbane, Australia and accused a local television station of passing on footage of his side training to the Wallabies. Prior to a Test versus England at Twickenham Stadium in 2013, a British journalist managed to gain access to their team room in London and reported on the motivational messages which were written on a whiteboard. One of the messages read: 'We are the most dominant team in the history of the world.'

Did You Know That?

Daniel Craig, who played the world's most famous spy, 007 James Bond, in several movies, played rugby for Hoylake RFC.

I WILL!

The morning after England beat Australia 20-17 after extra time in the 2003 Rugby World Cup Final at Telstra Stadium, Sydney, Australia, the England hooker, Steve Thompson, proposed to his girlfriend, Fiona McArthur, on Manly Beach. She said yes!

THE GIANT FROM GRENOBLE

Olivier Brouzet played for France in three Rugby World Cup final tournaments: 1995 (finished in third place), 1999 (finished runners-up to Australia, 35-12) and 2003 (finished in fourth place). Standing 6ft 7in tall and weighing 117kg, he was a man mountain. At club level he represented FC Grenoble, Club Athlétic Bordeaux-Bègles, Northampton Saints, ASM Clermont Auvergne and Stade Francais Paris. He won a total of 72 caps for *Les Bleus* from 1994–2003 and scored 10 points. He is the son of shot putter Yves Brouzet who held the French national record for 34 years (20.20m which he achieved in July 1973 in Colombes, France).

Did You Know That?

When he was a teenager, André the Giant (André René Roussimoff) played rugby in Grenoble until he took up professional wrestling. He was already 6ft 6in tall when he started playing rugby (he grew up to become 7ft 4in).

NOT THAT 'SORRY' REALLY

Following their 34-17 victory over Australia in the 2015 Rugby World Cup Final at Twickenham Stadium, England, the victorious New Zealand players were photographed dancing to Justin Bieber's song 'Sorry'.

THE PROFESSIONALS

The International Rugby Board opened the sport to professionals in August 1995, after the completion of the 1995 Rugby World Cup finals held in South Africa. In 1886, Ireland, Scotland and Wales formed the International Rugby Football Board (IRFB) after unsuccessful attempts to unify and formalise rugby's rules. The new organisation introduced a points structure of three points for a goal and one for a try. The three member nations of the IRFB agreed not to play England until they joined the IRFB. England eventually became a member in 1890.

Did You Know That?

In 1930, the four member nations agreed that they would play all future rugby matches under the laws of the IRFB. In 1998, the IRFB changed its name to the International Rugby Board (IRB) and then in 2014, it changed its name again to the current World Rugby (WR).

BY ROYAL APPOINTMENT

France and Australia met at the Millennium Stadium, Cardiff, on 6 November 1999 to contest the Rugby World Cup Final. The Wallabies beat *Les Bleus* 35–12 to become the first team to win the Webb Ellis Cup twice (also winners in 1991). The trophy was presented by Queen Elizabeth II to the Australian captain, John Eales.

RUGBY WORLD CUP QUOTES

'At the end of the day people don't remember how we won it, they remember that we did win it. I'd probably have gone to my grave with regrets had we not won that day.'

Australian captain, Nick Farr-Jones, after the Wallabies defeated England 12-6 in the 1991 Rugby World Cup Final played at Twickenham Stadium, London

THE IRISH RUGBY FOOTBALL UNION

In 1874, the Irish Football Union was formed in southern Ireland and the Northern Football Union was formed in Northern Ireland. Five years later, in 1879, both unions amalgamated to become the Irish Rugby Football Union. Ireland played their first international on 15 February 1875. They lost by two goals to nil against England at the Kennington Oval, London in the 1874/75 Home Nations Championship which was contested by England, Ireland and Scotland. The matches for the 1874/75 Home Nations Championship were decided on goals scored. A goal was awarded for a successful conversion after a try, for a dropped goal or for a goal from a mark. If a game ended in a draw, any unconverted tries were added up to give a winner. If there was still no clear winner, the match was declared a draw. Wales did not enter the competition until the 1882/83 season.

Did You Know That?

England beat Ireland in the first ever international match featuring 15 players rather than the previous 20-a-side fixtures. The game was played at Kennington Oval, London on 5 February 1877 with England winning the game by two goals to nil.

Did You Know That?

The first rugby match under floodlights took place in Salford, Greater Manchester, England between Broughton and Swinton on 22 October 1878. It was played at Broughton's Yew Street ground in Salford and the floodlights used were two Gramme's lights, suspended from 30ft poles. Broughton won the game by two goals, three tries, and three touchdowns to Swinton's none. Following this experimental game, another floodlit game took place later the same month in Liverpool, England which led to increased demand from fans for evening kick-offs as the electric companies attempted to overturn the monopoly previously enjoyed by the gas companies.

FIJI WELCOMES THE ALL BLACKS

Fiji participated in the inaugural Rugby World Cup in 1987 which was won by New Zealand. This was more than 100 years after rugby was first played in Fiji by European and Fijian soldiers of the Native Constabulary at Ba, on Viti Levu Island in 1884. A rugby union was founded in Fiji in 1913 for the European settlers. In December 1913 New Zealand were on their way back home following a successful tour of California, USA, during which they had played a total of 16 games, winning every one, including a 51-3 Test victory over the United States at California Field, Berkeley on 15 November 1913. The Fiji Rugby Football Union contacted the New Zealand Rugby Union and arranged a representative game which was played at Albert Park, Suva, Fiji. It was the first representative game played in the colony with the All Blacks defeating their hosts, who were all born in Europe, 67-3.

> ### Did You Know That?
> In 1914, a 'native rugby competition' was started in Fiji and the following year, 1915, a Fiji Native Union was formed and became affiliated to the Fiji Rugby Football Union.

THE NEW ZEALAND BEAVER

Stephen Donald (25 appearances, 2008–11, 116 points) scored a penalty in the 2011 Rugby World Cup Final which effectively sealed the All Blacks' 8-7 victory over France at Eden Park, Auckland, New Zealand on 23 October 2011. Donald, nicknamed 'the Beaver', made his Test debut on 14 June 2008 in a 37-20 win over England at Eden Park, Auckland, New Zealand. The 2011 Rugby World Cup Final was the last time he pulled on the famous All Blacks jersey. After the final, he was hailed as the player that won the 2011 Rugby World Cup for New Zealand and became a national hero overnight. Two weeks before the final Donald had been on a fishing holiday and he was called into New Zealand's 2011 Rugby World Cup finals squad as a result of injuries to other players. 'My preparation wasn't ideal but it was an unreal experience. To pretty much come from nowhere and find yourself playing in a World Cup Final is an unreal experience – it just feels funny. I was out with a mate white-baiting. We'd had a good day, hauling in around 11 kilos, but it got a lot better. I didn't get any of Ted's (Graham Henry's) calls because my phone was switched off, and it was only when I spoke to someone else later I found out they had been trying to contact me. Luckily, I had his number in my phone. You always dream about things like playing in World Cups, but as number four in line you start to give that up a bit. But when I got the call I felt like the dream just got that much closer to reality again. It hasn't sunk in yet, and it's the same for the rest of the guys. They were just sitting around the changing room, not moving much and not saying much. The coaches said to me to be ready because it could come down to me having to kick the winning goal, and that is exactly how it panned out,' said the unlikely hero. A biopic on Donald's journey to the 2011 Rugby World Cup Final entitled *The Kick* screened on TVNZ on 10 August 2014.

> ### *Did You Know That?*
> Donald's local rugby club in Waiuku renamed their home ground Beaver Park in his honour.

BLOW YOUR WHISTLE!

Referee Craig Joubert's handling of the 2011 Rugby World Cup Final was heavily criticised by the French media and some of the French players. Following France's 8-7 loss to New Zealand at Eden Park, Auckland, New Zealand, the French media pointed to numerous occasions when All Blacks players were off their feet or not releasing and were not punished for doing so. They also said there were three occasions when blatant high tackles went unpunished, one of which led to Donald's penalty which ultimately decided the outcome of the match. Although the French journalists did not claim that Joubert's decisions, and in some cases lack of them, won the game for the home side, he did make some crucial calls that shaped the game.

The French pair of Dimitri Szarzewski and Maxime Mermoz also criticised the performance of Joubert. Szarzewski was in no doubt that Joubert was to blame, accusing the South African official of favouritism towards the host nation. '(Jerome) Kaino committed a lot of fouls, (Richie) McCaw was doing what he wanted and they were not penalised. Unless the fault was really rough, they were not punished. Mr Joubert was not brave. It was a World Cup Final. I wanted things to be fair. And that was not the case,' said the hooker. Meanwhile, Mermoz claimed that he had been struck by All Blacks scrum-half Piri Weepu and suggested that Joubert had ignored the assault. 'I took a punch from Weepu right in the ear. I couldn't hear anything and I still can't hear well now. And the referee didn't whistle,' said the centre.

Les Bleus' fly-half Morgan Parra spoke about being forced off with a head injury. 'I was bleeding a bit, I took a knock and I was a bit dazed. I was trying to get out from under the ruck, I took a knee to the face. It wasn't when (Ma'a) Nonu tackled me but afterwards. Did he (McCaw) mean it? I don't know. I haven't seen the footage. But it wasn't from Nonu.'

ULTIMATE RIVALS

Before their 2015 Rugby World Cup semi-final encounter with South Africa, New Zealand centre Conrad Smith described the Springboks as the All Blacks' 'ultimate rival'. New Zealand and South Africa had last met in Rugby World Cup combat 12 years previously, when an All Blacks team comprising the likes of Richie McCaw, Carlos Spencer, Doug Howlett and Justin Marshall defeated the Springboks 29-9 in a Melbourne quarter-final. Since that meeting in 2003, New Zealand had beaten the Springboks 18 times in 27 encounters. Smith, who faced South Africa on 17 separate occasions during his 92-cap Test career, said: 'They are a special opponent, and it's a very special rivalry. I grew up during the apartheid era, when Australia were the traditional foes, but now South Africa have come back into it and I think it's got back to where it was and they are our ultimate rival. There is something special about playing them, and playing them in a semi-final will be extra special.' New Zealand first played South Africa in a Test match on 13 August 1921 in Carisbrook, Dunedin, New Zealand which the All Blacks won 13-5. Up until the start of the professional era, post the 1995 Rugby World Cup finals in South Africa, the Springboks won 21 Tests to New Zealand's 18. In the 57 Tests since, the All Blacks lead their head-to-head 42-15. Since 2004, the two rugby giants have contested the Freedom Cup, which was originally to be a one-off Test match to commemorate the tenth anniversary of South African democracy. The Springboks won the inaugural Freedom Cup 40-26 at Ellis Park, Johannesburg, South Africa. However, the Freedom Cup has been included as part of the Tri-Nations/Rugby Championship since 2006, with New Zealand winning 21 of their encounters to South Africa's tally of nine during this period.

THE PUMAS, NOT THE JAGUARS

In May and June 1965, Argentina toured Rhodesia (an unrecognised state in southern Africa from 1965 to 1979 which is now known as Zimbabwe) and South Africa. They played 16 matches on the tour, winning 11, drawing one and losing four. One of the wins was a 16-11 victory over the Junior Springboks (South Africa's Under-20 team) at Ellis Park, Johannesburg on 19 June 1965. This game was classed by the Argentine Rugby Union as an official Test. Argentina are nicknamed the Pumas and the nickname was born on the 1965 tour. Carl Kohler was sent by his newspaper, *Die Transvaler* (based in Johannesburg), to report on the games. Kohler's newspaper wanted him to refer to the tourists by a nickname and not just 'the Argentine Rugby Union Football Team', in a similar way to Australia being known as the Wallabies and New Zealand as the All Blacks. After one of the games Kohler was running late in submitting his match report and he asked Isak van Heerden, the coach of the Natal Rugby team at the time, for ideas. The Natal coach had been asked by the South African Rugby Board to assist with the tour. Kohler and van Heerden saw a photograph of a type of lion with spots on the Unión Argentina de Rugby (UAR, formerly the River Plate Rugby Union) crest on the players' jerseys. Kohler was aware that the Americas had jaguars and pumas but without having the time to check with the team which big cat it was, he made a guess and referred to them as the Pumas in his match report. In fact the animal was a jaguar, a native of north-eastern Argentina which was chosen as the symbol of the team in 1941. The mistake stuck, and was eventually adopted by the Argentines themselves (although the UAR crest still depicts a jaguar).

Did You Know That?

The inaugural South American Rugby Championship was held in Buenos Aires, Argentina from 9-16 September 1951 and was contested by Argentina, Brazil, Chile and Uruguay. It was originally called the Torneo Internacional ABCU, using the initials of the four countries participating in it. Argentina's Uriel O'Farrell scored 11 tries against Brazil on 13 September 1951 in a 72-0 victory, an individual try record in a match which still stands today. The Pumas won the inaugural tournament.

MOST EXPERIENCED EVER SIDE

Australia's starting XV in their 91-3 win over Japan at Stade de Gerland, Lyon, France in Pool B at the 2007 Rugby World Cup finals was the most experienced starting team in the sport's history in terms of the greatest number of international caps. The Wallabies' side had earned a combined total of 798 caps.

Did You Know That?

The head coach of Japan for the 2007 tournament was John Kirwan, who won the inaugural Rugby World Cup as a player with New Zealand in 1987.

HABANA RACES A CHEETAH

In April 2007, South Africa's flying winger, Bryan Habana, made headlines around the world when he raced a cheetah in a 100 metres race. He agreed to the challenge as part of a De Wildt awareness campaign to highlight that the animal was an endangered species. The race ended in a photo finish. However, Bryan was given a 50 metres head start as a cheetah can reach speeds of up to 70mph, 0-60 in three seconds, in comparison to a human's top speed of 22mph. The race organisers used a leg of lamb tied to a teddy bear to ensure the cheetah was not distracted and wouldn't decide to run after Habana instead. A few years later he raced a British Airways A380 Airbus which had four Rolls-Royce Trent 900 engines, each one producing 70,000 pounds of thrust meaning the plane is airborne when it reaches 140mph (it can fly at 600mph in the air). And the Springbok flying machine beat the plane across the line before saluting it as it lifted into the air.

Did You Know That?
Habana was once timed for the 100m at 10.2 seconds. To put this into perspective, Jesse Owens (USA) won the 100m gold medal at the 1936 Olympic Games in Berlin, West Germany in a time of 10.3 seconds.

PURE RUGBY GOLD – JONAH LOMU

Jonah Tali Lomu was born to Tongan parents on 12 May 1975 and came from very humble beginnings, growing up in Mangere, south Auckland, New Zealand. He spent some of his early childhood in Tonga with his Aunt Longo and Uncle Mosese. At school, Wesley College (Auckland), he was an athletics star and excelled at rugby. He started out as a lock and then as a loose forward and from an early age he intimidated opponents with his size, strength and blistering speed. Up until he was 14 years old he played rugby league before making the switch to rugby union. Before too long he became a New Zealand age-group representative. Lomu began his senior international rugby career in the New Zealand Sevens team and impressed at the 1994 Hong Kong Sevens tournament, helping his side to a 32-20 win over Australia in the final.

The All Blacks coach at the time, Laurie Mains, liked what he saw and selected him on the left wing for the mid-year series against France. On 26 June 1994, aged just 19 years and 45 days, he pulled on the All Blacks shirt for the first time to make his international Test debut and become the youngest All Black ever (the record had stood since 1905). The All Blacks lost 22-8 to France in Christchurch, New Zealand.

Lomu scored the first of his 37 tries for New Zealand in a 43-19 win over Ireland in the All Blacks' opening Pool C game at the 1995 Rugby World Cup finals (he scored two tries in the win at Ellis Park, Johannesburg, South Africa). The All Blacks won their pool and he also scored a try in the 48-30 quarter-finals win over Scotland at Loftus Versfield, Pretoria. In the semi-finals the All Blacks faced England at Newlands, Cape Town and it was in this match, more than any other, the world witnessed Lomu's extraordinary talent and devastating running power. He scored four tries in the All Blacks' 45-29 demolition of England including one try where he bulldozed his way through the opposition's defence and simply trampled over Mike Catt. After the game the England captain, Will Carling, was asked about Lomu's performance and he said: 'He is a freak, and the sooner he goes away the better.' The All Blacks lost the 1995 Rugby World Cup Final to the host nation, South Africa, a 15-12 defeat after extra-time at Ellis Park, Johannesburg.

Lomu's health problems first came to light in 1996 and in 1997 he was diagnosed with a kidney condition (nephrotic syndrome) resulting in him missing most of the season. In 1998 he was a member of the New Zealand Sevens team which won the gold medal at the Commonwealth Games in Kuala Lumpur. The following year he scored eight tries at the 1999 Rugby World Cup finals, making him the tournament's all-time leading try scorer with 15 (equalled in 2015 by Bryan Habana of South Africa). Lomu's other shining moment came in a Tri-Nations game dubbed the 'Match of the Century'. On 15 July 2000, the All Blacks faced Australia in front of a world record rugby crowd of 110,000 at Sydney's new Olympic Stadium. The All Blacks won 39-35 thanks to a try scored by Lomu in the last minute after he managed to evade desperate tacklers while somehow remaining in the field of play. On 23 November 2002, he pulled on an All Blacks shirt for the 64th (57 starts) and final time in a 43-17 victory over Wales at the Millennium Stadium, Cardiff. He was only 27 years old and bowed out of first-class rugby the following year, by which time he needed dialysis three times a week. In 2003 he dropped out of the Super 12 early in the campaign and made a brave attempt to resume first-class rugby in the National Provincial Championship for Wellington but it was evident that his health was failing and his career was coming to a premature end. However, a kidney transplant in 2004 enabled him to play sporadically until 2010, but he was a pale shadow of the magnificent athlete he had been. As his playing career wound down, he became an advocate for health charities such as Kidney Kids. He was made a Member of the New Zealand Order of Merit in 2003 and that same year he was presented with a Special Merit Award at the International Rugby Players' Association's (IRPA) awards ceremony for his contribution to the international game. Only two other players had been presented with this very prestigious award – Jason Leonard (England) and John Eales (Australia). Lomu was presented with the award four days before the start of the 2003 Rugby World Cup in Sydney, Australia by one of his heroes, France's Serge Blanco. Lomu said he was extremely humbled to be given such an honour and added that it meant even more to him coming through recognition from his fellow players. He was appointed as a Member of the New Zealand Order of Merit in the Queen's Birthday Honours list in June of 2007 and the same year he was inducted into the International Rugby Hall of Fame in 2007. Lomu was a member of the Champions for Peace club, a group of 54 famous elite athletes committed to serving peace in the world through sport and, in 2011, he was inducted into the IRB Hall of Fame.

On 18 November 2015, Jonah Lomu lost his brave battle for life after suffering a heart attack associated with his kidney condition. His sudden death came just a few weeks after he returned to New Zealand having watched his beloved All Blacks win back-to-back Rugby World Cups. People around the world were moved by his sudden death at such a young age, 40. The Argentinian Pumas donned number 11 jerseys before a match; Britain's *Telegraph* eulogised him as 'a force of nature' and 'a man apart'. A crowd of 10,000 people attended a memorial service at Eden Park. He was the sport's biggest drawcard, a global superstar.

At club level he played for Counties Manukau (1994–99 – 28 games, 19 tries), Blues (Super Rugby 1996–98 – 22 games, 13 tries – winning two Super Rugby titles), Chiefs (Super Rugby 1999 – eight games, two tries), Wainuiomata Rugby Football Club (2000–01 – two games), Hurricanes (Super Rugby 2000–03 – 29 games, 11 tries), Wellington (2000–03 – 21 games, 13 tries), North Harbour (2006 – three games), Cardiff Blues (2005/06 – ten games, one try) and Marseilles (2009/10 – three games). He also represented the New Zealand Sevens from 1994–2001. Despite being 196cm tall and weighing nearly 120kg, he possessed lightning pace (he could run the 100m in 10.8 seconds) and exquisite balance and caused havoc among defenders all over the world. With 37 Test tries he is ranked sixth on the All Blacks' all-time list. There is no question that his legacy is that he was a rugby phenomenon, a folk hero and one of the greatest players ever to play the game. Jonah is survived by his wife Nadene and their two sons, Brayley and Dhyreille.

Did You Know That?

In the 2006 Tri-Nations Series, the Freedom Cup was played for in all three New Zealand-South Africa games. The All Blacks won two of the games (one home 35-17 and one away 45-26) meaning they won the Freedom Cup for the first time. However, during the post-match presentation after the third game, which was won 21-20 by South Africa, a TV presenter for Supersport actually presented the Freedom Cup to the captain of the Springboks, John Smit, who gladly accepted it before millions of television viewers. Thankfully, the error was subsequently corrected off-air when the trophy was handed over to the skipper of the All Blacks, Richie McCaw.

IN HIS OWN WORDS

'Jonah single-handedly destroyed teams and is undoubtedly the single player who has grown the profile of the game the most and on the broadest scale.'

Joel Stransky (Rugby World Cup winner with South Africa in 1995) speaking about the legendary All Black, Jonah Lomu

---

Did You Know That?

Jonah Lomu entered into a number of marketing contracts with commercial giants such as McDonald's, Adidas, Reebok and Heineken (which he promoted at the 2015 Rugby World Cup, just before his death).

ARGENTINA's WORLD CUP RECORD

1987 Pool Stage
1991 Pool Stage
1995 Pool Stage
1999 Quarter-Finals
2003 Pool Stage
2007 Third
2011 Quarter-Finals
2015 Fourth
Union – Argentine Rugby Union
Home – Estadio Jose Amalfitani, Liniers, Buenos Aires
Most Caps – Felipe Contepomi (87)
Top Points Scorer – Federico Nicolás Sánchez (655)
Top Try Scorer – José María Núñez Piossek (30)

Emblem – Jaguarete (a feline in South America related to the jaguar)
Nickname – Los Pumas
High – Their 17-12 win over the 2007 host nation, France, in the opening game of the tournament at Stade de France. Los Pumas topped their pool (they also beat Ireland, Georgia and Namibia) and finished in third place overall after losing their semi-final encounter with South Africa but winning the third place play-off 34-10 against France to claim the bronze medal.
Low – Their performances in the 1995 edition when they lost all three of their pool games to England (24-18), Italy (31-25) and Western Samoa (32-26) to finish bottom of Pool B.
National anthem – 'The Argentine National Anthem'
Alternative national anthem – 'Don't Cry For Me Argentina' by Julie Covington

---

Did You Know That?

Argentina have won every match against South American national teams, including 41 against Uruguay, 38 against Chile, 17 against Paraguay and 13 against Brazil. In 2018, Argentina defeated both Australia and South Africa for the first time in a single calendar year. In contrast, they have never beaten New Zealand, but did secure one draw against the All Blacks.

AUSTRALIA'S WORLD CUP RECORD

1987 Fourth
1991 Winners
1995 Quarter-Finals
1999 Winners
2003 Runners-Up
2007 Quarter-Finals
2011 Third
2015 Runners-Up
Union – Rugby Australia
Home – Various venues
Most Caps – George Gregan (139)
Top Points Scorer – Michael Lynagh (911)
Top Try Scorer – David Campese (64)
Emblem – Wallaby
Nickname – The Wallabies
High – Their 12-6 win over the tournament hosts, England, at Twickenham in the 1991 final.
Low – Losing the 2003 final 20-17 to England at the Telstra Stadium, Sydney when Jonny Wilkinson scored a dropped goal late in the game.

National anthem – 'Advance Australia Fair'
Alternative national anthem – 'Australia' by the Manic Street Preachers

---

Did You Know That?
The Wallabies hold the record for the biggest ever Rugby World Cup win, defeating Namibia 142-0 in the 2003 edition of the tournament.

CANADA'S WORLD CUP RECORD
1987 Pool Stage
1991 Quarter-Finals
1995 Pool Stage
1999 Pool Stage
2003 Pool Stage
2007 Pool Stage
2011 Pool Stage
2015 Pool Stage
Union – Rugby Canada
Home – Various venues
Most Caps – Aaron Carpenter (80)
Top Points Scorer – James Pritchard (607)
Top Try Scorer – DTH van der Merwe (35)
Emblem – Maple leaf
Nickname – Canucks/Les Rouges
High – Reaching the quarter-finals in 1991 after finishing runners-up to France in Pool 4 with victories over Fiji (13-3) and Romania (19-11). They lost their quarter-final encounter 29-13 to the All Blacks played at Villeneuve-d'Ascq, Lille, France.
Low – Losing 79-15 to New Zealand in a 2011 Rugby World Cup Pool A game played at Regional Stadium, Wellington, New Zealand.
National anthem – 'O Canada'
Alternative national anthem – 'My Heart Will Go On' by Celine Dion

---

Did You Know That?
Canada have participated at every Rugby World Cup finals tournament and only failed to win a game at two of them, in 2007 and 2015.

ENGLAND'S WORLD CUP RECORD
1987 Quarter-Finals
1991 Runners-Up
1995 Fourth

1999 Quarter-Finals
2003 Winners
2007 Runners-Up
2011 Quarter-Finals
2015 Pool Stage
Union – Rugby Football Union
Home – Twickenham Stadium
Most Caps – Jason Leonard (114)
Top Points Scorer – Jonny Wilkinson (1,179)
Top Try Scorer – Rory Underwood (49)
Emblem – Red rose
Nickname – England does not have a nickname
High – Winning the Webb Ellis Cup on Australian soil in 2003 when they beat the hosts 20-17 after extra time thanks to a dropped goal from Jonny Wilkinson with only 26 seconds of the game remaining at Telstra Stadium, Sydney.
Low – Exiting the 2015 edition at the pool stage when they were the host nation. England won two and lost two of their Pool A games to finish third behind group winners Australia and runners-up, Wales.
National anthem – 'God Save the Queen'
Alternative national anthem – 'Swing Low Sweet Chariot'

Did You Know That?

Steve Thompson, who was once England's most capped hooker and won the Rugby World Cup in 2003, is a former national roller-skating champion. In 1989, he won the Junior Boys 6-10 years 500 Metres British Championship at Tatem Park, when he was known as Steve Walter (Silver Blazers R.S.C.).

FIJI's WORLD CUP RECORD

1987 Quarter-Finals
1991 Pool Stage
1995 Did Not Qualify
1999 Quarter-Final Play-Offs
2003 Pool Stage
2007 Quarter-Finals
2011 Pool Stage
2015 Pool Stage
Union – Fiji Rugby Union
Home – ANZ National Stadium, Suva
Most Caps – Nicky Little (71)
Top Points Scorer – Nicky Little (670)
Top Try Scorer – Sanivalati Laulau (20)

Emblem – Palm

Nickname – The Warriors

High – Beating Wales 38-34 in Nantes, France to finish second in their pool behind Australia and eliminate Wales from the 2007 competition. Fiji lost 37-20 to South Africa in the quarter-finals.

Low – Their performances in the 1991 edition when they lost all three of their pool games to France (33-9), Canada (13-3) and Romania (17-15) to finish bottom of Pool B. They then failed to qualify for the 1995 Rugby World Cup.

National anthem – 'God Bless Fiji'

Alternative national anthem – 'Orinocco Flow (Sail Away)' by Enya (with the line: 'From Fiji to Tiree and the Isles of Ebony')

Did You Know That?

The *Bole* is a war dance performed by the Fiji rugby team before each Test match.

FRANCE'S WORLD CUP RECORD

1987 Runners-Up

1991 Quarter-Finals

1995 Third

1999 Runners-Up

2003 Fourth

2007 Fourth

2011 Runners-Up

2015 Quarter-Finals

Union – French Rugby Federation

Home – Stade de France, Saint Denis

Most Caps – Fabien Pelous (118)

Top Points Scorer – Frédéric Michalak (436)

Top Try Scorer – Serge Blanco (38)

Emblem – Gallic rooster

Nickname – *Les Bleus*

High – Unquestionably *Les Bleus*' semi-final win in 1999 over the tournament's favourites, New Zealand, at Twickenham Stadium, England. France trailed 17-10 at half-time but came back strongly in the second half to win the match 43-31.

Low – The opening match of the 2007 Rugby World Cup as the host nation. France lost 17-12 to Argentina at Stade de France, Saint Denis in Pool D.

National anthem – 'La Marseillaise'

Alternative national anthem – 'Oxygène' by Jean-Michel Jarre

GEORGIA'S WORLD CUP RECORD

1987 Did Not Qualify
1991 Did Not Qualify
1995 Did Not Qualify
1999 Did Not Qualify
2003 Pool Stage
2007 Pool Stage
2011 Pool Stage
2015 Pool Stage
Union – Georgian Rugby Union
Home – Mikheil Meskhi Stadium, Tbilisi
Most Caps – Merab Kvirikashvili (115)
Top Points Scorer – Merab Kvirikashvili (838)
Top Try Scorer – Mamuka Gorgodze (26)
Emblem – Borjgali (a Georgian symbol of the sun)
Nickname – The Lelos
High – Georgia has only ever won four Rugby World Cup matches (one in 2007, one in 2011 and two in 2015) but their high point was a 14-10 loss to Ireland in a Pool D match played at Stade Chaban-Delmas, Bordeaux, France in 2007.
Low – Their debut game in the Rugby World Cup (2003) when they were beaten 86-4 in a Pool C match at the Subiaco Oval, Perth by the tournament's eventual winners, England.
National anthem – 'Freedom'
Alternative national anthem – 'Georgia On My Mind' by Ray Charles

IRELAND'S WORLD CUP RECORD

1987 Quarter-Finals
1991 Quarter-Finals
1995 Quarter-Finals
1999 Quarter-Final Play-Offs

2003 Quarter-Finals
2007 Pool Stage
2011 Quarter-Finals
2015 Quarter-Finals
Union – Irish Rugby Football Union
Home – Aviva Stadium, Dublin
Most Caps – Brian O'Driscoll (141)
Top Points Scorer – Ronan O'Gara (1,083)
Top Try Scorer – Brian O'Driscoll (46)
Emblem – Shamrock
Nickname – Ireland does not have a nickname
High – Their Pool C shootout with Wales at the 1995 Rugby World Cup to determine which nation would join the pool winners, New Zealand, in the quarter-finals. Ireland won a pulsating encounter 24-23 at Ellis Park, Johannesburg, South Africa.
Low – Losing 28-24 to Argentina at Stade Bollaert-Delelis, Lens, France in the quarter-final play-offs at the 1999 Rugby World Cup. Ireland led 15-9 at half-time.
National anthem – Whilst 'The Soldier's Song' is the national anthem of the Republic of Ireland and is sung before every Ireland home game, 'Ireland's Call' is also sung before home games as the Ireland team also includes players from Northern Ireland. Only 'Ireland's Call' is played before away games.
Alternative national anthem – 'The Luck of the Irish' by John Lennon

---

Did You Know That?
Along with Italy, Ireland are the only Tier 1 nation never to have reached the semi-final stages of a Rugby World Cup.

ITALY'S WORLD CUP RECORD
1987 Pool Stage
1991 Pool Stage
1995 Pool Stage
1999 Pool Stage
2003 Pool Stage
2007 Pool Stage
2011 Pool Stage
2015 Pool Stage
Union – Italian Rugby Federation
Home – Stadio Olimpico, Rome
Most Caps – Sergio Parisse (134)
Top Points Scorer – Diego Dominguez (983)

Top Try Scorer – Marcello Cuttitta (25)
Emblem – Italian flag
Nickname – The Azzurri
High – Defeating Fiji 18-15 in their second game in Pool 3 at the inaugural Rugby World Cup at Lancaster Park, Christchurch, New Zealand.
Low – An embarrassing 101-3 Pool C loss to the All Blacks in the 1999 Rugby World Cup hosted by Wales. The match was played at McAlpine Stadium, Huddersfield, England.
National anthem – 'The Song of the Italians'
Alternative national anthem – 'Three Coins in the Fountain' by Frank Sinatra

---

Did You Know That?

Italy's Fabio Ongaro holds the record for the most sin bins in the history of the Rugby World Cup with three.

JAPAN'S WORLD CUP RECORD

1987 Pool Stage
1991 Pool Stage
1995 Pool Stage
1999 Pool Stage
2003 Pool Stage
2007 Pool Stage
2011 Pool Stage
2015 Pool Stage
Union – Japan Rugby Football Union
Home – Chichibunomiya Rugby Stadium, Tokyo
Most Caps – Hitoshi Ono (98)
Top Points Scorer – Ayumu Goromaru (708)
Top Try Scorer – Daisuke Ohata (69)
Emblem – Sakura (cherry blossom)
Nickname – The Brave Blossoms
High – A remarkable 34-32 victory over South Africa in their opening Pool B game of the 2015 Rugby World Cup at Brighton Community Stadium, Brighton, England. Prior to this Japan had only one other victory in the history of the competition, a 52-8 win over Zimbabwe at Ravenhill, Belfast, Northern Ireland in the 1991 edition.
Low – A quite humiliating 145-17 loss to New Zealand at Free State Stadium, Bloemfontein, South Africa in 1995. The All Blacks' points tally against Japan is a Rugby World Cup record for a single game.
National anthem – 'His Majesty's Reign'
Alternative national anthem – 'Japanese Boy' by Aneka

NAMIBIA'S WORLD CUP RECORD

1987 Did Not Qualify
1991 Did Not Qualify
1995 Did Not Qualify
1999 Pool Stage
2003 Pool Stage
2007 Pool Stage
2011 Pool Stage
2015 Pool Stage
Union – Namibia Rugby Union
Home – Hage Geingob Rugby Stadium, Windhoek
Most Caps – Eugene Jantjies (61)
Top Points Scorer – Theuns Kotzé (430)
Top Try Scorer – Gerhard Mans (27)
Emblem – African fish eagle
Nickname – Welwitschias
High – They have never won a Rugby World Cup game but did achieve a highly creditable 32-17 Pool D loss against Ireland at Stade Chaban-Delmas, Bordeaux, France in 2007.
Low – a 142-0 whitewash by Australia in their Pool A match at the Adelaide Oval on 25 October 2003.
National anthem – 'Land of the Brave'
Alternative national anthem – 'Home of the Brave' by Toto

NEW ZEALAND'S WORLD CUP RECORD

1987 Winners
1991 Third
1995 Runners-Up
1999 Fourth
2003 Third
2007 Quarter-Finals
2011 Winners

2015 Winners
Union – New Zealand Rugby Union
Home – Various venues
Most Caps – Richie McCaw (148)
Top Points Scorer – Dan Carter (1,598)
Top Try Scorer – Doug Howlett (49)
Emblem – Silver fern frond
Nickname – All Blacks
High – Becoming the first, and to date only, nation to win the Rugby World Cup three times (1987, 2011 and 2015) and the first to retain the Webb Ellis Cup when they lifted the trophy in 2015.
Low – In 1999, the All Blacks looked set to reach their third final in the first four Rugby World Cups when they led France 24-10 in their semi-final encounter (17-10 at half-time). However, the unfancied French came battling back to claim a famous 43-31 win at Twickenham Stadium, London.
National anthem – 'God Defend New Zealand'
Alternative national anthem – 'I Got You' by Split Enz

Did You Know That?

The All Blacks have scored a try in their last 26 Rugby World Cup games dating back to the 2003 edition of the tournament (a 40-13 third place play-off win against France). They lost 22-18 in the 1999 third place play-off match versus South Africa with Andrew Mehrtens scoring all 18 points from six penalty kicks.

ROMANIA'S WORLD CUP RECORD

1987 Pool Stage
1991 Pool Stage
1995 Pool Stage
1999 Pool Stage
2003 Pool Stage
2007 Pool Stage
2011 Pool Stage
2015 Pool Stage
Union – Romanian Rugby Federation
Home – Stadionul Național de Rugby Arcul de Triumf, Bucharest (being demolished to make way for a new stadium in 2019)
Most Caps – Florin Vlaicu (111)
Top Points Scorer – Florin Vlaicu (837)
Top Try Scorer – Cătălin Fercu (32)
Emblem – An oak leaf
Nickname – Oaks

High – Beating the USA for the first time in their history. Romania won their 1999 Rugby World Cup Pool E game 27-25 at Lansdowne Road, Dublin, Ireland (Wales were the host nation). Kevin Dalzell missed a late conversion which would have sealed victory for his side.
Low – A 90-8 mauling by Australia in a Pool A game played at Suncorp Stadium, Brisbane, Australia in 2003.
National anthem – 'Wake Up Romanian!
Alternative national anthem – 'Wake Me Up Before You Go-Go' by Wham!

Did You Know That?
Romania hold the unwanted record of scoring the fewest points at a Rugby World Cup, just 14 in 1995 when South Africa was the host nation. They lost all three of their Pool A games: Canada 34-3, South Africa 21-8 and Australia 42-3.

RUSSIA'S WORLD CUP RECORD
1987 Declined invitation to participate
1991 Did not participate in qualifying
1995 Did Not Qualify
1999 Did Not Qualify
2003 Banned from qualifying for breaches of eligibility rules
2007 Did Not Qualify
2011 Pool Stage
2015 Did Not Qualify
Union – Rugby Union of Russia
Home – Sochi Central Stadium
Most Caps – Yuri Kushnarev (101)
Top Points Scorer – Yuri Kushnarev (733)
Top Try Scorer – Vasily Artemyev (28)
Emblem – Russian bear
Nickname – The Bears
High – Beating the Barbarians 27-23 in Moscow, Russia on 6 June 1992 which was their first international as Russia (formerly the Soviet Union and CIS).
Low – A 75-3 loss to Japan in Tokyo, Japan on 6 November 2000, their record defeat.
National anthem – 'State Anthem of the Russian Federation'
Alternative national anthem – 'Back in the USSR' by The Beatles

---

Did You Know That?
The Rugby Union of the Soviet Union was founded in 1936, although the national side did not play its first official international until 1974.

SAMOA'S WORLD CUP RECORD
1987 Did Not Qualify
1991 Quarter-Finals
1995 Quarter-Finals
1999 Quarter-Final Play-Offs
2003 Pool Stage
2007 Pool Stage
2011 Pool Stage
2015 Pool Stage
Union – Samoa Rugby Union
Home – Apia Park, Apia
Most Caps – Brian Lima (64)
Top Points Scorer – Tusi Pisi (219)
Top Try Scorer – Brian Lima (29)
Emblem – Southern cross
Nickname – Manu Samoa
High – A 16-13 win as Western Samoa over one of the co-host nations, Wales, at Cardiff Arms Park in a Pool 3 game in 1991. The win helped the Samoans to qualify to the quarter-final stages of the tournament as group runners-up to the eventual 1991 Rugby World Cup winners, Australia.
Low – Their 60-10 defeat at the hands of South Africa in a Pool C game at Suncorp Stadium, Brisbane, Australia on 1 November 2003.
National anthem – 'The Banner of Freedom'
Alternative national anthem – 'Freedom' by George Michael

Did You Know That?
Samoa hold the unwanted record of having the biggest Rugby World Cup half-time lead only to go on and lose the game. On 10 October 1999, the Samoans led Argentina 16-3 at half-time in their Pool D game played at Stradey Park, Llanelli, Wales only to lose the game 32-16.

SCOTLAND'S WORLD CUP RECORD
1987 Quarter-Finals
1991 Fourth
1995 Quarter-Finals
1999 Quarter-Finals
2003 Quarter-Finals
2007 Quarter-Finals
2011 Quarter-Finals
2015 Quarter-Finals

Union – Scottish Rugby Union
Home – Murrayfield Stadium, Edinburgh
Most Caps – Ross Ford (110)
Top Points Scorer – Chris Paterson (809)
Top Try Scorer – Ian Smith and Tony Stanger (24)
Emblem – Thistle
Nickname – Scotland does not have a nickname
High – Winning all three of their Pool 2 games at the 1991 edition when they were one of the co-hosts, which included a 24-15 win over Ireland at Murrayfield Stadium, Edinburgh.
Low – A humiliating whitewash to New Zealand in the 2007 Rugby World Cup, losing 40-0 before a packed home crowd at Murrayfield Stadium, Edinburgh (France were the host nation of the 2007 edition but some matches were also staged in Scotland and Wales).
National anthem – 'Flower of Scotland'
Alternative national anthem – 'I Guess That's Why They Call It The Blues' by Elton John

---

Did You Know That?
Scotland have never beaten New Zealand and have been put out of four of the previous eight Rugby World Cups by the All Blacks; 1987 quarter-finals 30-3, 1995 quarter-finals 48-30, 1999 quarter-finals 30-18 and the 40-0 pool stage loss in 2007. Scotland also lost 13-6 in the third-place play-off match against the All Blacks in 1991.

SOUTH AFRICA'S WORLD CUP RECORD
1987 Banned
1991 Banned
1995 Winners
1999 Third
2003 Quarter-Finals
2007 Winners
2011 Quarter-Finals
2015 Third
Union – South African Rugby Union
Home – Various venues
Most Caps – Victor Matfield (127)
Top Points Scorer – Percy Montgomery (893)
Top Try Scorer – Bryan Habana (67)
Emblem – Springbok and Protea
Nickname – Springboks
High – Winning the 1995 edition as the host nation when they were

welcomed back into the rugby fold after being banned for years as a result of their apartheid regime. Nelson Mandela attended the final wearing a replica Francois Pienaar shirt.

Low – A narrow 20-18 defeat to New Zealand in the 2015 semi-finals.

National anthem – 'National Anthem of South Africa'

Alternative national anthem – 'Africa' by Toto

Did You Know That?
South Africa have not beaten Australia or New Zealand at a Rugby World Cup since 1995.

TONGA'S WORLD CUP RECORD
1987 Pool Stage
1991 Did Not Qualify
1995 Pool Stage
1999 Pool Stage
2003 Pool Stage
2007 Pool Stage
2011 Pool Stage
2015 Pool Stage
Union – Tonga Rugby Football Union
Home – Teufaiva Sport Stadium, Nuku'alofa
Most Caps – Nili Latu (43)
Top Points Scorer – Kurt Morath (338)
Top Try Scorer – Fetu'u Vainikolo (15)
Emblem – White dove
Nickname – Sea Eagles
High – A 19-14 upset win over France in their final Pool A game of the 2011 Rugby World Cup at Regional Stadium, Wellington, New Zealand.
Low – A 101-10 mauling by England at Twickenham, England in the 1999 Rugby World Cup. The host nation ran in 13 tries.
National anthem – 'Song of the King of the Tonga Islands'
Alternative national anthem – 'Living on an Island' by Status Quo

---

Did You Know That?
Ten countries have seen at least one of their players dismissed at a Rugby World Cup, with Canada and Tonga both having lost three members of their team.

URUGUAY'S WORLD CUP RECORD
1987 Did Not Qualify

1991 Did Not Qualify
1995 Did Not Qualify
1999 Pool Stage
2003 Pool Stage
2007 Did Not Qualify
2011 Did Not Qualify
2015 Pool Stage
Union – Uruguayan Rugby Union
Home – Estadio Charrúa, Montevideo
Most Caps – Diego Magno (82)
Top Points Scorer – Federico Sciarra (261)
Top Try Scorer – Diego Ormaechea (33)
Emblem – Southern lapwing
Nickname – Los Teros
High – Beating Georgia 24-12 at the Aussie Stadium, Sydney, Australia in the 2003 tournament, to record only their second ever win at a Rugby World Cup finals. In the 1999 edition in Wales they defeated Spain 27-15 at Netherdale, Galashiels, Scotland.
Low – Five days after the win over Georgia, they were beaten 111-13 by England at Suncorp Stadium, Brisbane with England scoring 17 tries.
National anthem – 'National Anthem'
Alternative national anthem – 'S.S. in Uruguay' by Serge Gainsbourg

---

Did You Know That?

Uruguay won the South American Rugby Championship in 1981, the only time (pre-2014) that a team other than Argentina won the tournament (1951–2014). They have won three of the last five editions of the South American Rugby Championship in 2014, 2016 and 2017 (it became known as the South American Six nations in 2018 which was won by Brazil).

USA'S WORLD CUP RECORD

1987 Pool Stage
1991 Pool Stage
1995 Did Not Qualify
1999 Pool Stage
2003 Pool Stage
2007 Pool Stage
2011 Pool Stage
2015 Pool Stage
Union – USA Rugby
Home – Various venues
Most Caps – Todd Clever (76)

Top Points Scorer – Mike Hercus (465)
Top Try Scorer – Vaea Naufahu Anitoni (26)
Emblem – American bald eagle
Nickname – The Eagles
High – Winning their first Rugby World Cup match at the first attempt, a 21-18 victory against Japan in a Pool 1 game played at Ballymore, Australia in the inaugural Rugby World Cup in 1987.
Low – A humiliating whitewash to South Africa in the 2015 Rugby World Cup, losing 64-0 in a Pool B match at the Olympic Stadium, London.
National anthem – 'Star Spangled Banner'
Alternative national anthem – 'America' by Neil Diamond

Did You Know That?
The USA has only ever won three Rugby World Cup matches. They have defeated Japan twice, the 21-18 win in 1987 and a 39-26 Pool B victory in 2003 followed by a 13-6 Pool C win over Russia in 2011.

WALES'S WORLD CUP RECORD
1987 Third
1991 Pool Stage
1995 Pool Stage
1999 Quarter-Finals
2003 Quarter-Finals
2007 Pool Stage
2011 Semi-Finals
2015 Quarter-Finals
Union – Welsh Rugby Union
Home – Principality Stadium, Cardiff
Most Caps – Gethin Jenkins (129)
Top Points Scorer – Neil Jenkins (1,049)
Top Try Scorer – Shane Williams (58)
Emblem – Prince of Wales's feathers
Nickname – Dragons
High – Beating England 16-3 in the quarter-finals of the inaugural Rugby World Cup in 1987 at Ballymore, Brisbane, Australia (co-hosts Australia and New Zealand).
Low – A 9-8 loss to France in the semi-finals of the 2011 Rugby World Cup. The game was played at Eden Park, Auckland, New Zealand.
National anthem – 'Land of my Fathers'
Alternative national anthem – 'Green Green Grass of Home' by Tom Jones

GERMAN RUGBY FEDERATION

Although it is the oldest Rugby Union (German Rugby Federation – Deutscher Rugby-Verband) in continental Europe, formed in 1900, Germany has never qualified for a Rugby World Cup finals. Germany's greatest achievement in men's rugby is arguably the silver medal they won at the 1900 Olympic Games in Paris, France. The German team was mostly made up of players from FC 1880 Frankfurt. Only two games were played with France defeating Germany 27-17 and Great Britain 27-8. France claimed the gold medal with Germany and Great Britain both awarded a silver medal (there was no bronze medal at the inaugural Olympic Games rugby competition). The Great Britain side was represented by players from Aston Old Edwardians, Coventry and Moseley Wanderers. In all, 47 athletes from the three nations competed. Germany competes in the Championship Division, the top tier of the Rugby Europe International Championships, which is the senior men's rugby tournament for European nations below the Six Nations.

UNLUCKY 13 FOR *LES BLEUS*

The 1999 Rugby World Cup Final was contested by Australia and France on 6 November 1999 at the Millennium Stadium, Cardiff, Wales. The two nations had first met on 28 January 1928 at Stade Olympique Yves-du-Manoir, Colombes, Paris, France during a New South Wales Waratahs tour of the British Isles, France and Canada. The stadium was named in honour of Yves du Manoir, a French rugby player and during the 1924 Olympic Games hosted by Paris, it was used for the athletics competitions and also for some of the cycling, football, gymnastics, horse riding, modern pentathlon (fencing and running) tennis and the rugby which was won by the USA. The tourists won the first meeting 11-8. The 1999 Rugby World Cup Final was the 29th time the pair had met with 13 wins each and two draws (14-14 in Sydney,

171

Australia in 1972 and in Clermond-Ferrand, France in 1983). But the 1999 Rugby World Cup Final proved to be 'unlucky 13' for Les Bleus as they lost 35-12.

Did You Know That?

Stade Olympique Yves-du-Manoir was portrayed in the 1981 movie, *Escape to Victory*, starring Michael Caine and Sylvester Stallone although the stadium used in the filming was actually the Hungária Körúti Stadion in Budapest, Hungary.

TRY-LESS RUGBY WORLD CUP WINNERS

South Africa won both of their Rugby World Cups without scoring a try in either final. In 1995, the Springboks defeated New Zealand 15-12 on home soil (Ellis Park, Johannesburg) with Joel Stransky scoring three penalties and two dropped goals and in 2007, they beat England 15-6 at Stade de France, Paris, France (Percy Montgomery scored four penalties with Francois Steyn adding a fifth). Every other final, including the All Blacks' narrow 8-7 victory over France in the 2011 final at Eden Park, Auckland, New Zealand, saw at least one try being scored.

Did You Know That?

Including the 2015 edition, nine teams have failed to score a single point in a Rugby World Cup match: Scotland 89-0 Ivory Coast (1995); South Africa 20-0 Canada (1995); Scotland 48-0 Spain (1999); Australia 142-0 Namibia (2003); South Africa 36-0 England (2007); Scotland 42-0 Romania (2007); New Zealand 40-0 Scotland (2007); Georgia 30-0 Namibia (2007); South Africa 87-0 Namibia (2011); Wales 66-0 Fiji (2011) and South Africa 64-0 USA (2015).

SHIRT NUMBERING

In 1897, New Zealand and Queensland became the first teams to display a number on their jerseys, 1-15 for New Zealand and 16-30 for Queensland in a game played in Brisbane, Queensland, Australia. The match organisers thought that numbering the jerseys would help the spectators identify the players. However, the practice was not immediately adopted throughout rugby and it wasn't until 1921 when the issue was brought before the International Rugby Board (IRB) by the English and Welsh Rugby Unions. The IRB left it up to the teams to decide whether to wear numbers. In 1928, Scotland adopted numbering for a game against France but did not continue with it whilst the Welsh actually used a lettering system during the 1930s.

It wasn't until the 1950s when all of the home nations (England, Ireland, Scotland and Wales) used the numbering system. England, Scotland and Wales used 1-15 and 16-30 whilst the Irish (and the French) used 1-15 for both teams. However, in season 1960/61 the 1-15 numbering system for both teams was adopted for international matches.

Did You Know That?

When England played Scotland in the Calcutta Cup at Twickenham Stadium, London on 17 March 1928 (England won 6-0) it is claimed that King George V asked the president of the Scottish Football Union, James Aikman Smith, why the Scottish players were not wearing numbers. Smith's reply was, 'This, sir, is a rugby match, not a cattle sale.'

THE CONDORS

The Chile national rugby union team has never reached a Rugby World Cup finals.

Nicknamed Los Cóndores (the Condors), Chile were the first South American nation outside Argentina to play international rugby union. They played their first Test against Argentina in Valparaíso, Chile on 18 September 1936 and lost 29-0.

Did You Know That?

In 2012, two Scottish-Chilean players, Donald and Ian Campbell, were inducted into the IRB Hall of Fame. Donald and Ian, once described as 'the most skilful player in South America', both played club rugby for the Prince of Wales Country Club, Santiago and international rugby for Chile. Ian appeared in every international match Chile played between 1948 and 1961. Their father, Colin, was a Scottish-born emigrant, businessman and amateur football player, who played international football for Argentina (one cap in 1907) and Chile (three caps in 1910).

THE FRENCH CHEETAH

In January 2019, France international Wesley Fofana confirmed that he will retire from international rugby at the end of the 2019 Rugby World Cup. Fofana made his debut for France on 4 February 2012 scoring a try in a 30-12 win over Italy at Stade de France, Paris in the Six Nations. The 31-year-old who has played for Clermont Auvergne since 2008, said he is convinced about his decision to quit international rugby at the end of 2019 whether or not he is picked for the showpiece event in Japan but assured his fans he will continue playing for his club. 'It's all pleasure now, I'm making the most of it because after the World Cup I will stop. I'm doing everything I can to be there, of course, and then I will retire from France. Even if I'm not picked for the World Cup, whatever happens, I'll stop,' said Fofana, who won the French Top 14 title with Clermont Auvergne in 2010. In France he is known as 'Le Guépard' (the Cheetah) for his pace.

Did You Know That?
Fofana is of Malian descent.

NO WASPS

In December 2018, Fiji international Frank Lomani turned down an offer from Gallagher Premiership club Wasps in order to focus on the 2019 Rugby World Cup in Japan. 'The Wasps deal didn't work out. I just want to come back home and spend time with my family and rest after two years of non-stop rugby. My focus now is the 2019 RWC, prepare well and do my family and country proud. I have always wanted to make my family proud every time I play, make my hometown proud and at the same time challenge youths that nothing is impossible,' Lomani told the *Fiji Sun*. Fiji are grouped in Pool D alongside Australia, Wales, Georgia and Uruguay in the 2019 Rugby World Cup.

A HISTORIC VICTORY

Fiji's first ever win over France, a 21-14 victory at Stade de France, Paris on 24 November 2018 meant Fiji gained 1.55 rating points and edged past Argentina and France to eighth place in World Rugby's Top 10 Rankings. Ten of Fiji's 23-man squad play in the French Top 14 and four others came from the Championship-winning Fijian Drua side that takes part in the Australian National Rugby Championship. New Zealand ended 2018 as the No.1 ranked side with 92.54 rating points with their only defeat in the year coming against Ireland who were the No.2 ranked side with 91.17 rating points. The third and fourth places remained unchanged, Wales and England respectively, with South Africa fifth.

Did You Know That?
Fiji have now played France ten times, losing the other nine.

COVER UP

A famous hot spa resort is offering an online map showing 'onsen' spots such as spas, beaches, gyms and hundreds of facilities opening their doors to visitors who have tattoos ahead of the 2019 Rugby World Cup in Japan. Tattoos are typically frowned upon in Japan as such body markings are associated with the 'Yakuza', the Japanese mafia. World Rugby had earlier advised the teams and supporters attending that they would need to cover up any tattoo markings in public places for fear of causing offence. The city office of Beppu in the World Cup host prefecture of Oita, where the All Blacks will play during the 2019 tournament, has prepared the online map on the website titled '100 Tattoo-allowed Hot Springs'. 'We don't want to disappoint people who come all the way (from overseas) as the operators of many public baths refuse guests with tattoos,' a city official said, explaining why the city created the Google Maps-based guide. On the Beppu map onsens have been colour coded either blue, orange or dark blue, with the 50 in blue allowing visitors with tattoos in their large baths, the 40 in orange asking the ink-wearers to use private pools and ten in dark blue allowing only the soaking of hands and feet in tubs. 'It's difficult to distinguish between gangsters and other guests when both have tattoos,' an accommodation facility representative told the agency. Tattoos are part of traditional culture in countries such as New Zealand whose national rugby team will play in Oita, near Beppu, during the 2019 tournament.

ASIA'S RUGBY WORLD CUP FEVER

World Rugby's initiative to drive the game into Asia resulted in 900,000 new rugby participants as part of World Rugby's ambitious Asia 1 Million legacy project. The governing body was determined to make the maximum out of the 2019 World Cup in Japan, the first time that the tournament will be held outside the traditional European and southern hemisphere nations. With a partnership of Asia Rugby and the Japan Rugby Football Union, 30,000 new rugby participants joined 'Get Into Rugby' programmes across Japan with a further 200,000 schoolchildren in Rugby World Cup host cities introduced to tag rugby following its inclusion in the physical education curriculum of 1,982 schools in the Rugby World Cup host cities. However, Japan's preparations were not without difficulties too. As the national stadium in Tokyo would not be ready before the event, the final was shifted to Yokohama while a broken roof during the June 2018 Test between Japan and Georgia saw fans soaked.

TOP OF THE POPS 2003

When England won the fifth Rugby World Cup Final on 22 November 2003, the No.1 song in the UK pop charts was 'Crashed The Wedding' by Busted. This was the second UK No.1 hit for the North London trio.

It spent one week in the top slot before being ousted by Westlife with 'Mandy', the 12th UK No.1 song for the Irish boy band.

Did You Know That?

Japan Rugby received over 38,000 applications for the volunteer programme for the 2019 Rugby World Cup. This represents a record as the largest number of volunteer applications and the largest volunteer workforce for any Rugby World Cup. Japan Rugby received four times the number of applications compared to the number of positions available, which is a fantastic achievement.

OCEANIA/EUROPE PLAY-OFF

Samoa progressed to the 2019 Rugby World Cup in Japan following their victories over Germany in the Oceania/Europe play-offs. Samoa sealed a 42-28 victory in Heidelberg after already completing a 66-15 win in the first leg in Apia to take their aggregate to 108-43. They will play in Pool A in the showpiece event alongside Ireland, Japan, Russia and Scotland.

David Kirk, the captain of the All Blacks, holds aloft the Webb Ellis Cup after New Zealand's 29-9 victory over France in the inaugural Rugby World Cup Final at Auckland's Eden Park, New Zealand – 20 June 1987

Australia's Michael Lynagh scores the match-winning try during the Wallabies' Rugby World Cup semi-final match against Ireland at Lansdowne Road, Dublin, Ireland on 20 October 1991. Australia won the game 19-18 and went on to beat England 12-6 in the final.

Australian scrum-half and captain, Nick Farr-Jones (left), and winger David Campese lift the Webb Ellis Cup after Australia's 12-6 victory over England in the 1991 Rugby World Cup Final at Twickenham Stadium, London – 2 November 1991.

All Blacks legend Jonah Lomu charges through the tackle of Mike Catt of England to score a try during their 1995 Rugby World Cup semi-final at Newlands Stadium, Cape Town, South Africa. New Zealand won the match 45-29 on 18 June 1995.

Joel Stransky of South Africa scores the winning drop goal during the 1995 World Cup Final against New Zealand played at Ellis Park, Johannesburg, South Africa. The Springboks won the match 15-12 after extra time on 24 June 1995.

South African president Nelson Mandela, dressed in a No 6 Springbok jersey, congratulates the Springbok captain Francois Pienaar after South Africa beat New Zealand 15-12 after extra time at Ellis Park, Johannesburg, South Africa to win the 1995 Rugby World Cup Final – 24 June 1995.

South African captain Francois Pienaar is carried on Hennie Le Roux's shoulders with the Webb Ellis Cup after the Springboks defeated New Zealand 15-12 after extra time to win the 1995 Rugby World Cup Final at Ellis Park, Johannesburg, South Africa – 24 June 1995.

Australian lock and captain John Eales holds up the Webb Ellis Cup after the 1999 Rugby World Cup Final. The Springboks defeated France 34-12 at the Millennium Stadium, Cardiff, Wales on 6 November 1999.

England's Jonny Wilkinson kicks the winning drop-goal against Australia in the 2003 Rugby World Cup final at the Telstra Stadium, Sydney, Australia on 22 November 2003. England defeated the host nation 20-17 after extra time.

The captain of South Africa, John Smit, and his team-mates are joined by the South African president, Thabo Mbeki, after winning the 2007 Rugby World Cup Final. The Springboks beat England 15-6 at Stade de France, St Denis, Paris, France on 20 October 2007.

Former South Africa president Nelson Mandela poses with South Africa captain John Smit and the Webb Ellis Cup during the Springboks' visit to Nelson Mandela at his residence in Houghton, Johannesburg, South Africa on 27 October 2007. One week earlier the Springboks defeated England 15-6 at Stade de France, St Denis, Paris, France in the 2007 Rugby World Cup Final.

New Zealand captain, Richie McCaw, celebrates the All Blacks' 8-7 victory over France in the 2011 Rugby World Cup Final played at Eden Park, Auckland, New Zealand on 23 October 2011.

New Zealand perform the haka prior to the 2015 Rugby World Cup Final played at Twickenham Stadium, London on 31 October 2015. The All Blacks defeated Australia 34-17 to become the first country to win the Webb Ellis Cup three times.

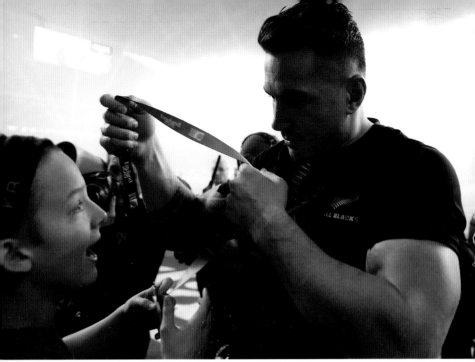

The All Blacks' Sonny Bill Williams gives his Rugby World Cup Final winning medal to a young fan, Charlie Lines, following their 2015 win over Australia. The All Blacks defeated the Wallabies 34-17 at Twickenham Stadium, London, England on 31 October 2015.

Pyrotechnics explode as the New Zealand captain, Richie McCaw, lifts the Webb Ellis Cup following their 34-17 victory against Australia in the 2015 Rugby World Cup Final at Twickenham Stadium, London, England on 31 October 2015.

THE 2007 RUGBY WORLD CUP FINALS

The 2007 Rugby World Cup finals were hosted by France. It was the sixth edition of the quadrennial international rugby union tournament. A total of 20 nations competed for the Webb Ellis Cup which saw 48 matches over 44 days; 42 matches were played in ten cities throughout France plus four in Cardiff, Wales and two in Edinburgh, Scotland. The eight quarter-finalists from the 2003 tournament (Australia, England, France, Ireland, New Zealand, Scotland, South Africa and Wales) automatically qualified for the 2007 tournament and the remaining 12 places went to the successful teams in the regional qualifying competitions (Argentina, Canada, Fiji, Georgia, Italy, Japan, Namibia, Romania, Samoa, Tonga, USA and Portugal, who were making their Rugby World Cup finals debut). South Africa won Pool A (won all four games) with the reigning world champions, England, runners-up; Australia topped Pool B with four wins and Fiji pipped Wales to runners-up position; Pool C went to form with New Zealand winning all four of their games including a 40-0 win over the runners-up, Scotland. Pool D, comprising Argentina, France, Georgia, Ireland and Namibia threw up several surprises with Argentina winning all four of their games and Ireland losing out to France for runners-up spot. In a repeat of the 2003 Rugby World Cup Final, England beat Australia 12-10 in the quarter-finals and were joined in the semi-finals by France (beat the All Blacks 20-18), South Africa (defeated Fiji 37-20) and Argentina (beat Scotland 19-13). The first semi-final saw the host nation getting knocked out of the tournament by England (14-9) with South Africa reaching the final after defeating the Pumas 37-13. Argentina won the bronze final match by beating France 34-10.

Final – 20 October 2007
Stade de France, Saint-Denis, Paris, France
South Africa 15-6 England

South Africa met England in the final five weeks after beating them 36-0 in their Pool A encounter at Stade de France, Saint-Denis, Paris. But the rematch proved to be a very defensive game as neither side could breach their opponents' stubborn defence. So it came down to the boots of the kickers and the Springboks led 9-3 at half-time thanks to the reliable kicking of Percy Montgomery. Jonny Wilkinson, the hero of the 2003 Rugby World Cup Final replied with a penalty in the first half in a game of tactical high kicking and little open play. Early into the second half England went very close to scoring a try through Mark Cueto but following a lengthy deliberation by the TV match official, the England winger was ruled to have been in touch when he crossed over the line in the corner. Wilkinson, who missed two drop goal attempts, made the score 9-6 with his second successful penalty in the 44th minute and seven minutes later Montgomery made it a six-point gap once again with his fourth score of the game. South Africa were awarded a penalty in the 62nd minute and Francois Steyn took over the kicking duties and slotted the ball between the uprights from 46 metres out. This was the end of the scoring and South Africa became the second nation to win the Webb Ellis Cup twice following Australia's triumphs in 1991 and 1999. South Africa's captain, John Smit, accepted the famous gold trophy from Nicolas Sarkozy, the President of France. Several Springboks players carried the President of South Africa, Thabo Mbeki, on their shoulders as the beaming president held aloft the Webb Ellis Cup.

'It's important for our country and I think everyone back home is rejoicing. It's unbelievable. To see the president of our country sitting on the players' shoulders, it doesn't get much better than that,' said South Africa coach, Jack White. Meanwhile, Smit said: 'We have had the responsibility of carrying the hopes of a nation on our shoulders and now we have a team that is taking the trophy back home to the nation. I certainly hope that being able to lift this cup and take it back home can create a scenario that everyone binds together and we start forgetting about counting numbers and colours. Twelve years ago, I sat watching the final at Ellis Park and wondered whether it was possible to do it again. Dreams come true. It was a colossal game, but to be able to win a World Cup, I think I'll only realise in a couple of days' time.'

South Africa: Percy Montgomery; JP Pietersen, Jaque Fourie, Francois Steyn, Bryan Habana; Butch James, Fourie Du Preez; Os Du Randt, John Smit, CJ van der Linde, Bakkies Botha, Victor Matfield, Schalk Burger, Juan Smith, Danie Rossouw.

Replacements: Bismarck du Plessis, Jannie du Plessis, Johan Muller, Wikus van Heerden, Ruan Pienaar, Andre Pretorius, Wynard Olivier.

England: Jason Robinson; Paul Sackey, Mathew Tait, Mike Catt, Mark Cueto; Jonny Wilkinson, Andy Gomarsall; Andrew Sheridan, Mark Regan, Phil Vickery, Simon Shaw, Ben Kay, Martin Corry, Lewis Moody, Nick Easter.

Replacements: George Chuter, Matt Stevens, Lawrence Dallaglio, Joe Worsley, Peter Richards, Toby Flood, Dan Hipkiss.

South Africa	England
Pens Montgomery 4, Steyn	Pens Wilkinson 2

Referee: Alain Rolland (Ireland)
Attendance: 80,430

Did You Know That?

Stade de France became the first stadium to host a FIFA Football World Cup Final (1998) and a Rugby World Cup Final.

A HEFTY PRICE TO PAY

In May 2018, Russia progressed to the 2019 Rugby World Cup as Europe 1 after World Rugby sanctioned Spain, Belgium and Romania for fielding ineligible players during qualifying matches. Spain lodged a complaint following their shocking 18-10 defeat to Belgium in Brussels that resulted in Romania qualifying for the 2019 showpiece event. However, the panel confirmed that all three countries breached eligibility rules resulting in deduction of points. As a result, Russia joined Ireland, Scotland and Japan in Pool A.

A statement from the sport's governing body read: 'While the independent disputes committee has determined that mistakes were not made in bad faith by Rugby Europe and some participating unions, World Rugby is extremely disappointed with the unfortunate and avoidable events, as expressed when announcing the convening of the independent committee. Regulation 8 covering eligibility is essential to maintaining the unique characteristics and culture of elite competitions between unions, and the integrity of international matches depends on strict adherence to eligibility criteria set out in the regulation.

'The committee's decision and findings clearly demonstrate issues with the processes adopted by some of the participating unions relating to the eligibility of players as well as the delivery and organisation of the Rugby Europe Championship. World Rugby is committed to addressing these issues and will lead a review of European tournament delivery in the context of Rugby World Cup qualifying in full partnership with Rugby Europe. This will include the organisation's processes for eligibility compliance and match official appointments in order to prevent a repeat of these unfortunate events. In addition, World Rugby has already formally reminded all unions and regional associations of their obligations regarding Regulation 8 and will reiterate at the Annual Meeting of Council this week, while World Rugby will also oversee match official appointments at all stages of future Rugby World Cup qualifiers.' In 2003, Russia were expelled from qualifying for that year's Rugby World Cup for breaching eligibility rules.

LET'S MAKE IT BIGGER

In September 2018, World Rugby chief executive Brett Gosper stated that the board is considering expansion of the Rugby World Cup to allow 24 teams to compete in the showpiece event. The competition started with 16 teams in 1987, expanded to 20 from the fourth edition in 1999 and could now grow even bigger in time for the 2023 finals in France. 'We're always looking from an expansive point of view rather than reducing so it's just a question of when rather than if. We want to make sure the teams are competitive enough to move to a 24-team tournament. We have assumed 20 for 2023 but we could change that between now and 2023. The tendency for us is to try and look to expand. It's about growing the global game – getting interest from fans and commercial interest in new markets. But you've got to make sure you've got the teams. We're definitely in an expansive mindset, is how I'd put it,' said Gosper. An increase in the number of sides could see some mismatches between the teams but Gosper is confident that the teams are given proper support to be competitive at the highest level. 'We'll work hard after that team qualifies to ensure they've got all the technical coaches they need – as we do for each World Cup. We are confident that teams that qualify will be competitive enough, even against the All Blacks,' added Gosper.

THREE DRAGONS MAKE RUGBY WORLD CUP HISTORY

On 17 October 2015, a new Rugby World Cup record was set when Taulupe Faletau, Dan Lydiate and Sam Warburton (captain) formed the Wales back row against South Africa, starting together in the tournament for a seventh time to overtake the mark of six held by England's famed combination of Neil Back, Lawrence Dallaglio and Richard Hill. Wales lost their quarter-final 23-19 to the Springboks at Twickenham Stadium, London.

HABANA'S TRY-SCORING RECORD UNDER THREAT

In December 2018, South African rugby legend Bryan Habana backed New Zealand wing Rieko Ioane to break his Rugby World Cup record for most tries in a single tournament. Habana scored eight tries during the 2007 edition in France and was critical to the Springboks winning the title, while he also won the IRB Player of the Year Award. His eight tries in the tournament, including four against Samoa and two against Argentina, equalled the record set by Jonah Lomu during the 1999 showpiece event. Nevertheless, the 35-year-old believed Ioane with his terrific try-scoring ability of 22 touchdowns from 24 Tests has a better chance of breaking the record. 'To be brutally honest, I think it is written on the wall for Rieko to break the Rugby World Cup record of the most tries in one competition. He has a phenomenal strike rate and has every opportunity to beat the record, and records are there to be broken,' said Habana.

Did You Know That?
Bryan Habana was not selected for South Africa's Olympic Rugby Sevens squad for the 2016 Olympic Games hosted by Rio de Janeiro, Brazil. Rieko Ioane played for New Zealand in the tournament.

CANADA ON THEIR WAY TO JAPAN

Canada claimed the final spot to compete in the 2019 Rugby World Cup in Japan after they managed to defeat Hong Kong 27-10 in the final game of the repechage tournament in Marseille, France on 23 November 2018. This also means Canada will head into Pool B that already has New Zealand, Italy, South Africa and Namibia. The qualification process for the 2019 tournament began in St Vincent and the Grenadines on 5 March 2016 and 188 games were played in a span of 994 days. A total of 71 teams were involved as they amassed 10,355 points with only USA, Uruguay, Russia, Fiji, Tonga, Samoa, Namibia and Canada progressing to the mega event. The qualifying tournament also saw Germany finishing second with nine points while Hong Kong and Kenya occupied the third and fourth spots respectively. Canada captain Phil Mack was delighted with the result and is excited about competing with the top teams in the 2019 Rugby World Cup. 'We're over the moon. Coming into this we knew it would be tough. We knew each game would be a different task. But all the support from home and the way the boys have dug in and got all the work done building up to this in the last year has been awesome,' said Mack.

TOP 10 WORLD RUGBY RANKINGS - 1 JANUARY 2019

Rank	Team	Rating Points
1	New Zealand	92.54
2	Ireland	91.17
3	Wales	87.24
4	England	86.22
5	South Africa	84.58
6	Australia	82.40
7	Scotland	81.84
8	Fiji	77.95
9	France	77.33
10	Argentina	77.05

TATTOO BAN

In September 2018, the 2019 Rugby World Cup organisers issued an instruction to players and fans to cover their tattoos during the showpiece event to avoid causing offence. The players participating in the tournament are asked to wear a vest when they are in gyms or pools. Tournament organising director Alan Gilpin said the teams have responded positively to the request. 'When we raised it with the teams a year or so ago, we were probably expecting a frustrated reaction from them, but there hasn't been at all,' said Gilpin.

Did You Know That?
The South Africa Amateurs are the amateur national rugby union team of South Africa and played in the Rugby Africa Gold Cup until 2007.

RUGBY AFRICA GOLD CUP WINNERS

Namibia progressed to the 2019 Rugby World Cup in Japan after they defeated Kenya 53-28 to win the Rugby Africa Gold Cup in Windhoek on 18 August 2018. As a result, Namibia were slotted into Pool B along with New Zealand, South Africa, Italy and Canada. This will also be the second consecutive time the All Blacks will face Namibia in Rugby World Cups after previously playing them in the 2015 edition in England, where Steve Hansen's men registered a 58-14 victory. Namibia have won the Rugby Africa Gold Cup more times than any other nation – eight (2002, 2004, 2009, 2014, 2015, 2016, 2017 and 2018). The Rugby Africa Gold Cup has been contested annually since 2000 and features South Africa Amateurs (three wins), Kenya (two wins), Morocco (two wins), Namibia, Tunisia, Uganda and Zimbabwe (one win).

GLOBAL APPEAL

Rugby has 793 million followers globally, with more than 338 million considering themselves fans, an increase of 24% since 2013. India, China and the USA alone constitute almost 33% of the population, according to the largest-ever market research into fan trends and perceptions conducted by World Rugby. The study was published when the Rugby World Cup 2019 Trophy Tour visited India in August 2018 where there are 25.7 million rugby fans. The research undertaken by Nielsen Sports paints a picture of a vibrant, growing sport that is increasingly broadening its global appeal. The research, undertaken across 88 markets, reflected participation trends, with significant increases in rugby interest driven by emerging markets since rugby's Olympic Games inclusion in Rio de Janeiro, Brazil in 2016.

> ### *Did You Know That?*
> The average age of a rugby fan is 36. This has fallen by two years since 2013, while the sport is increasingly attracting a younger audience in emerging rugby markets. Some 36% of rugby fans globally are women or girls.

TELEVISON MATCH OFFICIALS

World Rugby confirmed in July 2018 that the sport's governing body is examining the role of Television Match Officials (TMO) in the game and is considering how to give full control back to the on-field referees. The TMO's authority now covers the scoring (or not) of tries, probable infringements in the run-up to a score, and unnoticed foul play. Although the TMO system has its benefits, it also has an impact on the games becoming stop-start affairs in a sport that already struggles with scrum sequences sometimes taking an age. The ever-growing authority of the TMO might also lead one to think that the referees are being undermined. During the 2015 Rugby World Cup, several times there seemed like an incessant wait for a TMO's decision that stunted the natural flow of the game. A total of 132 decisions were sent upstairs which resulted in games lasting longer than their expected time-frame. Regardless of all the criticism, the TMO has become a key part of the game. Their decisions on the validity of tries are seldom questioned and the TMO has led to more foul play being penalised mid-game instead of with post-match citings. However, the slow-motion replays presented to the referees quite often misconstrue high-paced, mistimed tackles and cause frequent resentment among fans. The fact that referees can award a try, but then catch a glimpse of a replay on one of the stadium's screens and call for a review is also flawed.

A SIGN OF THE TIMES

After England beat Australia 20-17 after extra time in the 2003 Rugby World Cup Final at Telstra Stadium, Sydney, Australia on 22 November 2003, an article in *The Times* newspaper described the team's open top bus tour of London as 'A sweet natured version of the Nuremberg Rally'. In 2003, Rupert Murdoch, who was born in Melbourne, Australia, owned *The Times* and many British journalists were not surprised by the article.

Did You Know That?

The Nuremberg Rally was the annual rally of the Nazi Party in Germany and was held from 1923 to 1938. They were large Nazi propaganda events, particularly after Adolf Hitler's rise to power as Fuhrer in 1933.

RUGBY WORLD CUP VERSUS FOOTBALL WORLD CUP

Just as the Rugby World Cup showcases the best rugby stars, the FIFA Football World Cup brings together the world's best footballing nations for a month of high-class action. Of course, the different game codes are the main differences between the tournaments, but there are several other subtle differences that demonstrate the traditions and values of each code. The beauty of the FIFA World Cup is that even the most established footballing nations are at risk of being eliminated from the tournament in the qualification process. Only the host nation gets a bye into the World Cup finals, meaning the highest-ranked nations get exposed to many of the lower-ranked nations who see these countries as significant thorns in their respective qualifying groups. Unlike in football, the Rugby World Cup doesn't give the smaller, developing nations that exposure. By comparison, the FIFA World Cup has 32 entrants and there's even been talk of them extending that number further in future tournaments. On the flip side, there have been murmurings about the Rugby World Cup even reducing its numbers further still to 16 to maintain its competitiveness. Without a doubt, the tiered qualification process has meant that there is an increased disparity between the haves and have-nots in the world of rugby than in football.

Another area in which the Rugby World Cup and FIFA World Cup differ is their advertising campaigns, as the two sports attract many different brands during the tournaments. The FIFA World Cup appeals more to brands that want to stand out as the best and focus firmly on the competition. The likes of Adidas and Nike feature prominently. Meanwhile, the Rugby World Cup and the essence of rugby is about working and standing together. Subsequently, brands and sponsors of the Rugby World Cup tend to be more all-inclusive, age-wise, with Land Rover one of the most prominent sponsors of the last finals. What's great about both tournaments is that they have their own audiences. The success of the FIFA World Cup does not mean the failure of the Rugby World Cup. They can both coexist and hopefully, inspire the next generation of fans and players alike.

Did You Know That?
England is the only nation to have won both the FIFA Football World Cup (1966) and the Rugby World Cup (2003).

WHEN IRISH EYES WERE NOT SMILING

Three rugby unions submitted bids to World Rugby to play host to the 2023 Rugby World Cup: France, Ireland and South Africa. Italy was also in the fray to host the tournament but with government not promising any support, they lost their bid. The World Rugby Board recommended South Africa's bid taking into consideration the vision, tournament scheduling, and organising process, infrastructure, venues for the tournament and financial commitments presented by the three countries. South Africa ranked the highest with 78.97 per cent, with France on 75.88 per cent and Ireland 72.25 per cent. On the day of the voting process, 15 November 2017, Ireland had a shocking day as they were eliminated in the first round with just eight votes as compared to France and South Africa that had 18 and 13 respectively. In the second round, France gained 24 votes as compared to South Africa's 15 to win the rights for hosting the showpiece event in 2023. This will be the third time France will play host to the Rugby World Cup after previously hosting it in 1991 and 2007.

Did You Know That?
Brian O'Driscoll, Ireland's record international cap holder with 133, was Ireland's bid ambassador for the 2023 Rugby World Cup.

FIJI SECURE A PLACE AT THE BIG TABLE

On 8 July 2017, Fiji confirmed their berth in the 2019 Rugby World Cup after securing the top spot in the World Rugby Pacific Nations Cup 2017 tournament when they defeated Tonga 14-10 in Nuku'alofa, Tonga. Leone Nakarawa's try and three Ben Volavola penalties proved enough as Fiji went on to claim 12 points while Tonga and Samoa managed six and five points respectively. Fiji joined Pool D as Oceania 1 Qualifier in the 2019 showpiece event alongside Australia, Wales, Georgia and Uruguay.

TOP OF THE POPS 2007

When South Africa won the sixth Rugby World Cup Final on 20 October 2007, the second time they lifted the Webb Ellis Cup (1995), the No.1 song in the UK pop charts was 'About You Now' by Sugababes. This was the sixth UK No.1 hit for the British girl band. The song spent four weeks in the top slot before being ousted by Leona Lewis with 'Bleeding Love', the second UK No.1 for the winner of the 2006 *X Factor* TV show.

RUGBY ON THE RISE IN THE LAND OF THE RISING SUN

The organisers of the 2019 Rugby World Cup in Japan believe the historic victory achieved by the country in the previous edition of the marquee tournament against South Africa created an unprecedented interest in the tournament. On 19 September 2015, the Brave Blossoms shocked the rugby fraternity after Karne Hesketh scored a last-gasp try to ensure a historic 34-32 victory over South Africa at the Brighton Community Stadium, Brighton, England. The victory is considered as one of the greatest sporting achievements in the history of the nation. In July 2016, the organisers sold a pure gold rugby ball weighing 2.8kg for 38 million yen (around £275,000) in honour of Japan's magnificent 2015 Rugby World Cup triumph and an event was held in Tokyo to celebrate the anniversary of the victory over the Springboks. The chief executive of Japan Rugby 2019, Akira Shimazu, urged the fans all over the country to show their support and make the event a successful one. 'Rugby World Cup 2019 will be a global tournament, but it will also be a tournament for all of Japan, hosted by 12 cities the length and breadth of the nation. We will welcome hundreds of thousands of people from all over the world to Japan, but we are also welcoming all of Japan to be part of this great celebration of rugby and friendship,' said Shimazu.

> ### Did You Know That?
> The most expensive item of sports memorabilia ever sold is a New York Yankees baseball jersey worn by the legendary Babe Ruth in 1920. The jersey sold for $4,415,658 (£3,400,108).

A COSTLY DECISION

Referee Craig Joubert admitted with hindsight he would have reconsidered his decision to award Australia a contentious penalty in the last minute of the game which saw the Wallabies edge Scotland 35-34 in the quarter-finals of the 2015 Rugby World Cup at Twickenham Stadium, London, England. The South African also admitted he ran off the pitch after blowing the final whistle to avoid confrontation with the players. World Rugby later announced Joubert had made the wrong decision and should have awarded a scrum but it was the 38-year-old's decision to run off the pitch which angered many. 'In my head was a desire to avoid any possible unseemly confrontation that would mar what had been a wonderful occasion. I had it in my mind somewhere that there had been an incident between the official and the England coaches (Andy Farrell and Graham Rowntree) in their match against Australia and I just didn't want any of that to happen, not because I don't understand the emotions of the moment for players and coaches, their desire for answers to questions, but just because I did not want that to become another possible incident. That was my thinking, not for myself but for the situation,' said Joubert in an interview with the *Daily Telegraph*. On the late penalty, Joubert added: 'In hindsight, would I have reconsidered that decision? Absolutely.'

> ### *Did You Know That?*
> Joubert retired from refereeing at the end of 2016 to take up a role as a referee talent development coach at World Rugby.

THE TIME WAS RIGHT TO GO

Just three days after coaching South Africa to a Bronze medal victory over Argentina in the 2015 Rugby World Cup finals, the coach of the Springboks, Heyneke Meyer resigned. South Africa defeated the Pumas 24-13 at the Olympic Stadium, London, England. The South African Rugby Union said that Meyer had advised SARU president, Oregan Hoskins, and chief executive Jurie Roux, of his desire to step down. Meyer's contract was due to expire in four weeks' time after he had taken charge of the Springboks in January 2012 on a four-year contract. South Africa's third place finish represented a reasonable recovery after his team suffered a shock 34-32 defeat against opening Pool B opponents Japan. Meyer's Springboks reign delivered 34 victories in 50 Tests, which included one win against the 2011 World champions, New Zealand, and two runners-up finishes in the Rugby Championship. He had previously enjoyed prolonged success with the Pretoria-based Bulls, while he also spent time in charge of Aviva Premiership club Leicester. 'I have always put the Springboks first in my time as coach, and since returning from England I have realised that as much as I believe I still have a lot to offer, the time has come for change. My integrity has always been very important, and I feel I can leave with my head held high. I've always maintained that my only motivation was to serve my country and to do what was best for the Springboks. The Springboks are a special team, and carrying the hopes of a nation is a huge responsibility and great privilege,' Meyer told www.sarugby.net.

Did You Know That?

Meyer made his first international appearance as a coach in 1999 when he coached the Emerging Springboks. He later became forwards coach for the Springboks ahead of the 1999 Rugby World Cup. South Africa finished top of their group, and made it to the semi-finals after beating England 44-21. In the last four, South Africa lost to Australia after extra time, 27-21. He remained with the Springboks between his club commitments, until 2001, when he returned to Pretoria as a full-time coach with the Bulls and Blue Bulls.

THE CHEAP SEATS

The cheapest tickets for the 2015 Rugby World Cup final played at Twickenham Stadium, London cost £150 with the most expensive costing £715. However, tickets for some of the pool stage matches were priced at as little as £7. A total of 1 million of the 2.3 million tickets available went on sale at £100 or less, with 500,000 selling at £50 or less. Adult ticket prices started at £15 for pool matches and child tickets were made available from £7 at 41 of the 48 matches.

Did You Know That?

The cost of viewing the men's 100m final at the 2012 Olympic Games in London ranged from £50 to £725 while tickets to see the women's 100m final ranged from £50 to £450. Tickets for the opening ceremony cost between £20.12 and £2,012.

CARTER'S TREBLE OF GONGS

New Zealand fly-half Dan Carter followed up his man of the match performance in the 2015 Rugby World Cup Final by being crowned World Rugby Player of the Year for 2015. Carter, who kicked 19 points including a sublime drop goal in the 34-17 victory over Australia at Twickenham Stadium, London was recognised with the game's most prestigious individual award for a third time (2005 and 2012), a mark also held by All Blacks captain Richie McCaw (winner in 2006, 2009 and 2010). The 33-year-old beat New Zealand teammate Julian Savea, Australia flanker Michael Hooper and the Wallabies' No 8 David Pocock, Wales second-row Alun Wyn Jones and Scotland scrum-half Greig Laidlaw to the accolade. New Zealand were inevitably named Team of the Year after becoming the first nation to defend the Webb Ellis Cup, triumphing for an unprecedented third time.

Michael Cheika was recognised as Coach of the Year after inheriting an Australia squad that was beset by disciplinary problems 12 months previously before turning them into World Cup runners-up. New Zealand wing Nehe Milner-Skudder was named Breakthrough Player of the Year. All of the winners were selected by an independent panel of judges, chaired by Australia's 1999 World Cup-winning captain John Eales and made up of former internationals, media and the current tournament's participating teams. Carter and McCaw jointly hold the record for the most World Rugby Player of the Year awards.

> ### Did You Know That?
> On 16 November 2013, Carter became only the fifth All Black to win 100 Test caps when New Zealand defeated England 30-22 at Twickenham Stadium in a tour match.

CHASING GREAT

In 2016, a sports documentary was released entitled *Chasing Great*. It follows New Zealand captain, Richie McCaw, through his final season (2015) as he attempts to become the first player to skipper a country to back-to-back Rugby World Cup Final victories. But it's not just a story about his rugby exploits, which were already well documented, as the viewer is taken inside Richie's world and learns about his life. The directors, Justin Pemberton and Michelle Walshe, were given unprecedented access to Richie and his remarkable family video archive. *Chasing Great* is the story of how a shy farm boy went on to be a sporting legend and a hero to a nation. What emerges is a very personal insight into high level international sport and a psychological profile of the mind of a champion.

> ### Did You Know That?
> Fabio Ongaro played for the Italian youth teams as a flanker.

TOP OF THE POPS 2011

When New Zealand won the sixth Rugby World Cup Final on 23 October 2011, the second time they lifted the Webb Ellis Cup (1987), the No.1 song in the UK pop charts was 'We Found Love' by Rihanna featuring Calvin Harris. It was Rihanna's sixth UK No.1 hit and the fourth for Harris, a Scottish artist and music producer. It spent three weeks in the top slot before being ousted by Professor Greene featuring Emeli Sande with 'Read All About It'.

THE 2011 RUGBY WORLD CUP FINALS

The 2011 Rugby World Cup was the seventh edition of the world famous tournament and for the second time, New Zealand was chosen as the host nation. The International Rugby Board selected New Zealand ahead of Japan and South Africa. Once again the tournament featured 20 nations with only one change from the 2007 tournament with Russia taking Portugal's place. It was the biggest sporting event ever held in New Zealand.

Pool A was dominated by the host nation who won all four of their matches including a 37-17 victory over the runners-up, France. England topped Pool B with four wins and were joined in the quarter-finals by Argentina, who squeezed Scotland into third place. Pool C saw Ireland finish in top spot with a 100% record including a 15-6 victory over Australia who finished runners-up. The remaining two quarter-final spots went to Pool D winners South Africa who won all of their games, and Wales.

The quarter-final games were played in Auckland (Eden Park) and Wellington. The first two games brought Six Nations rivals together with Wales beating Ireland 22-10 at Regional Stadium, Wellington and France defeating England 19-12 at Eden Park, Auckland. Australia won their encounter with Tri-Nations rivals South Africa, a narrow 11-9 victory at Regional Stadium, and New Zealand saw off Argentina 33-10 at Eden Park to claim the final semi-final berth. Eden Park played host to both semi-finals, France squeezing Wales out with a 9-8 win and the hosts defeating their southern hemisphere rivals, Australia, 20-6. The bronze final was a close game which saw Australia beat Wales 21-20 at Eden Park.

Final – 23 October 2011
Eden Park, Auckland, New Zealand
New Zealand 8–7 France

The All Blacks went into the 2011 Rugby World Cup Final versus France as red hot favourites following impressive performances during the tournament which saw them win five games in a row including a 37-17 Pool A match victory over France. The men in black looked set to break their 24-year Rugby World Cup bogey, despite having arguably less depth than in previous tournaments and losing one of their best players Daniel Carter to injury. They hadn't won the Webb Ellis Cup since 1987, despite being the best team in the world for long periods of time. In 1999 and 2007 *Les Bleus* had spoiled the All Blacks' dreams of glory with dramatic come-from-behind victories whilst this match was a re-enactment of the inaugural Rugby World Cup final in 1987. Both sides were playing in their third Rugby World Cup Final (France 1987 and 1999, New Zealand 1987 and 1995). Such was the dominance of the host nation in this tournament that if they beat France in the final, it would be France's third loss of the tournament (they lost 19-14 to Tonga in Pool A) and the All Blacks' sixth win in a row. Simply getting into the final was a great achievement for France, who had only shown glimpses of form up until then. It was difficult to know if this was something to fear or not, given that the All Blacks had been stung twice by France in previous tournaments. If France could put together 80 minutes of what they did in about 40 minutes against England (won 19-12 in the quarter-finals) and for the opening 15 minutes in their pool match against New Zealand, then an upset could be on the cards. The unpredictable nature of France made picking the outcome of the final difficult, although the bookmakers made them rank outsiders priced at 7-1 to win the final. The All Blacks had played France 50 times since 1906, with 37 wins to the All Blacks, 12 to France and one draw. The teams had played five times at the Rugby World Cup, with New Zealand having a 3-2 advantage. Eden Park, Auckland was a fortress for the All Blacks, with them not having lost on their largest ground since 1994 when France scored 'the try from the end of the world'.

The French advanced on the pre-match haka and seldom took a backward step thereafter in the final. However, playing in front of a delirious crowd, New Zealand ended 24 years of hurt as they narrowly edged out France 8-7. France started the game very confidently, and they certainly seemed to settle down faster than the host nation. *Les Bleus* showed a willingness to move the ball wide and really take the game to the All Blacks. But, as in the pool stages, for all of France's possession and territory they were unable to gather any points and they were made to pay. After Piri Weepu won a penalty at the breakdown, the All Blacks sent the kick deep into the French 22. From the line-out Jerome Kaino took the ball and with the softest of touches flicked it down to Tony Woodcock, who had the biggest of holes to run through and touch down. The most unlikely of scorers (66/1 with most bookmakers) had opened the scoring for the favourites. Weepu missed the conversion, but a 5-0 lead had been established.

France then lost their fly-half Morgan Parra who took a huge blow to the head from Richie McCaw's knee and was replaced by Francois Trinh-Duc. Weepu had the chance to extend the lead after 25 minutes but sliced his kick well wide. New Zealand were starting to get into their stride and probing kicks from Israel Dagg and Weepu kept the pressure on the French line-out. Kieran Read was becoming more and more prominent, carrying the ball with great power and giving his side real impetus going forward. The curse of the New Zealand number ten jersey struck again after 30 minutes, when Aaron Cruden suffered what looked like a very nasty knee injury and he was replaced by Bath-bound Stephen Donald. Towards the end of the half Trinh-Duc made a brilliant break from inside his own half, and only a wonderful effort from Weepu stopped the fly-half, who showed great pace to break the All Blacks' line. France were unrecognisable from the team that had struggled in their pool games and forced the All Blacks to dig deeper than they had had to in earlier games. The collisions were bone-shaking as both fly-halves found out.

At the start of the second half Dimitri Yachvili had a chance to get France on the board, but like Weepu he dragged his first kick wide of the posts. They were again made to pay when Donald stepped up to the tee and made it 8-0, with a simple penalty attempt. But France didn't have to wait long to register their first points of the game as great work by Trinh-Duc saw him once again break the line. He got a brilliant offload to Aurélien Rougerie who was held up just a couple of metres from the line. The French then recycled the ball and their inspirational captain, Thierry Dusautoir, crashed through the line to score under the posts. Yachvili added the simple conversion to make the score 8-7.

France grew in confidence with each minute that passed. Thierry Dusautoir, Julien Bonnaire and Imanol Harinordoquy were superb for *Les Bleus*, really putting their bodies on the line. Dusautoir was again showing the form of 2007, making 20 tackles in the opening 60 minutes. Harinordoquy was ruling the line-out with ease, calling the shots and giving France a real advantage in that area. They had chances to take the lead but Trinh-Duc missed a long-range penalty attempt with 15 minutes to go. After the visitors had enjoyed all the second-half possession and territory, but let themselves down with errors at crucial times, New Zealand just saw out the final few minutes and ended all those years of waiting. It wasn't the prettiest of games but they ground out the win. As one journalist put it: 'The All Black aristocrats survived the French Revolution.' Substitute Stephen Donald had been called back from holiday and was visibly not at peak fitness. However, he became an unlikely hero by kicking a wobbly penalty that ultimately secured victory. The real hero of the hour was the All Blacks' captain, Richie McCaw, who played the knockout matches with a broken bone in his foot.

After lifting the Webb Ellis Cup, the All Blacks' captain, Richie McCaw, was asked how he felt and said: 'I think at some stage some team was going to do it and this group of 30 had the opportunity. You just have to keep getting up and believing in the mate beside you and trust in him and make sure you do your job. Everyone around New Zealand has given this team so much over the past six weeks and now we've repaid them. There's going to be a lot of stories told as we get older but no one here can take it away from this group. They're tough men and I think the whole country should be very proud of every single one of them.'

Thierry Dusautoir, the captain of France, who was named man of the match, said: 'We read a lot of stuff this week but I thought we showed we know how to play rugby. We are really disappointed. I am really proud of my boys and what they did in the World Cup. We did our utmost, and fell short by a point.'

'People have always said and thought that the All Blacks were the greatest team of all time. But tonight I think it's France that was great, and even immense. It's tough to take, we needed a little bit more,' said the departing French head coach, Marc Lievremont. Meanwhile, New Zealand head coach, Graham Henry, said: 'Marvellous. The people have been outstanding in support of the team and the Rugby World Cup. I'm so proud to be a New Zealander standing here.'

The final was Henry's last as head coach of the All Blacks and a fitting end to his eight-year reign in charge which included defeat by France in the quarter-final stages of the 2007 Rugby World Cup finals.

New Zealand: Israel Dagg; Cory Jane, Conrad Smith, Ma'a Nonu, Richard Kahui; Aaron Cruden, Piri Weepu; Tony Woodcock, Keven Mealamu, Owen Franks, Sam Whitelock, Brad Thorn, Jerome Kaino, Richie McCaw (capt), Kieran Read.

Replacements: Stephen Donald, Ali Williams, Andrew Hore, Andy Ellis, Sonny Bill Williams, Ben Franks, Adam Thomson.

France: Maxime Médard; Vincent Clerc, Aurélien Rougerie Maxime Mermoz, Alexis Palisson; Morgan Parra, Dimitri Yachvili; Jean-Baptiste Poux, William Servat, Nicolas Mas, Pascal Papé, Lionel Nallet, Thierry Dusautoir (capt), Julien Bonnaire, Imanol Harinordoquy.

Replacements: François Trinh-Duc, Damien Traille, Dimitri Szarzewski, Fabien Barcella, Julien Pierre, Jean-Marc Doussain, Fulgence Ouedraogo.

New Zealand	France
Try Woodcock	Try Dusautoir
Pen Donald	Con Trinh-Duc

Referee: Craig Joubert (South Africa)
Attendance: 60,000

ROLLING IN THE MONEY

The Rugby Football Union (RFU) made a profit of £15 million from hosting the 2015 Rugby World Cup tournament in England. The RFU managed to exceed the revenue target of £250 million which it knew would cover the £80 million it had to pay to World Rugby for hosting the tournament, leaving an extra £15 million for the RFU. It was a tournament of record attendances and sell-out matches. Wembley Stadium, London twice broke the record for the biggest ever Rugby World Cup attendance. The match venues were packed for every match whilst the 15 fanzones were also a huge success with more than 1 million people passing through them. A total of 2.47 million tickets were sold for England 2015, achieving 98% of the capacity of its venues overall.

> ### Did You Know That?
> The 2014 FIFA Football World Cup helped create a record revenue of $2 billion (£1.54 billion) for FIFA, with $337 million (£260 million) in profits coming from the four-year cycle leading up to the finals in Brazil.

TRUTH OR FICTION

History tells us that in 1823, William Webb Ellis, a pupil at Rugby School with a fine disregard for the rules of football, took the ball in his arms and ran with it, originating the game of rugby football. However, others think he was merely playing caid (which is now used by people in some parts of Ireland to refer to modern Gaelic football). William's father, James, served as a cornet in the 7th and 3rd Dragoon Guards and it is claimed that during his early life William's father was stationed in Ireland where William played caid with his friends. Although the story of William inventing rugby has become firmly entrenched in the sport's folklore, most rugby historians discount it as an origin myth.

> ### Did You Know That?
> Shane Horgan had a background in Gaelic football, a Meath minor (Under-18 level) who played for Bellewstown GAA Club before becoming an Irish rugby international, winning 65 Test caps between 2000–09, scoring 105 points.

A LOAD OF BALLS

It is claimed that 900 rugby balls were used during the matches at the 2003 Rugby World Cup finals in Australia in 11 stadiums across ten cities and players and officials drank 132,000 litres of sports drinks. An estimated 1.87 million people watched the 48 games across the 44 days and it is claimed that the home fans purchased 91% of the available match tickets. Tourism Australia estimated that some 44,000 tourists flocked down under on 400 jumbo jets to attend the tournament.

> ### *Did You Know That?*
> Bars in Adelaide reported nightly takings 30 times higher than normal whilst Heineken exported 30,000 kegs of beer from the Netherlands.

RUGBY'S GROUP OF DEATH

Fiji had a difficult draw in the 2015 Rugby World Cup finals, being placed in Pool A which contained three tier one teams with world rankings of fourth (England), fifth (Australia) and sixth (Wales), making it the most challenging pool in Rugby World Cup history. The Fijians were ranked at No.12 in the world whilst the fifth team in Pool A was Uruguay who had a world ranking of 20th place, making it a tally of 47 points for world rankings placings. Uruguay's performance at the 2015 Rugby World Cup finals was most noteworthy. After conceding an average of 92 points at the 2003 Rugby World Cup finals, their last tournament before 2015, they managed to almost halve their margin of defeat (54 points) despite the fact that 90% of their 31-man squad were amateurs and having to play in the most demanding pool ever. Romania's pool (D) contained three tier one teams for the third consecutive time: Ireland: France and Italy.

> ### *Did You Know That?*
> Pool B also comprised teams with a collective world rankings tally of 47 points: South Africa - 2nd, Scotland - 8th, Samoa - 10th, Japan - 11th and USA - 16th.

THE TWO GREATEST EVER ALL BLACKS HANG UP THEIR BOOTS

Dan Carter admitted his man of the match performance that helped the All Blacks to a historic third Rugby World Cup triumph over Australia in the 2015 World Cup Final was the perfect way to bow out of a glittering international career. Carter scored 19 points including a stunning drop goal as the All Blacks kept Australia at arm's length throughout their 34-17 final victory, at Twickenham Stadium, London. It was Carter's 112th cap for his native New Zealand and the success was even sweeter having missed their last World Cup triumph – four years earlier in France – through injury. After the game he told ITV:

'This win is right up there with everything I've done in my career – it is the ultimate achievement. It has been an amazing career and to finish like this is hard to believe. This victory means a lot – it was a dark place four years ago and I've had to work extremely hard to be here today. I'm proud of the boys and what they have achieved. Becoming the first team to retain the trophy shows how special this side is.'

New Zealand captain Richie McCaw also hung up his boots after a world-record 148 caps and the head coach of the All Blacks, Steve Hansen, said his skipper and Carter were the greatest All Blacks of all time. Hansen said: 'Richie is the best All Black we have ever had and Dan is a close second. The only thing that separates them is Richie has played 148 matches at flanker, which is unheard of – you put your body on the line every time you go out there. The challenge for the other guys now is to try and become as great as him and Dan.'

McCaw himself said becoming the first nation to retain the World Cup felt 'special' – and different to 2011 when the overwhelming emotion the team felt upon lifting the cup was relief. He said: 'It is a different feel to 2011 when the final was tighter, and it was a massive relief four years ago. This time it was an opportunity that we really wanted to take and rather than a huge sense of relief it was a sense of satisfaction at having got the job done. I feel pretty warm inside and proud and I'm going to spend the next couple of days enjoying the company of these men. We said four years ago after the last one that we'd get on the road again and our goal was to play here at Twickenham in the World Cup Final. I'm so proud of the way the guys have done it today.

'We lost a bit of momentum in the second half but kept our composure and came home strong, which has been a hallmark of this team for the last four years.' Hansen also paid tribute to Australia for putting up a strong fight in the second half. He added: 'On a night like this it's extremely tough for the loser but I thought Australia were magnificent in the way they approached the game, they never laid down. At 21-3, you could be fooled into thinking the game was over but at 21-17 they could easily have come back. Whilst we are very proud of what we have achieved as a group we would like to say well done to Australia as well.'

Did You Know That?

In the 2012 *Mega Kiwi Sex Survey*, Richie McCaw was voted as the most desirable man by New Zealand women, ahead of fellow All Blacks Dan Carter and Sonny Bill Williams.

RUGBY WORLD CUP QUOTES

'We had to dig deeper than ever before and it's hard to get it to sink in, but I am so proud of every single one of them. We couldn't have been under more pressure at times but we stuck to our guns and got there in the end.'

Richie McCaw after captaining New Zealand to Rugby World Cup glory in 2011

Did You Know That?

In November 2006, the New Zealand government announced that it had decided against building a new stadium on Auckland's waterfront to host the 2011 Rugby World Cup Final and opted instead to upgrade Eden Park. The new waterfront stadium was to cost NZ$497 million (£262,417,319) compared to the upgrade of Eden Park which would cost NZ$385 million (£203,280,167).

SOUTH AFRICA'S RUGBY WORLD CUP WINNING LIONS

South Africa's 1995 Rugby World Cup squad was dominated by players from Transvaal (later changed its name to the Gauteng Lions and now known as the Golden Lions) including their inspirational captain, Francois Pienaar. No fewer than 12 of the 26-man squad were from the Johannesburg-based club whilst at the time of the tournament, James Small (wing, 69 caps between 1988 and 1999, 42 tries and 192 points) and Adriaan Richter (loose forward, 27 caps between 1988 and 1991, six tries and 24 points) were not Transvaal players but both did play for them before and after the finals.

Balie Swart, prop, 108 caps between 1992 and 1999, six tries and 30 points

Chris Rossouw, hooker, 48 caps between 1994 and 1997, 15 tries and 75 points

James Dalton, hooker, 76 caps between 1992 and 2000, 20 tries and 100 points

Kobus Wiese, lock, 128 caps between 1988 and 1998, 21 tries and 102 points

Hannes Strydom, lock, 116 caps between 1993 and 2000, eight tries and 40 points

Hennie le Roux, centre, 153 caps between 1992 and 2000, 63 tries and 561 points

Japie Mulder, centre, 113 caps between 1991 and 2001, 32 tries and 159 points

Christiaan Scholtz, centre, 54 caps between 1994 and 1997, 14 tries and 73 points

Pieter Hendriks, wing, 138 caps between 1990 and 2000, 89 tries and 422 points

Gavin Johnson, full-back, 77 caps between 1993 and 1997, 30 tries and 821 points

Rudolf Straeuli, loose forward, 61 caps between 1993 and 1996, 14 tries and 70 points

Johan Roux, scrum-half, 111 caps between 1993 and 1998, 40 tries and 412 points

NB – caps relate to games played for the club, not the national side.

James Dalton and Pieter Hendriks were banned from the 1995 Rugby World Cup finals for fighting in the Springboks' Pool A match against Canada, which they won 20-0, and were replaced by Naka Drotske and Chester Williams respectively. Williams joined the Golden Lions in 1999 and in his two seasons with the club (1999–2000) he won 23 caps, scoring 11 tries and 55 points.

Did You Know That?

Brazil has never qualified for a Rugby World Cup finals but did compete in the inaugural Rugby Sevens competition at the Summer Olympic Games held in Rio de Janeiro, Brazil. Brazil currently rank third in South America (behind Argentina and Uruguay) and fifth in the Americas region.

MIRRORING STADE DE FRANCE

In 1998, Stade de France, Saint Denis, Paris, France played host to the 1998 FIFA Football World Cup Final which saw the host nation defeat the tournament favourites, Brazil, 3-0. Nine years later Stade de France hosted the 2007 Rugby World Cup Final, when South Africa defeated England 15-6. On 30 June 2002, the International Stadium, Yokohama, Japan, played host to the 2002 FIFA Football World Cup Final which Brazil won 2-0 against Germany. The 2019 Rugby World Cup Final will be played at Yokohama Stadium which will result in this stadium becoming only the second ever to host a football and a rugby World Cup Final. England and South Africa have also hosted both tournaments. England hosted the 1966 FIFA Football World Cup Final at Wembley Stadium, London and the 1991 Rugby World Cup Final at Twickenham Stadium, London. South Africa hosted the 1995 Rugby World Cup Final at Ellis Park, Johannesburg and the 2010 FIFA Football World Cup Final which was played at Soccer City, Johannesburg.

THE INCREDIBLE BULKS

According to the 2015 Rugby World Cup Statistical Report published by World Rugby the average weight of a forward at the 2015 Rugby World Cup finals was 112kg (17st 9lbs), the average weight of a back was 95kg (14st 13lbs) and the average weight of a half-back was 86kg (13st 8lbs). A total of 11 of the 20 nations competing at the tournament exceeded or equalled the average weight for a squad member which was 103kg (16st 3lbs): 1. Wales – 106kg (16st 9lbs), 2=. France – 105kg (16st 7lbs), 2=. New Zealand – 105kg (16st 7lbs), 2=. Samoa – 105kg (16st 7lbs), 2=. South Africa – 105kg (16st 7lbs), 2=. Tonga – 105kg (16st 7lbs), 7=. Ireland 104kg (16st 5lbs), 7=. Scotland 104kg (16st 5lbs), 9=. England 103kg (16st,3lbs), 9=. Italy 103kg (16st 3lbs) and 9=. USA 103kg (16st 3lbs). But the tag of 'The Biggest Player at the 2015 Rugby World Cup' went to a player who is actually nicknamed 'Weeny', the France prop forward, Uini Atonio who weighed a formidable 155kg (24st 5lbs) and stands 197cm tall. Atonio was closely followed on the scales by Will Skelton (Australia, 140kg – 22st) and Census Johnston (Samoa, 138kg – 21st 10lbs). However, the record for the heaviest ever international rugby union player goes to Fiji's Bill Cavubati, not surprisingly nicknamed 'Big Bill', who weighed a mammoth 165kg (25st 13lbs – 6ft 1in). The 620 players at the 2015 Rugby World Cup finals averaged over 6ft in height.

THE FOREIGN INFLUENCE

A total of 620 players made up the 20 squads at the 2015 Rugby World Cup finals in England. No fewer than 223 (36%) of them played their club rugby outside their own country. Only four nations had a full squad, 31 players, who played their rugby at home: England, France, Ireland and New Zealand. Three nations were made up of less than three home based players: Tonga 1 (3%), Fiji 2 (6%) and Samoa 3 (10%). The remainder had the following number of overseas players: Australia

2, Japan 4, Uruguay 4, Scotland 8, Romania 9, Wales 9, Argentina 11, South Africa 11, Canada 14, Italy 15, USA 15, Georgia 18 and Namibia 18.

Did You Know That?

The first overseas-based player to play in the Rugby World Cup finals was Rodolfo Ambrosio. On 22 May 1987, he made his debut for Italy against New Zealand in the opening game of the inaugural Rugby World Cup finals, 1987. Italy lost the game 70-6. Ambrosio was born on 27 December 1961 in Córdoba, Argentina and when he was called into the Italy squad for the 1987 tournament he was playing for Tala Rugby Club in his home city. He was the first Italia-Argentinian to represent Italy.

NAMIBIA'S MOST HISTORIC TRY

On 24 September 2015, New Zealand defeated Namibia 58-14 at the Olympic Stadium, London, England in Pool C of the 2015 Rugby World Cup finals. In the 51st minute of the game, Johan Deysel scored a try for Namibia, his country's first ever try at a Rugby World Cup finals tournament. The try, which saw three All Blacks all trying in vain to pull Deysel down, is considered the most historic try in the history of rugby union in Namibia. Not surprisingly, Deysel was swamped by his teammates whilst his extremely proud father, Johan Snr, looked down from the stands on his son. 'Dad's here and he'll be very proud. He might have scored some tries but he never played against the All Blacks,' said Johan Jnr after the game.

Did You Know That?

Johan Snr played in 16 Tests for Namibia from 1990–92 and scored 20 points.

TIER 1 VERSUS TIER 2 IMBALANCES

High-scoring wins by Tier 1 sides over Tier 2 sides have been a regular feature of all eight Rugby World Cup finals tournaments to date. The following list shows the top ten victories by highest number of points scored.

No.	RWC	Tier 1 Nation	Tier 2 Nation	Score
1.	1995	New Zealand	Japan	145-17
2.	2003	Australia	Namibia	142-0
3.	2003	England	Uruguay	111-13
4.	2007	New Zealand	Portugal	108-13
5.	1999	New Zealand	Italy	101-3
6.	1999	England	Tonga	101-10

7.	2007	Australia	Japan	91-3
8.	2003	New Zealand	Tonga	91-7
9.	2003	Australia	Romania	90-8
10.	1995	Scotland	Ivory Coast	89-0

Did You Know That?

The biggest ever winning margin in a rugby union Test match is Argentina's 152-0 demolition of Paraguay in the South American Championship played at Mendoza Rugby Club, Mendoza, Argentina on 1 May 2002. The score was 69-0 at half-time: Tries were scored by Bouza 2, Gaitan, Legora, Nannini, Nunez Piossek 4, Phelan, Senillosa 3, Soler 4, Sporleder 4 and Stortoni 3. Jose Cilley converted 16 of the 24 tries. This beat the previous record winning margin by a single point; Hong Kong defeated Singapore 164-13 in a 1995 Rugby World Cup qualifier/Asian Championship (Asia Pool 2) in Kuala Lumpur, Malaysia on 27 October 1994. The score was 83-3 at the interval whilst winger, Ashley Billington, scored ten tries in the game. The cumulative total of 177 points remains the highest scored in a Test match. Other notable scores are: England 143 Romania 0 (2002, Charlie Hodgson scored 44 points), Japan 134 Chinese Taipei 6 (1998), New Zealand 145 Japan 17 (1995), Zimbabwe 130 Botswana 10 (1996), Luxembourg 3 Sweden 116 (2001), Brazil 3 Argentina 114 (1993), England 110 Holland 0 (1998) and Hong Kong 108 Sri Lanka 0 (1980).

GOING DUTCH

The Netherlands have never played at a Rugby World Cup finals. The Dutch Rugby Federation was founded on 7 September 1920 but folded in 1923 due to a lack of clubs. However, the Netherlands played their first international on 1 July 1930, a 6-0 loss to Belgium in The Hague. On 1 October 1932, the Dutch Rugby Union (Nederlandse Rugby Bond) was formed just four months after their second international game, a 6-6 draw versus Belgium on 1 July 1932 in Amsterdam, Netherlands. In 1988, the Dutch Rugby Union was affiliated to the International Rugby Board. They are nicknamed 'Oranje'.

TOP OF THE POPS 2015

When New Zealand won the seventh Rugby World Cup Final on 31 October 2015, and became the first nation to lift the Webb Ellis Cup three times (1987 and 2011), the No.1 song in the UK pop charts was 'Turn The Music Louder (Rumble)' by KDA featuring Tinie Tempah and Katy B. It was KDA's (Kris Di Angelis) only UK No.1 hit. It spent one week in the top slot before being ousted by Adele with 'Hello'.

THE DOUBLE ALL BLACK

Jeffrey 'Goldie' William Wilson MNZM won 60 Test caps (71 games in total) for New Zealand from 1993–2002 and scored 234 points (44 tries, one conversion, three penalty goals, and one drop goal). He represented the All Blacks at the 1995 and 1999 Rugby World Cup finals at full-back and as a winger. Wilson played provincial rugby for Otago (1993–2002) and Southland (1992) and Super Rugby for the Highlanders (1996–2002). Wilson made his Test debut for New Zealand on 20 November 1993 (the day before he celebrated his 20th birthday) against Scotland at Murrayfield, Edinburgh, Scotland, scoring three tries and one conversion in the All Blacks' 51-15 victory. On 25 August 2001, he played his last game for his country, a 26-15 win over South Africa at Eden Park, Auckland, New Zealand in the Tri-Nations. He hung up his rugby boots in 2002 aged just 28 and resurrected his cricket career. Wilson played provincial cricket as an all-rounder for Otago, a hard-hitting right-handed batsman and a right-arm fast-medium pace bowler. He played six one-day internationals (scored 103 runs and took four wickets) and one Twenty20 international (scored 18 runs) for New Zealand's cricket team, nicknamed 'The Black Caps'. Amazingly, his first and last appearances for the Black Caps were 12 years apart. During the 1992/93 season, he played in four ODIs in a series versus Australia and played his last game on 1 March 2005 in an ODI versus Australia in Wellington, New Zealand. The tourists won the game by seven wickets and Wilson scored one run and took one wicket in the game. The 12-year gap between his appearances in the 1992/93 season and his return to international cricket on 17 February 2005 (a T20 versus Australia in Auckland) is a world record for the longest gap between two consecutive ODIs. Not surprisingly he also holds the record for the most consecutive ODI matches missed for a team by a player with 271 ODIs. Wilson retired from cricket at the end of the 2004/05 season due to persistent injury.

A TREBLE FOR THE ALL BLACKS

Although international rugby has been played for well over a century, the Rugby World Cup is a relatively recent phenomenon. In a country where rugby became a surrogate for religion, New Zealand hosting (co-hosts with Australia) and then winning the first Rugby World Cup was a big deal. For much of the 20th century New Zealand's All Blacks vied with South Africa's Springboks for the unofficial title of the best team in international rugby. Without a Rugby World Cup to bring the top teams together in a single competition, such claims were difficult to prove. Just how the inaugural Rugby World Cup came about is less well known but unquestionably the struggle between the amateur ideal and creeping professionalism, tensions between the British rugby unions and their southern hemisphere counterparts, and international protests over sporting contacts with South Africa all played their part. When the All Blacks won the first Rugby World Cup (the final was held at Eden Park, Auckland on 20 June 1987, with the home team beating France 29-9), the Springboks were absent because of the country's apartheid policy.

The All Blacks' failure to repeat this success at subsequent World Cup tournaments weighed increasingly heavily on several generations of New Zealand fans. Photographs of the winning All Blacks captain, David Kirk, holding the Webb Ellis Cup aloft in 1987 became one of the nation's most famous sporting images. The 2011 tournament was the first since 1987 to be hosted by New Zealand (this time without Australia as co-hosts). The same four teams made the semi-finals – New Zealand, Australia, Wales and France – and once again New Zealand and France squared off in the final at Eden Park. After a much closer game than most people expected, the All Blacks prevailed 8-7 in the lowest-scoring final in the tournament's history. In 2015, the All Blacks threw off the burden of 1987 entirely when they became both the first team to win back-to-back Rugby World Cups and the first to taste victory three times. Richie McCaw is the only captain to have triumphantly hoisted the Webb Ellis Cup twice. This final, at London's Twickenham Stadium, was the highest-scoring so far, with New Zealand beating Australia 34-17.

A LATE START

Finau Maka made his international debut for Tonga at the 2007 Rugby World Cup finals aged 30. He won the man of the match award in Tonga's opening Pool A game versus the USA and scored a try in the second minute of the game in his country's 25-15 victory at Stade de la Mosson, Montpellier, France. He had hoped to follow in his brother Isitolo's footsteps and play for New Zealand (four caps in 1998) before deciding to try and get a place in the France squad for the 2007 tournament. He qualified to play for France on residency grounds having played club rugby for Toulouse since 2001. However, when the head coach of France, Bernard Laporte, did not select him for his squad he turned his attention to playing for the country where he was born. Four years later he captained Tonga at the 2011 Rugby World Cup finals and led his country to the biggest upset in Rugby World Cup history at the time, a 19-14 Pool A victory over France at the Regional Stadium, Wellington, New Zealand (Japan surpassed that, defeating South Africa 34-32 at the 2015 Rugby World Cup finals hosted by England). His brother was the head coach of Tonga during the tournament. Maka's trademark afro hairstyle made him a distinctive figure on and off the field. He won eight caps for Tonga (2007–11) and scored five points, plus one cap for the Pacific Islanders in 2008.

PERCY SETS NEW SPRINGBOKS' CAPS RECORD

When South Africa beat England 36-0 in their Pool A match at the 2007 Rugby World Cup finals at Stade de France, Saint-Denis, Paris, France, Percy Montgomery equalled Joost van der Westhuizen's record for most caps by a Springbok with 89. Montgomery scored three conversions and four penalties in the win over the reigning world champions. This was the first time England had failed to score in a Rugby World Cup finals game and the first time a Rugby World Cup winning nation had failed to score in a game at the tournament. Montgomery then surpassed van der Westhuizen's caps tally in South Africa's next game, a 30-25 victory over Tonga at Stade Bollaert-Delelis, Lens (he scored one conversion and one penalty).

> ### Did You Know That?
> It was only the fifth time a side had failed to score in a Rugby World Cup match, after Canada, Spain, Namibia and Romania. Scotland became the sixth nation to fail to score at the 2007 tournament when New Zealand beat them 40-0 in a Pool C encounter.

THE PUKPUKS
Papua New Guinea have never qualified for a Rugby World Cup finals. They participated in the Oceania World Cup qualifying tournaments for the 2007 and 2011 Rugby World Cup finals but failed to qualify. They are nicknamed 'The Pukpuks'.

> ### Did You Know That?
> A pukpuk is a form of crocodile.

WORLD RECORD TRY SCORER
Daisuke Ohata played for Japan in the 1999 (scored one try) and 2003 Rugby World Cup finals (scored one try). He made his international debut on 9 November 1996, scoring three tries in Japan's 41-25 victory against Korea at the Municipal Stadium, Taipei in the Asian Championship. On 14 May 2006, he scored another hat-trick of tries when Japan beat Georgia 32-7 at Hanazono Field, Higashiōsaka, Osaka, Japan to claim Australian David Campese's world record for most Test tries which had stood at 64. Ohata's three tries put him on 65 and he achieved this total in 55 Tests in comparison to Campese's 101 Tests. 'I doubt (Campese) would have expected a Japanese player to break his record. There was a weird kind of pressure on me to do it, so I'm happy to get it done,' said the 30-year-old Ohata when asked about making rugby union history. However, some rugby journalists failed to recognise Ohata's achievement as only 25% of his tries were scored against major rugby union playing nations. He brought the curtain down on his international career three Tests later, a 54-0 win

over the same nation he made his debut against and once again, he scored three tries versus Korea. The game, an Asia 3 Rugby World Cup qualifier (2007), was played at Football Club, Hong Kong. He played a total of 59 Tests for Japan and scored 69 tries (1996–2006). He was forced into retirement in January 2011 following a serious knee injury and in November 2016, he was inducted into the World Rugby Hall of Fame.

Did You Know That?

The Japan Rugby Football Union (JRFU) presented Ohata with a gold-striped shirt after the 32-7 win over Georgia to commemorate his achievement.

NO CHANCE

The opening game of the inaugural Rugby World Cup finals in 1987 brought together two nations who had never previously met in a Test match before. On 22 May 1987, New Zealand, co-hosts of the tournament with Australia, beat Italy 70-6 in Pool 3 at Eden Park, Auckland, New Zealand. The result is New Zealand's biggest winning margin over the *Azzurri* on home soil (they won 70-6 in Bologna, Italy on 28 October 1995). Since then they have met on a further 13 occasions, including during the 1999, 2003, 2007 and 2011 Rugby World Cup finals, with the All Blacks leading their head-to-head encounters 14-0 (820 points to 131 points). New Zealand won three games on home soil, seven in Italy and four at a neutral venue. An Italy XV played a New Zealand XV on 28 November 1979 in Rovigo, Italy during the All Blacks' tour of England, Scotland and Italy. The tourists won 18-12 in a match which was recognised as a Test match by the Italian Rugby Federation but none of the All Blacks' players were awarded a cap.

Did You Know That?

The first 11 meetings between the two sides were never played at the same venue, whilst their last three meetings have all been played at Stadio Olimpico, Rome, Italy.

THE RUGBY WORLD CUP'S BAD BOY

The Italian hooker, Fabio Ongaro, holds the unwanted Rugby World Cup record for being given the most yellow cards, three (no red cards). He played in a total of nine games (includes four from the substitutes' bench) in the tournament (2003, 2007 and 2011). No player has been handed more than one red card at a Rugby World Cup finals.

THE 2015 RUGBY WORLD CUP FINALS

The 2015 Rugby World Cup was the eighth edition of rugby union's most prized tournament and was the third time England hosted matches (1991 and 1999). Once again the tournament featured 20 nations with only one change from the 2011 tournament, Uruguay replacing Russia. This was the first Rugby World Cup with no new teams competing.

The host nation were in Pool A but failed to make it to the quarter-final stages after losing 28-25 to Wales who finished runners-up and 33-13 to Pool A winners, Australia who won all four of their matches. Pool B was won by South Africa who were sensationally beaten 34-32 by Japan in their opening game. Scotland took the other quarter-final spot after finishing second to the Springboks. The reigning world champions, New Zealand, won all four of their Pool C games with Argentina finishing in the runners-up spot. The Pumas actually scored five points more than the All Blacks in their games. Three Six Nations rivals battled out Pool D along with Canada and Romania. Ireland topped Pool D with a 100% record which included a 24-9 win over France in the last game to decide which nation would finish top. France were Pool D runners-up, Italy third with Romania fourth having defeated the bottom side, Canada 17-15.

Twickenham Stadium, London and the Millennium Stadium, Cardiff, Wales hosted the four quarter-final games. South Africa defeated Wales 23-19 at Twickenham Stadium and in a repeat of the 2011 final, the All Blacks demolished France 62-13 in the Welsh capital. Argentina caused a major shock by progressing to the semi-finals at the expense of Ireland, winning 43-20 in Cardiff. The last quarter-final was the closest of the four with the Wallabies edging Scotland out of the tournament by winning 35-34 in London. The first semi-final paired together fierce rivals New Zealand and South Africa. The All Blacks squeezed past their southern hemisphere rivals with a 20-18 victory at Twickenham Stadium. The Wallabies beat the impressive Pumas 29-15 in London to set up an Antipodes final. The Olympic Stadium, London played host to the bronze final, which saw South Africa defeat Argentina 24-13.

Final – 31 October 2015
Twickenham Stadium, London
New Zealand 34-17 Australia

New Zealand made sporting history at Twickenham Stadium, London on 31 October 2015 when they became the first team to be crowned Rugby World Cup winners for a second successive time.

Tries in each half by wing Nehe Milner-Skudder and centre Ma'a Nonu, followed by a late Beauden Barrett breakaway score, plus 19 points from All Blacks fly-half Dan Carter – including an important late drop goal – in his 112th and final Test before joining French club Racing 92, saw New Zealand defeat their great trans-Tasman rivals, Australia, 34-17. It extended their record Rugby World Cup winning run to 14 Tests.

But the All Blacks were briefly given a second-half scare as Australia threatened a remarkable fightback from 18 points adrift after 42 minutes as No 8 David Pocock and centre Tevita Kuridrani scored tries, with fly-half Bernard Foley converting both touchdowns that followed an earlier penalty. It proved to be a pulsating final, brilliantly refereed by Welshman Nigel Owens, but New Zealand had enough in the tank to guarantee a winning farewell to Test rugby for the likes of Carter, Nonu, Conrad Smith and 148 times-capped Captain Marvel Richie McCaw. The tournament's best two teams played out a thrilling spectacle, with the Wallabies often giving as good as they got, but the All Blacks ultimately possessed a mastery of the key moments as they dug deep into rich resources of experience to see them home.

New Zealand dominated the early exchanges, with Nonu proving a particular threat, and it was no surprise when Carter booted the All Blacks into a seventh-minute lead through an angled penalty. While Carter's accuracy was never in doubt, there were more concerns surrounding All Blacks No 8 Kieran Read, who required treatment for a foot injury before appearing to run things off in back-play and being able to continue. It was Australia who suffered the first major injury blow – albeit after Foley had tied things up with a penalty – when lock Kane Douglas limped off following prolonged treatment and he was replaced by former Exeter captain Dean Mumm. The All Blacks continued to dominate in terms of territory, but their attacking plays were met by immense Australian defence as each player hit the opposite number ferociously.

Carter restored New Zealand's advantage through a 26th-minute penalty, with the Wallabies forced to regroup after centre Matt Giteau went off for a head injury assessment. And unfortunately for Giteau, it proved to be the end of his Rugby World Cup with Kurtley Beale replacing him. Beale went on to the wing, with wing Adam Ashley-Cooper moving into midfield.

But the closing stages of the opening period were dominated by New Zealand, with Carter completing his penalty hat-trick before New Zealand finally breached Australia's defence. Slick passing ended with centre Conrad Smith finding McCaw in support, and the skipper's off-load resulted in Milner-Skudder collecting his sixth try of the tournament. Carter's touchline conversion gave the All Blacks a 16-3 interval advantage, and there appeared no way back for Australia, who had offered little in attack. New Zealand made an interval switch, sending on Sonny Bill Williams for Conrad Smith, but the Wallabies knew they had to score first or face being dumped out of the contest.

Inevitably, the All Blacks had other ideas, and they surged further ahead when Nonu gathered loose ball and set off on an arcing run that led to him claiming a superb opportunist try. Despite Carter drifting his conversion attempt narrowly wide, New Zealand led by 18 points, meaning that Australia required one of rugby's greatest comebacks to deny the All Blacks another world title. New Zealand, though, did not help themselves when full-back Ben Smith was yellow-carded for a clumsy tackle on Wallabies' wing Drew Mitchell, and Australia capitalised immediately with a close-range try for Pocock that Foley converted. And it got better for the Wallabies just 11 minutes later when Kuridrani was worked clear in space, and his power took him to the line for a try that Foley again converted, making it 21-17 inside the final quarter. Carter, though, sealed the deal, landing a drop goal and then a long-range penalty as he stepped up to the plate when it mattered in his first Rugby World Cup Final, before Barrett's runaway score as the clock ticked down finished Australia off. It was, though, an occasion to savour, and gave a memorable England 2015 tournament an outstanding finish.

'It is my proudest moment. So proud of the way the guys have done it. We played damn good rugby here. We lost a bit of momentum in the second half but we came back strong which has been the hallmark of this team. I knew the momentum was against us and it was a matter of not panicking and do the simple things right. I still don't want to quit. I want to enjoy the moment,' said Richie McCaw after lifting the Webb Ellis Cup.

When asked after the game about his crucial drop goal, Carter said: 'I practised a few in the back garden with my old man! I was pleased it went over, I was yelling at the ball to go over and it did. It gave us breathing space.'

New Zealand No 8 Kieran Read was interviewed on ITV: 'This is pretty surreal. Not just to win the World Cup once, but twice, it's a dream.' On All Blacks teammates Dan Carter and Richie McCaw, Read said: 'They're going to go down in history as the greats of this game. This victory is deserved for them.'

Australia captain Stephen Moore said: 'It's all about New Zealand tonight – they thoroughly deserved to win. They have been the best team in the tournament and they played really well tonight. There are no excuses from us, I'm proud of the effort we put in and the way we fought our way back into the match. Sometimes you just come up against a better team and that was the case tonight.' Meanwhile, Australia's head coach, Michael Cheika said: 'We fought back bravely, but they're the world champions and they deserve to be. I always believed, even at the end – but it wasn't to be that way. I'm really proud of my lads and I really want to thank the Australian public, both here and in Australia, for getting behind rugby. New Zealand won fair and square and they've been the form team since the last World Cup. We wanted to challenge them tonight, and I think we did, but we just came up short.'

The final brought a few tournament firsts: New Zealand were the first side to win back-to-back Rugby World Cups; this was the All Blacks' first Rugby World Cup title outside of New Zealand, with their 1987 and 2011 victories both coming on home soil; New Zealand's Ma'a Nonu, 33, became the oldest player to score a try in a Rugby World Cup Final; this was the highest scoring final in Rugby World Cup history, and the tally of five tries was also a record. Dan Carter ended his international career having scored 126 points at Twickenham Stadium, more than any other non-England player and the eighth of anyone. The side leading at half-time had now won all eight Rugby World Cup Finals.

New Zealand: Ben Smith; Nehe Milner-Skudder, Conrad Smith, Ma'a Nonu, Julian Savea; Dan Carter, Aaron Smith; Joe Moody, Dane Coles, Owen Franks, Brodie Retallick, Sam Whitelock, Jerome Kaino, Richie McCaw, Kieran Read.

Replacements: Beauden Barrett, Sonny Bill Williams, Tawera Kerr-Barlow, Ben Franks, Keven Mealamu, Charlie Faumuina, Victor Vito, Sam Cane.

Sin Bin: Ben Smith (52).

Australia: Israel Folau; Adam Ashley-Cooper, Tevita Kuridrani, Matt Giteau, Drew Mitchell; Bernard Foley, Will Genia; Scott Sio, Stephen Moore, Sekope Kepu, Kane Douglas, Rob Simmons, Scott Fardy, Michael Hooper, David Pocock.

Replacements: Kurtley Beale, Matt Toomua, Nick Phipps, James Slipper, Tatafu Polota-Nau, Greg Holmes, Dean Mumm, Ben McCalman.

Australia (3) 17	New Zealand (16) 34
Tries Pocock (52), Kuridrani (63)	Tries Milner-Skudder (38), Nonu (41), Barrett (78)
Cons Foley (53, 64)	Cons Carter (40, 79)
Pen Foley (13)	Pen Carter (7, 26, 35, 74)
Drops none	Drops Carter (69)

Attendance: 80,125
Referee: Nigel Owens (Wales)

Did You Know That?

Dan Carter's 19-points tally in the 2015 Rugby World Cup Final has only been bettered by Australia's Matt Burke, who scored 25 points when the Wallabies defeated France 35-12 in the 1999 final at the Millennium Stadium, Cardiff, Wales, kicking two conversions and seven penalties.

THE RUGBY WORLD CUP FINALS RECORD MAKERS

SAMOA BLOW BIGGEST EVER HALF-TIME LEAD

Samoa holds the unwanted record of holding the biggest half-time lead in a Rugby World Cup game without winning the game. Samoa led Argentina 16-3 in their Pool D game at Stradey Park, Llanelli, Wales on 10 October 1999 but ended up losing 32-16.

Did You Know That?

Samoa also holds the record for scoring the most points in the first half without winning the game. On 10 October 2015, they led Scotland 26-23 at the interval in a Pool B game at St James' Park, Newcastle, England but lost the game 36-33.

ALL OVER IN THE FIRST HALF

New Zealand holds the record for scoring the most first-half points in a Rugby World Cup game. On 4 June 1995, they led Japan 84-3 at Free State Stadium, Bloemfontein, South Africa in a Pool C encounter and ran out 145-17 winners. The half-time score is also a Rugby World Cup finals score for the biggest lead by a team by the interval, 81 points.

Did You Know That?

Not surprisingly, the All Blacks also set the Rugby World Cup finals record for scoring the most conversions in a game. The 145-17 mauling of Japan produced 21 tries with Simon Culhane successfully converting 20 of them and he scored a try.

MOST TRIES SCORED WITHOUT WINNING THE GAME

Wales holds the unwanted record for scoring the most number of tries in a Rugby World Cup game without winning it. On 29 September 2007, they lost 38-34 to Fiji at Stade de la Beaujoire, Nantes, France despite scoring five tries in the match. Fiji scored four tries in the Pool B game.

Did You Know That?

Wales also holds the Rugby World Cup finals record for scoring the most points in a match without winning it. On 2 November 2003, they were defeated 53-37 by New Zealand at Telstra Stadium, Sydney, Australia in Pool D.

DROP GOAL KINGS

South Africa and Jan 'Jannie' Henrik de Beer hold the Rugby World Cup finals record for coring the most number of drop goals in a match. On 24 October 1999, the Springboks' fly-half scored five drop goals in their 44-21 win over England at Stade de France, Saint-Denis, Paris, France in the quarter-finals. He also scored two conversions and five penalties in the game whilst his opposite No.10, Paul Grayson, successfully kicked six penalties (England's Jonny Wilkinson also scored a penalty).

> ### Did You Know That?
> Although he only played in 13 Tests (1997–99), de Beer scored 181 points (two tries, 33 conversions, 27 penalties and eight drop goals) for the Springboks, an impressive average of 14 points per game.

LETHAL KICKING

Four nations hold the joint-record for scoring the most penalties in a Rugby World Cup finals game, eight; Gavin Hastings kicked eight penalties for Scotland in their 41-5 win over Tonga in the 1995 tournament (he also scored a try and a conversion in the game), Thierry Lacroix kicked eight penalties for France in their 36-12 win over Ireland in the 1995 tournament (he also scored a conversion in the game), Gonzalo Quesada kicked eight penalties for Argentina in their 32-16 win over Samoa Tonga in the 1999 tournament (he also scored a drop goal in the game) and Matt Burke kicked eight penalties for Australia in their 27-21 win over South Africa in the 1999 tournament (Jannie de Beer scored all of the Springboks' points, six penalties and a drop goal).

> ### Did You Know That?
> Gonzalo Quesada also scored seven penalties versus Japan (Argentina won 33-12) and seven penalties plus one conversion versus Ireland at the 1999 Rugby World Cup finals (David Humphreys scored seven penalties and one drop goal for Ireland in their 28-24 loss). Not surprisingly, Quesada ended the 1999 tournament as the leading points scorer with 102 points to his name.

MOST TRIES IN A GAME

Australia holds the record for scoring the most number of tries in a Rugby World Cup game. On 25 October 2003, the Wallabies beat Namibia 142-0 (69-0 at half-time) in a Pool A game at the Adelaide Oval, Sydney, Australia. The game produced 22 tries, five were scored by Chris Latham, and 16 conversions from Mat Rogers.

THE UNDEFEATED

Going into the 2019 Rugby World Cup finals, New Zealand holds the record for the most consecutive wins, 14. The All Blacks won all seven of their games in the 2011 and 2015 tournaments and have not lost a Rugby World Cup finals game since France defeated them 20-18 at the Millennium Stadium, Cardiff, Wales in the quarter-finals of the 2011 tournament. The 14-game winning run is also the tournament's best ever undefeated record.

NEVER ON THE WINNING SIDE

On 1 October 1999, Namibia played in their inaugural match at a Rugby World Cup finals and lost 67-18 to Fiji in a Pool 3 game at Stade de la Méditerranée, Béziers, France. They then lost their remaining two pool games. At the 2003 Rugby World Cup finals, they lost all four Group A games including a tournament record 142-0 loss to Australia which is the tournament record for a points margin defeat. The 2007 tournament brought four more defeats in Pool D followed by another whitewash in four Pool D games when New Zealand played host to the 2011 Rugby World Cup finals. At the 2015 tournament, hosted by England, despite one again losing all four of their Pool C games, they went home as a greatly improved side after going down 58-14 to the defending World Champions, New Zealand, 35-21 to Tonga, a close 17-16 defeat by Georgia and a 64-19 loss to Argentina. Their 19-game losing sequence is a tournament record which they hope to bring to an end when they play in the 2019 Rugby World Cup finals hosted by Japan where they will face New Zealand, South Africa, Italy and Canada. Japan were on an 18-game winless run when they faced Canada on 27 September 2011 at McLean Park, Napier, New Zealand.

They brought their winless streak to an end by drawing the game 23-23. Namibia's 19 defeats is also a Rugby World Cup finals record for the most consecutive losses away from home, which is also the record for the most number of consecutive games away from home without a victory.

IMPREGNABLE HOME FORTRESSES

New Zealand holds the Rugby World Cup finals record for the most consecutive victories on home soil. The inaugural tournament was co-hosted by Australia and New Zealand in 1987 and the All Blacks won all three of their Pool 3 games, which were played in Auckland, Christchurch and Wellington. They played in the 1987 quarter-finals in Christchurch but their semi-final win over Wales took place at Ballymore Stadium, Brisbane, Australia. They won the 1987 Rugby World Cup at Eden Park, Auckland, New Zealand. The 2011 tournament was hosted by New Zealand and they won all seven of their games including the final at Eden Park to stretch their consecutive victories at home tally to 12.

A LEAKY HOME DEFENCE

Wales holds the Rugby World Cup finals record for the most consecutive matches on home soil without a win, three (which is also the record for the most number of consecutive losses at home). Wales hosted the 1999 tournament and lost their third and final Pool D game 38-31 at the Millennium Stadium, Cardiff. Wales then met Australia in the quarter-finals at the Millennium Stadium, Cardiff and lost the game 24-9. The 2007 tournament was hosted by France but some of the games were played in Cardiff and in Edinburgh, Scotland. Wales beat Canada in their opening Pool B encounter in Nantes, France but lost their second Pool B game at the Millennium Stadium, Cardiff, going down 32-20 to the Wallabies.

Did You Know That?

The heaviest home defeat for a nation which has played in a Rugby World Cup finals tournament belongs to Spain. On 1 November 2001, Australia beat Spain 92-10 at Campo Central, Madrid, Spain. The Wallabies, the reigning world champions at the time, were celebrating their 400th Test on the national holiday of All Saints Day. New Zealand tops the list for inflicting the most record home defeats, responsible for nine nations' blackest day. South Africa are next on the list with five, whilst Australia and England are joint-third having claimed four scalps each.

UNBEATEN ON THE ROAD

South Africa holds the Rugby World Cup finals record for the most consecutive wins away from home, 11 (which is also the record for the most number of consecutive undefeated games away from home). During the 2007 Rugby World Cup finals in France, the Springboks won all four of their Pool A games, their quarter-final and semi-final ties and defeated England 15-6 in the final at Stade de France, Saint-Denis, Paris. South Africa travelled to New Zealand for the 2011 tournament as the defending World Champions. The Springboks won all four of their Pool D games but exited the tournament at the quarter-final stages after losing 11-9 to Australia.

Did You Know That?

The last time the All Blacks failed to score a try in a Rugby World Cup finals game was during the 1999 tournament hosted by Wales. New Zealand met South Africa in the third-place play-off game at the Millennium Stadium, Cardiff and lost the game 22-18 to the defending world champions with Andrew Mehrtens scoring all of the All Blacks' points (six penalties).

LUCKY OPPONENTS

Four nations hold the Rugby World Cup finals record for the most number of consecutive wins over the same nation, five; New Zealand versus Italy (1987-2007), New Zealand versus Scotland (1987-2007), South Africa versus Samoa (1995-2015) and Australia versus Wales (1991-2015). This is also a tournament record for the most consecutive games unbeaten against the same opponent.

MASTER TRY SCORERS

The Rugby World Cup finals record for the highest number of consecutive matches in which a nation scored a try is 26. The record belongs to the All Blacks who set it between 11 October 2003 versus Italy in their opening Pool D game and their 2015 Rugby World Cup Final victory over Australia.

Did You Know That?

The Springboks' record 11-game winning streak took in five cities (Paris, Lens, Montpellier, Wellington, Auckland) and two countries (France and New Zealand).

LOOKING FOR A TRY

The Rugby World Cup finals record for most consecutive games without scoring a try is three and is held by four nations; England (1991–95), Spain (1999), Uruguay (1999–2003) and Scotland (2011).

Did You Know That?

Spain has only competed in one Rugby World Cup finals, 1999. They lost all three of their Pool 1 matches: 27-15 to Uruguay, 47-3 to South Africa and 48-0 to Scotland. They conceded 16 tries.

TRY AND TRY AGAIN

Fiji and Japan are the joint-holders of the Rugby World Cup finals record for the most number of consecutive games in which a nation has conceded a try, 28. Fiji's record dates from 24 May 1987 versus Argentina to Uruguay on 6 October 2015. Japan's record dates from 24 May 1987 versus USA to 11 October 2015 versus USA. Fiji have played in every Rugby World Cup finals since 1987 with the exception of 1995 when they failed to qualify, 25 Group/Pool games which includes two quarter-finals defeats (31-16 to France in 1987, a 37-20 loss to South Africa in 2007 and a 45-24 quarter-final play-offs loss to England in 1999). Japan have played in all eight Rugby World Cup finals, 28 Group/ Pool games.

Did You Know That?

Fiji won their inaugural game at a Rugby World Cup finals, a 28-9 victory over Argentina on 24 May 1987 at Rugby Park, Hamilton, New Zealand. Japan lost their inaugural game, a 21-18 loss to the USA on 24 May 1987 at Ballymore Stadium, Brisbane, Australia.

TIGHT AT THE BACK

South Africa holds the Rugby World Cup finals record for the most consecutive games without conceding a try, six. The Springboks' record began on 10 October 1999 versus Spain at Murrayfield, Edinburgh, Scotland (won 47-3) and came to an end after beating Uruguay 72-6 on 11 October 2003 at the Subiaco Oval, Perth, Australia.

Did You Know That?
No team has ever lost a Group/Pool game on their way to lifting the Webb Ellis Cup.

IT'S ALL ABOUT THE POINTS

New Zealand holds the Rugby World Cup finals record for a winning points deferential at a single tournament. In 2007, the All Blacks won four of their five games, scoring 327 points and conceding 55 for a plus points differential of 272.

Did You Know That?
On their way to winning Pool D at the 2011 tournament, Morné Steyn scored 44 points in their three victories; seven versus Wales, 19 versus Fiji and 18 versus Namibia. Steyn ended the 2011 tournament as the leading points scorer with 62.

Did You Know That?
The All Blacks hold the record for most points scored in a tournament, 361 in 2003 (won six, lost one).

NO WAY PAST

South Africa holds the Rugby World Cup finals record for conceding the fewest number of points, allowing a meagre 35 in 2011 (won four, lost one).

CROSSING THE WHITE LINE

At the 2003 Rugby World Cup finals, hosted by Australia and won by England, New Zealand set the tournament record for scoring the most number of tries. The All Blacks notched up 52 tries in their seven games, winning six and losing one. They also scored 40 conversions, six penalties and one drop goal for an overall total of 361 points (conceded 101).

Did You Know That?
The All Blacks also occupy second (48 tries in 2003) and third (43 tries in 1987) spot in the Top 3.

THE WOODEN SPOON WINNERS
No fewer than ten nations have lost every game they played in a Rugby World Cup finals. Georgia (2003), Japan (2003), Namibia (2003, 2007, 2011 and 2015), Tonga (2003), Portugal (2007), USA (2007 and 2015), Romania (2011), Russia (2011), Canada (2015) and Uruguay (2015) lost all four of their Group/Pool games.

Did You Know That?
If a team finishes bottom of a Group/Pool, they are classed as being the 'wooden spoon' winners.

BIG LOSERS
Namibia holds the unwanted Rugby World Cup finals record for a losing points deferential at a single tournament. In 2003, they lost all four of their games, scoring 38 points and conceding 310 for a minus points differential of 272. The 310 points against is also a tournament record for the highest number of points allowed by a nation. Their 47 tries against in 2003 is another unwanted tournament record they hold.

Did You Know That?
Namibia played their inaugural game at the tournament on 1 October 1999 and lost 67-18 to Fiji, conceding nine tries.

AN INEPT ATTACK
Romania holds the unwanted Rugby World Cup finals record for scoring the fewest number of points at a single tournament. In 1995, they lost all three of their games, scoring only a paltry 14 points and conceding 97.

Did You Know That?
In their opening Pool A game in 1995, they lost 34-3 to Canada at Boet Erasmus Stadium, Port Elizabeth, South Africa, a game in which Gareth Rees scored 19 points for Canada (four penalties, two conversions and one drop goal).

Y VIVA ESPANA

In 1999, Spain set the unwanted Rugby World Cup finals record for failing to score a try in any of their Group/Pool matches. They lost all three of their Pool A encounters: 27-15 to Uruguay, 47-3 to the reigning world champions, South Africa, and 48-0 to Scotland.

Did You Know That?

Only four players have a 100% winning record as captain: David Kirk (New Zealand), six games in 1987; Nick Farr-Jones (Australia), five games in 1991; Francois Pienaar (South Africa), five games in 1987; and John Eales (Australia), five games in 1999. All four players captained their team to Rugby World Cup glory.

A DECENT RECORD

Canada actually sits in fifth place in the table for least points conceded at a Rugby World Cup finals. South Africa leads the way with 35 (2011), followed by France with 44 (1991), England 48 (1987) and Samoa 49 (2011). At the 1995 Rugby World Cup finals in South Africa, Canada found themselves in Pool A alongside the host nation, which was making its Rugby World Cup debut, the reigning world champions, Australia, and Romania. Canada finished third in their Pool after beating Romania 34-3 in their opening game before losing 27-11 to the Wallabies and 20-0 to the Springboks.

Did You Know That?

Joel Stransky scored 32 points for South Africa in Pool A at the 1995 tournament and went on to score a drop goal in the final versus New Zealand to win the 1995 Rugby World Cup Final, a 15-12 victory after extra time. In fact, Stransky scored all of the Springboks' 15 points in the final, three penalties and two drop goals.

THE RECORD APPEARANCE MAKERS

1. Jason Leonard (England)   22 (18 starts)   1991–2003
2. Richie McCaw (New Zealand)   22 (18 starts)   2003–2015
3. Schalk Burger (South Africa)   20 (17 starts)   2003–2015
4. George Gregan (Australia)   20 (18 starts)   1995–2007
5. Keven Mealamu (New Zealand)   20 (12 starts)   2003–2015

Did You Know That?

Schalk Burger's father, also called Schalk Burger, won international honours for South Africa during their years of isolation in the 1980s. He was named World Player of the Year by the International Rugby Board in 2004.

CAPTAIN MARVEL

New Zealand's Richie McCaw holds the record for the most games as captain in the Rugby World Cup finals. The All Blacks' legendary flanker led his side out 13 times during a tournament (2007–15) winning 12 and losing just one. Five players are joint-second in this illustrious table with 11 games: Will Carling (England, 1991–95, winning seven and losing four); Raphael Ibanez (France, 1999–2007, winning seven and losing four); Martin Johnson (England, 1999–2003, winning nine and losing two); John Smit (South Africa, 2003–11, winning ten and losing one); and Sam Warburton (Wales 2011–15, winning seven and losing four). Namibia's Jacques Burger (2007–15) holds the unwanted record of leading his side out the most number of times during a Rugby World Cup finals, seven, without drawing or winning a single game. Takuro Muichi (2003–07) captained Japan in seven games, losing six and drawing one (a 23-23 draw with Canada on 27 September 2011).

> ### Did You Know That?
> Andriy Kovalenco scored all 15 (5 penalties) of their points versus Uruguay whilst Ferran Velazco Querol scored a penalty against the Springboks.

KEEPING IT IN THE FAMILY

Italy's Mauro Bergamasco holds the Rugby World Cup record for longevity. He was born on 1 May 1979 in Padova, Italy and made his tournament debut on 2 October 1999 in a 67-7 loss to England aged 20 years and 154 days. He played his 13th and last Rugby World Cup finals game on 4 October 2015 in a 15-9 defeat by Ireland aged 36 years and 156 days. His span of 16 years and two days taking in five tournaments beat the previous record held by Brian Lima of 15 years and 351 days. Lima played 18 matches in five tournaments from 1991–2007. Bergamasco's father, Arturo, was capped four times by Italy from 1973–78, whilst his younger brother, Mirco, won 89 caps from 2000–12 and scored 256 points (he played in the 2003, 2007 and 2011 Rugby World Cup finals – eight games).

THE YOUNGEST EVER PLAYER

Vasil Lobzhanidze (Georgia) is the youngest player to appear in a Rugby World Cup finals match. On 19 September 2015 he made his tournament debut aged 18 years and 340 days in Georgia's opening Pool C game versus Tonga at Kingsholm Stadium, Gloucester, England. Georgia won the game 17-10 to claim only their third ever win in the tournament. Lobzhanidze beat the previous record held by the USA's Thretton Palamo by just 33 days (Palamo was 19 years and eight days

old when he made his tournament debut on 30 September 2007 in a
64-15 loss to South Africa).

THE YOUNG WELSH DRAGON

Sam Warburton holds the Rugby World Cup finals record for being
the youngest player to captain his nation in a tournament. On 11
September 2011, aged 22 years and 341 days, he led Wales out for
their opening Pool D match versus the defending world champions,
South Africa, at Regional Stadium, Wellington, New Zealand. The
Springboks won the game 17-16. The youngest player to captain his
nation to a win at a Rugby World Cup finals was Australia's Sanchez
William Genia who was 23 years and 249 days old when the Wallabies
beat the USA 67-5 in a Pool C game at Regional Stadium, Wellington,
New Zealand on 23 September 2011. Genia was born on 17 January
1988 in Port Moresby, Papua New Guinea.

A QUITE UNIQUE TREBLE

Uruguay's Diego Ormaechea holds the Rugby World Cup finals record
for being the oldest player to captain his nation in a tournament. On
2 October 1999, aged 40 years and 13 days, he led Uruguay for their
opening Pool A match versus Spain. Uruguay won the game 27-15
with Ormaechea scoring a try. The game meant that Ormaechea also
became the oldest debutant in Rugby World cup history as well as the
oldest ever try scorer.

THE LONGEST RUGBY WORLD CUP DROP GOAL

Andrew (Andy) John Miller was born on 13 September 1972 in Te Puke, New Zealand. He began his career with Bay of Plenty, New Zealand in 1991 and in 1998 he joined Kobelco Steelers in Japan. In 1996, he played for Canterbury Crusaders in the inaugural Super 12 season. He left Kobelco Steelers in 2004 when he signed for Southland, New Zealand. In 1992, he played for New Zealand Colts (Under-21s) and scored 21 points. However, on 19 May 2002 Miller made his Test debut at fly-half for Japan versus Russia having qualified to play for the Cherry Blossoms through residency. He scored a try in Japan's 59-19 victory in Tokyo, Japan. Miller was a member of Japan's squad at the 2003 Rugby World Cup finals in Australia and kept Keiji Hirose, Japan's all-time leading points scorer, out of the side. On 23 October 2003, Miller scored (at the time) the longest drop goal in Rugby World Cup history, a 52-metre kick in his country's 41-13 Pool B loss to Fiji at Dairy Farmers Stadium, Townsville, Australia. Miller scored all of Japan's 13 points which also included a try, a conversion and a penalty, making it a four-way scoring feat. He made his tenth and final appearance for the Cherry Blossoms in their final Pool B game at the 2003 Rugby World Cup finals, a 39-26 defeat to the USA at Central Coast Stadium, Gosford, Australia. However, he never represented Japan again when the Japan Rugby Football Union briefly introduced a policy not to select foreign-born players in 2004. He played a total of ten times for Japan and scored 83 points.

THE LEADING RUGBY WORLD CUP POINTS SCORERS

1.	Jonny Wilkinson (England)	277 points	1999–2011	19 games
2.	Gavin Hastings (Scotland)	227 points	1987–1995	13 games
3.	Michael Lynagh (Australia)	195 points	1987–1995	15 games
4.	Dan Carter (New Zealand)	191 points	2003–2015	16 games
5.	Grant Fox (New Zealand)	170 points	1987–1991	10 games

MOST INDIVIDUAL TRIES AT RUGBY WORLD CUP FINALS

1. Jonah Lomu (New Zealand)	15 tries	1995–1999	15 games
2. Bryan Habana (South Africa)	15 tries	2007–2015	11 games
3. Drew Mitchell (Australia)	14 tries	2007–2015	13 games
4. Doug Howlett (New Zealand)	13 tries	2003–2007	10 games
5. David Campese (Australia)	10 tries	1987–1995	15 games
6. Rory Underwood (England)	11 tries	1987–1995	15 games
7. Brian Lima (Samoa)	10 tries	1991–2007	18 games
8. Chris Latham (Australia)	11 tries	1999–2007	7 games
9. Joe Rokocoko (New Zealand)	11 tries	2003–2007	8 games
10. Shane Williams (Wales)	10 tries	2003–2011	11 games
11. Vincent Clerc (France)	11 tries	2007–2011	13 games
12. Adam Ashley-Cooper (Australia)	11 tries	2007–2015	17 games

John Kirwan was the first player to score a try in a Rugby World Cup finals when he opened the scoring for the All Blacks in their 70-6 win over Italy (Pool 3) in the opening game of the inaugural tournament on 22 May 1987 at Eden Park, Auckland, New Zealand.

MOST INDIVIDUAL CONVERSIONS AT A RUGBY WORLD CUP FINALS

1. Dan Carter (New Zealand)   58   2003–2015   16 games
2. Gavin Hastings (Scotland)   39   1987–1995   13 games
3. Grant Fox (New Zealand)   37   1987–1991   10 games
4. Michael Lynagh (Australia)   36   1987–1995   15 games
5. Jonny Wilkinson (England)   28   1999–2011   19 games

Did You Know That?

Gavin Hastings, nicknamed 'Big Gav,' embarked on an American Football career in 1996 and played one season for the Scottish Claymores in NFL Europe, converting 24 of 27 'point after touchdown' attempts. In 1993, he was awarded the Order of the British Empire for services to rugby union, was inducted into the International Rugby Hall of Fame in 2003 and in 2013, he was inducted into the World Rugby Hall of Fame.

MOST INDIVIDUAL PENALTY GOALS SCORED AT RUGBY WORLD CUP FINALS

1. Jonny Wilkinson (England)   58   1999–2011   19 games
1. Gavin Hastings (Scotland)   36   1987–1995   13 games
2. Gonzalo Quesada (Argentina)   35   1999–2003   8 games
3. Michael Lynagh (Australia)   33   1987–1995   15 games
4. Andrew Mehrtens (South Africa)   33   1995–1999   10 games

MOST INDIVIDUAL DROP GOALS SCORED AT RUGBY WORLD CUP FINALS

1. Jonny Wilkinson (England)   14   1999–2011   19 games
2. Jannie de Beer (South Africa)   6   1999   5 games
3. Rob Andrew (England)   5   1987–1995   13 games
4. Gareth Rees (Canada)   5   1987–1999   13 games
5. Juan Hernandez (Argentina)   4   2003–2015   14 games

Did You Know That?

In 2011, Gareth Rees was inducted in the IRB World Rugby Hall of Fame as the first and only Canadian and along with his fellow 2011 inductee, Brian Lima of Samoa, became the first members from nations outside of the traditional top tier of the sport. In 2014, he was inducted in the Canada ports Hall of Fame as the first and only rugby player.

ALWAYS SCORES

Only two players in the history of the Rugby World Cup have scored a try in five consecutive games for their nation. During the inaugural tournament in 1987, Alan Whetton scored a try in each of New Zealand's three Pool 3 games, versus Italy, Fiji and Argentina. He then scored a try against Scotland in the quarter-finals and another in the All Blacks' semi-final victory over Wales. Despite starting the final versus France, he failed to make it six in a row in New Zealand's 29-9 victory. At the 1991 tournament, his fellow All Black, Jonah Lomu, scored two tries in New Zealand's opening Pool B win over Tonga, and scored again versus England followed by another double against Italy. In the quarter-finals he scored a try versus Scotland and two more in their semi-final loss to France but failed to cross the line in a 22-18 loss to South Africa in the third-place play-off match. Whetton also holds the record for most consecutive tries from making your debut in the tournament. Jonah Lomu made his tournament debut on 27 May 1995 and scored two tries in the All Blacks' 43-19 win over Ireland at Ellis Park, Johannesburg, South Africa but failed to score in his next game when New Zealand beat Wales 34-9 at the same venue.

Did You Know That?

New Zealand's John Kirwan was the first player to set the rugby union record of scoring eight tries in consecutive Tests, doing so in 1997/98. Since then only three other players have matched his feat, Christian Cullen (New Zealand, 2000), Daisuke Ohata (2002-03) and Nemani Nadolo (Fiji, 2013-14).

TRY AND TRY AGAIN

Sean Fitzpatrick holds the Rugby World Cup finals record of playing in the most number of games before scoring a try for his nation. He made his debut in the opening game of the inaugural Rugby World Cup finals, helping the All Blacks to a 70-6 win over Italy (Pool 3) on 22 May 1987 at Eden Park, Auckland, New Zealand. He scored his first try in the tournament 13 games later, a 48-30 victory over Scotland in the quarter-finals of the 1995 tournament at Loftus Versfeld Stadium, Pretoria, South Africa. Fitzpatrick won 92 Test caps for the All Blacks from 1987–97 and scored 11 tries.

Did You Know That?

Fitzpatrick captained New Zealand to a 2-1 series win over the British & Irish Lions in 1993.

A RECORD BARREN RUN

No player has played more matches in the Rugby World Cup finals than Jason Leonard. Not only is his 22 games (includes four as a substitute) for England a tournament record for the highest number of appearances but he also holds the Rugby World Cup finals record for playing the most games without scoring a try or any points for that matter.

Did You Know That?

Owen Franks holds the rugby union world record for winning the most number of Test caps without scoring a try. He played 106 times (includes 13 Rugby World Cup appearances) at prop for New Zealand from 2009–present.

BABY FACED TRY SCORER

George North is the youngest ever try scorer in the Rugby World Cup finals aged 19 years and 166 days. On 26 September 2011, he scored two tries for Wales in their 81-7 win over Namibia in Pool D at Stadium Taranaki, New Plymouth, New Zealand.

Did You Know That?

Robin Bredbury is the youngest try scorer in the history of rugby union. He scored two tries on his international debut for Hong Kong in his nation's 93-0 win over Thailand at Merdeka Stadium, Kuala Lumpur in a 1995 Rugby World Cup qualifier, Asia, Pool 2 game aged 17 years and 144 days.

LETHAL WEAPONS

Simon Culhane holds the Rugby World Cup finals record for scoring the most number of points in a game. On 4 June 1995, he scored 45 points in New Zealand's 145-17 victory over Japan in a Pool C match at Free State Stadium, Bloemfontein, South Africa. In the same game, Marc Ellis set the tournament record for scoring the most tries in a game, six (which is also a joint record for the most tries against a team in the tournament – Bryan Habana of South Africa scored six versus Samoa from 2007–15).

Did You Know That?

On 21 July 2002, Toru Kurihara set the world record for scoring the most number of points in an international match. He scored a mammoth 60 points (six tries and 15 conversions) for Japan in their 120-3 win over Chinese Taipei in a 2003 Rugby World Cup qualifier, Asia, Round 3 game played at Rugby Stadium, Tainan, Taiwan.

WE MEET AGAIN

Richie McCaw holds the Rugby World Cup finals record for playing the most number of games against the same opponent. Between the 2003 and 2015 tournaments, the All Black legend played against France five times (won four, lost one).

Did You Know That?

McCaw never lost a Test match versus Argentina (10 games), British & Irish Lions (2 games), Canada (2 games), Fiji (2 games), Georgia (1 game), Ireland (14 games), Italy (3 games), Japan (1 game), Namibia (1 game), Romania (1 game), Scotland (7 games), Samoa (1 game), Tonga (2 games) and Wales (11 games).

THE NEMESIS

Two players are joint Rugby World Cup finals record holders for scoring the most number of points against the same opponent. Simon Culhane scored 45 points for New Zealand on 4 June 1995 in their 145-17 win over Japan in a Pool C match at Free State Stadium, Bloemfontein, South Africa. His fellow All Black Dan Carter scored 45 points against France over four tournaments (2003 – eight points, 2007 – eight points, 2011 – 12 points & 2015 – 17 points).

Did You Know That?

In the 2015 Rugby World Cup final, Carter scored 17 points in New Zealand's 34-17 win over Australia at Twickenham Stadium, London, England. He successfully kicked four penalties, two conversions and a drop goal and was deservedly named 'Man of the Match'.

A HOME FROM HOME

Scotland's George Weir holds the Rugby World Cup finals record for playing the most number of games on the same ground. Between 1991 and 1999 he played in 14 Rugby World Cup finals games with nine (won six, lost three) of them staged at Murrayfield, Edinburgh, Scotland. In 1991, Scotland were one of five co-host nations and played all three of their Pool 2 matches at Murrayfield. In the quarter-finals they beat Western Samoa 28-6 at Murrayfield and followed this up with a 9-6 loss to England in the semi-finals at the same venue. Wales hosted the 1999 tournament although the majority of matches were played outside Wales (shared between England, France, Ireland and Scotland). All three of Scotland's Pool A games were played at Murrayfield (he missed the 43-12 victory versus Uruguay) as was their 35-20 quarter-final play-off win over Samoa and their 30-18 quarter-final loss to New Zealand.

> ### Did You Know That?
> Gethin Jenkins played 129 Tests for Wales (including 18 in the Rugby World Cup finals, 2003–15) and holds the rugby union world record for playing the most number of Tests at the same venue. Jenkins played 70 games for Wales at the Millennium Stadium, Cardiff, Wales. He actually made his international debut against Romania at the Racecourse Ground, Wrexham, Wales on 1 November 2002 (Wales won 40-3).

THE CABBAGE PATCH KIDS

Although Jonny Wilkinson holds the record for scoring the most rugby union points at the same venue, scoring 650 for England (1998–2011), Australia's Bernard Foley, nicknamed 'The Iceman', holds the Rugby World Cup finals record for most points scored at the same venue. During the 2015 tournament in England, the Wallaby played five games at Twickenham Stadium, nicknamed 'The Cabbage Patch', and scored a total of 69 points. Only two of Australia's four Pool A games were played at the stadium, a 33-13 win over England in which he scored 28 points and a 15-6 victory against Wales scoring all of his nation's points. The Wallabies defeated Scotland 35-34 in a highly controversial quarter-final game and Foley scored ten points. Foley then scored nine points in Australia's 29-15 win over Argentina in the semi-finals and seven points in the Wallabies' 34-17 loss to New Zealand in the final.

> ### Did You Know That?
> Victor Vito played his 100th and last game for the Hurricanes in the final of the 2016 Super Rugby. The Hurricanes beat the South African side, the Lions, 20-3 at Westpac Stadium, Wellington, New Zealand.

> ### Did You Know That?
> Foley scored 603 points in 68 Tests with 124 of them scored against Argentina.

A LUCKY GROUND

The most number of tries scored by a player at the same venue in a Rugby World Cup finals is six. On 4 June 1995, Marc Ellis scored six tries for New Zealand in their 145-17 victory over Japan in a Pool C match at Free State Stadium, Bloemfontein, South Africa. On 2 October 2015, Julian Savea scored three tries for the All Blacks when they beat Georgia 43-10 in a Pool C game at the Millennium Stadium,

Cardiff, Wales. In the quarter-finals New Zealand met France at the same venue and Savea scored another hat-trick of tries in a 62-13 victory for the All Blacks. One of his tries versus France subsequently won the 'Try of the Year' award. Savea was the leading try scorer at the 2015 tournament with eight (he also scored two versus Namibia in Pool C).

Did You Know That?
Julian Savea was named the 2010 IRB Junior Player of the Year.

SO YOU WIN AGAIN
Richie McCaw (New Zealand) has been on the winning side in a Rugby World Cup finals match more times than any other player.

1. Richie McCaw (NZ)   22 games (18 starts)   2003-2015 Won 20, Lost 2
2. Keven Mealamu (NZ)   20 games (12 starts)   2003-2015 Won 19, Lost 1
-3. Jason Leonard (E)   22 games (18 starts)   1991-2003 Won 16, Lost 6
-3. George Gregan (A)   20 games (18 starts)   1995-2007 Won 16, Lost 4
-3. Schalk Burger (SA)   20 games (17 starts)   2003-2015 Won 16, Lost 4

Did You Know That?
Schalk Burger played four times for the Barbarians: 2004 versus New Zealand XV, 2008 versus Australia XV, 2009 versus New Zealand XV and 2013 versus Fiji XV.

BIG LOSERS
Ovidiu Tonita (Romania) has been on the losing side in a Rugby World Cup finals match more times than any other player.

1. Ovidiu Tonita (R)   14 games (13 starts)   2003–2015 Lost 12, Won 2
-2. Romeo Gontineac (R)   14 games (14 starts)   1995–2007 Lost 11, Won 3
-2. Hugo Horn (N)   11 games (9 starts)   1999–2011 Lost 11, Won 0
-2. Jacques Burger (N)   11 games (11 starts)   2007–2015 Lost 11, Won 0
-2. Jamie Cudmore (C)   14 games (13 starts)   2003–2015 L 11, W 2, D1
-2. Tinus du Plessis (N)   11 games (7 starts)   2007–2015 Lost 11, Won 0
-2. Eugene Jantjies (N)   11 games (8 starts)   2007–2015 Lost 11, Won 0
-2. Merab Kvirikashvili (G) 15 games (10 starts)   2007–2015 Lost 11, Won 4
-2. Johannes Redelinghuys (N) 11 games (6 starts) 2007–2015 Lost 11, Won 0

Did You Know That?
When he was 15 years old, Ovidiu Tonita worked for the Coca-Cola Company.

THE UNDEFEATED

Only nine players have a 100% winning record in Rugby World Cup finals matches when having played ten games or more.

-1.	Ma'a Nonu (NZ)	15 games (12 starts)	2003–2015	Won 15
-1.	Conrad Smith (NZ)	15 games (14 starts)	2007–2015	Won 15
-3.	Jerome Kain0 (NZ)	14 games (14 starts)	2011–2015	Won 14
-3.	Samuel Whitelock (NZ)	14 games (13 starts)	2011–2015	Won 14
-3.	Sonny Bill Williams (NZ)	14 games (5 starts)	2011–2015	Won 14
6.	Owen Franks (NZ)	13 games (12 starts)	2011–2015	Won 13
-7.	Francois Steyn (SA)	11 games (9 starts)	2007–2011	Won 11
-7.	Kieran Read (NZ)	11 games (10 starts)	2011–2015	Won 11
9.	Victor Vito (NZ)	10 games (4 starts)	2011–2015	Won 10

2019 RUGBY WORLD CUP HOST CITIES

Japan is one of the most populated countries in the world with a population of approximately 127 million people. The area of Japan is comprised of over 6,000 different islands in the Pacific Ocean. However, only 430 of these islands are inhabited. Out of these 430 islands, the majority of the population live On four islands, which are Honshu, Hokkaido, Kyushu and Shikoku. A total of 12 cities spread across Japan will play host to the 2019 Rugby World Cup, the tenth edition of the tournament and the first to be staged in Asia.

The full list of venues is:

Sapporo Dome, Sapporo City

Kamaishi Recovery Memorial Stadium, Iwate Prefecture/ Kamaishi City

Kumagaya Rugby Ground, Saitama Prefecture/Kumagaya City

International Stadium Yokohama, Kanagawa Prefecture/ Yokohama City

Ogasayama Sports Park Ecopa Stadium, Shizuoka Prefecture

Toyota Stadium, Aichi Prefecture/Toyota City

Hanazono Rugby Stadium, Osaka Prefecture/Higashi Osaka City

Kobe City Misaki Park Stadium, Kobe City

Hakatanomori Football Stadium, Fukuoka City

Kumamoto Prefectural Athletic Stadium, Kumamoto Prefecture/Kumamoto City

Oita Stadium, Oita Prefecture
Tokyo Stadium, Tokyo

Sapporo is the fifth largest city in Japan with a population of 1,906,000 and hosted the 1972 Winter Olympic Games and several group games when Japan co-hosted the 2002 FIFA World Cup. Its annual Sapporo Snow Festival draws more than 2 million tourists from abroad (Sapporo Dome, capacity 41,410).

Iwate Prefecture and Kamaishi City is best known for its steel production (Kamaishi Unosumai Recovery Memorial Stadium, capacity 16,187).

Kumagaya City is a suburb on the outskirts of the country's capital city, Tokyo. It is often referred to as Japanese rugby's 'hallowed ground of the east' and plays host to the Spring All-Japan High School Rugby Championship (Kumagaya Rugby Stadium, capacity 24,000).

Kanagawa Prefecture and Yokohama City is the birthplace of rugby in Japan and with 3,690,000 residents is Japan's second largest city. In 1859, Yokohama opened its port to England, France, the Netherlands, Russia and the USA. British soldiers stationed in Yokohama began to play rugby in their spare time which led to the founding of Yokohama Football Club. In 1873, rival garrisons staged a game which saw English soldiers play an Ireland/Scotland combined side. Nissan Stadium (formerly known as Yokohama Stadium) hosted the final of the 2002 FIFA World Cup which saw Brazil beat Germany 2-0. It will stage the final of the 2019 Rugby World Cup (International Stadium Yokohama, capacity 72,327 – also known as Nissan Stadium).

Shizuoka Prefecture is one of Japan's biggest touri attractions with its hot spring resorts and tea orcha and is renowned for its beautiful scenery. It is one of two prefectures straddled by the iconic Mount Fuji

Shizuoka Rugby Club was founded in 1929 and play in the Japan Rugby Top League. Tag rugby is played at many of the schools in the prefecture (Ogasayama Sports Park Ecopa Stadium, capacity 50,889).

Toyota City is known as the 'City of Automobiles' as the Toyota car manufacturing company has its headquarters located there. Aichi Prefecture and Toyota City is situated in the middle of the country and is considered to be the home of Japanese rugby. Toyota Automobile Rugby Club was founded in 1941 in Toyota City and in 2004 changed its name to Toyota Verblitz when it entered the Top League. Toyota Verblitz have reached the All-Japan Rugby Football Championship on three occasions during the Top League era (2006, 2009 and 2010) but lost all three finals (Toyota Stadium, capacity 45,000).

Osaka is the third-largest city in Japan with 2,670,000 residents and is best known for the highly skilled craftsmen and artisans in its manufacturing companies, which is why it is referred to as the 'Craftwork City'. However, Higashi Osaka is also renowned for its rugby with Hanazono Rugby Stadium playing host to the winter All-Japan High School Championship. In 1929, the first rugby stadium was built in Hanazono leading to Higashi Osaka also being dubbed 'Rugby City' (Hanazono Rugby Stadium, capacity 30,000).

Kobe City is the sixth largest city in Japan with a population of 1,544,000 and is a major tourist attraction with its splendid mountain range on one side and Osaka Bay the other. The city hosted the 1985 Summer Universiade three games during the 2002 FIFA World Cup. The city made a full recovery from the disastrous earthquake struck it on 17 January 1995. Rugby is one of the sports in the city and is home to one of Japan's ered clubs, Kobe Steel Rugby Club (commonly he Kobelco Steelers). They were the first ever Top npions when the league started in the 2003/04